Berlioz on Bands

Books by David Whitwell

Philosophic Foundations of Education
Foundations of Music Education
Music Education of the Future
The Sousa Oral History Project
The Art of Musical Conducting
The Longy Club: 1900–1917
A Concise History of the Wind Band
Wagner on Bands
Aesthetics of Music in Ancient Civilizations
Aesthetics of Music on the Middle Ages

The History and Literature of the Wind Band and Wind Ensemble Series

Volume 1 The Wind Band and Wind Ensemble Before 1500
Volume 2 The Renaissance Wind Band and Wind Ensemble
Volume 3 The Baroque Wind Band and Wind Ensemble
Volume 4 The Wind Band and Wind Ensemble of the Classical Period (1750–1800)
Volume 5 The Nineteenth-Century Wind Band and Wind Ensemble
Volume 6 A Catalog of Multi-Part Repertoire for Wind Instruments or for Undesignated Instrumentation before 1600
Volume 7 Baroque Wind Band and Wind Ensemble Repertoire
Volume 8 Classic Period Wind Band and Wind Ensemble Repertoire
Volume 9 Nineteenth-Century Wind Band and Wind Ensemble Repertoire
Volume 10 A Supplementary Catalog of Wind Band and Wind Ensemble Repertoire
Volume 11 A Catalog of Wind Repertoire before the Twentieth Century for One to Five Players
Volume 12 A Second Supplementary Catalog of Early Wind Band and Wind Ensemble Repertoire
Volume 13 Name Index, Volumes 1–12, The History and Literature of the Wind Band and Wind Ensemble

www.whitwellbooks.com

David Whitwell

Berlioz on Bands

A Compilation of Berlioz's Writings on Bands and Wind Instruments

Second Edition

Edited by Craig Dabelstein

Whitwell Books • Austin, Texas, USA

Whitwell Publishing, Austin 78701
www.whitwellbooks.com

© 1992, 2012 by David Whitwell
All rights reserved. First edition 1992.
Second edition 2012

Printed in the United States of America.

Paperback ISBN-13: 978-1-936512-31-7
Paperback ISBN-10: 1936512319

Composed in Bembo

Foreword

SEVERAL OF BERLIOZ'S PROSE WORKS, including his *Memoirs* and the *Treatise on Instrumentation*, have been translated into English, published and available to the interested reader for many years. On the other hand, one of his books, his hundreds of newspaper articles, and thousands of his letters have never been made available in English.

Over a number of years, I have been collecting from among these materials copies of those which contain discussions of band and wind instruments, including for example more than one hundred of his newspaper articles between 1832–1862. My intent was simply to make available Berlioz's observations on these subjects which had never been available to the English student, presented together with excerpts from those works previously translated, to provide his unique perspective of music in the middle of the nineteenth century.

I would like to acknowledge the help of Professor Hugh Macdonald, of Washington University, who was generous with answers to my questions and contributed some of this material. I am especially grateful to Gaetan Martel, Research Coordinator for the 'Berlioz Project,' University of Maryland, who identified a number of newspaper articles dealing with bands which I had not previously found.

I would have never found the time to finish this book without the help of my two principal aides in translation, Mrs. Marian Lucille Strange, of Tempe, Arizona, and Robert Fienga, of Paris. I feel I must reveal the fact that neither of these scholars requested any payment whatsoever; theirs was a contribution to the art. The reader is in the debt of these rare and special people.

Finally, the reader is in the debt of Mr. Craig Dabelstein, of Brisbane, Australia, whose editorial help and general insights have not only improved this volume, but made it possible for it to return to print in a second edition.

David Whitwell
Austin, Texas

Contents

Part 1 On Wind Instruments and Wind Players

The Flute ... 3
The Oboe ... 9
The Clarinet ... 17
The Bassoon ... 23
The Saxophone ... 25
The Trumpet ... 29
The Horn ... 39
The Trombone ... 43
The Tuba and Bass Winds ... 49
Percussion Instruments ... 53

Part 2 On Wind Instrument Manufacture ... 65

Adolphe Sax ... 71

Part 3 On Bands ... 87

Bands in the German Speaking Countries ... 95
Bands in France ... 99
Bands and the Church ... 117
Bands and Opera ... 123

Part 4 On Performance Problems

On Acoustics ... 140
On Intonation ... 145

Part 5 Berlioz's Compositions for Winds

Early Compositions for Flute ... 155
Messe solennelle ... 159
Parody on the Symphonie Fantastique ... 163
Meditation religieuse ... 165
Le Dernier Jour du monde ... 167
Le Retour de l'armee d'Italie ... 169
Chant heroique ... 171
Le Jeune Pâtre breton ... 173

Fete musicale funèbre ... 175
Aubade ... 177
Symphonie funèbre et triomphale ... 179
Chasse a la grosse bete ... 221
Chant sacré ... 223

Part 6 On Composition ... 229

On Orchestration ... 239
Berlioz on other Composers ... 251
  Beethoven ... 251
  Reicha ... 253
  Rossini ... 255
  Bellini ... 255
  Spontini ... 256

Part 7 On Conducting

Berlioz as Conductor ... 261
On Conducting Technique ... 273
The Conductor's Duty to the Composer ... 277

Part 8 On Music Education ... 281

Part 9 Music in Society

France ... 293
Germany ... 301
Italy ... 307

Part 1

On Wind Instruments and Wind Players

The Flute

HECTOR BERLIOZ, in his letters, publications, and newspaper articles, commented extensively on the musical life of the first half of the nineteenth century. On no topic was his thinking more precise than on the subject of musical instruments and how these instruments were used by various composers in their scores.

One of the most striking characteristics of Berlioz's discussions of individual wind instruments was his interest in the character, the subjective nature, of the instrument itself. His comments reflect not only his careful attention to these qualities as a composer, but confirm and extend the awareness of the importance of instrumental choice, which had begun to become apparent in the generation or two before his own.

In addressing the particular nature of the flute he writes,

> The flute is endowed with a character peculiarly its own and with a special aptitude for expressing certain feelings, in which it is matched by no other instrument. For instance, if one desires to give an expression of desolation to a sad melody, combined with the feeling of humility and resignation, the weak medium tones of the flute, especially in C# minor and D minor, will certainly produce the intended effect. As far as I know, only one master knew how to avail himself of this pale tone-color—Gluck. When listening to the D minor melody of the pantomime in the Elysian-Fields scene in 'Orfeo,' one is immediately convinced that only a flute could play this melody appropriately. An oboe would be too child-like, and its tone not sufficiently clear. The English horn is too low. A clarinet would doubtless have been more suitable, but it would have been too strong for some of the passages; for even its softest tones cannot be reduced to the weak and veiled sound of the medium F and of the Bb above the stave, which imparts so much sadness to the flute in the key of D minor. Finally, neither the violin, nor the viola, nor the violoncello ... could express this sublime lament of a suffering and despairing spirit. It required precisely the instrument selected by the composer. Moreover, Gluck's melody is conceived in such a way that the flute can follow every impulse of this eternal grief, still imbued with the passions of earthly life. The voice starts almost inaudible, seemingly afraid to be overheard; then it sighs softly and rises to the expression of reproach, of deep pain, to the cry of a heart torn by incurable wounds; gradually it sinks back into a plaint, a sigh and the sorrowful murmur of a resigned soul. Gluck was, indeed, a great poet![1]

[1] Hector Berlioz, *Treatise on Instrumentation* (New York: Kalmus, 1948), 228.

Berlioz criticized composers who, insensitive to these qualities, included the flute rather automatically.

> Flutes are almost indispensable in instrumentation even though they are often featured in compositions where it would be better if they were not.[2]

[2] *Revue et gazette musicale*, January 2, 1842.

As a player himself during the early years of the nineteenth century when the flute, like all the woodwinds, experienced a period of extraordinary change in design and manufacture, Berlioz no doubt watched the various developments with interest. In an article on the results of the Universal Exhibition, in which Boehm of Munich was one of only four instrument makers awarded a gold medal, Berlioz reveals considerable knowledge of his subject.

> This eminent distinction given to Mr. Boehm, the only foreign maker receiving an award, was in recognition of the fact that he is the first to have applied a new bore system, as well as a new mechanism for fingering, to woodwind instruments such as flutes, oboes, clarinets and bassoons.
>
> Mr. Boehm makes the majority of his flutes of silver. The sound of these instruments is soft, crystal-clear but less full and loud than flutes made of wood. This new system has the advantage of giving the fingered woodwind instruments an almost perfect and precise intonation, and to allow the players to play without difficulty in keys virtually impossible with the old instruments.
>
> The fingering of Mr. Boehm's instruments is essentially different than the system used on other types of instruments; thus the opposition on the part of many musicians to put in place the new system. It would cost too much for them to restudy their instrument and even among the virtuosos … we find few who would take this initiative. However, there is no doubt in our minds that within a short period of time, the Gordon-Boehm system will triumph, and we congratulate the jury for recognizing this.[3]

[3] *Journal des Débats*, January 12, 1856.

Berlioz wrote little of the piccolo and, judging from his reference to Gluck's *Alceste*, perhaps it was not his favorite instrument.

> Nor does the piccolo at all figure in this work; everything being banished from it which is coarse, noisy or piercing …[4]

[4] Hector Berlioz, *Gluck & his Operas*, trans. Edwin Evans (London: Reeves, 1915), 78. Originally published as *Voyage musical en Allemagne et en Italie* (Paris, 1844).

His discussion of another member of the flute family, the flageolet, is interesting because this was the first instrument Berlioz studied. While he clearly distinguishes it from an actual flute in his discussion of this period, no one today is entirely sure what the actual instrument was—except, of course, as some member of the fife family. Among his series of newspaper articles which formed the basis of the eventual *Treatise on Instrumentation*, there is in fact a discussion of this instrument, although he elected to omit this discussion from the treatise itself.

> I have little to say about flageolets. Despite the really remarkable talent of certain virtuosi and the pleasure a well played flageolet solo can sometimes give, it is a fact that no masters of the art have ever used this silly little instrument, and they were right not to include it in their orchestras. In bright, sprightly dance pieces it is not out of place, however, although this is the only exception I would make in its favor.
>
> Its tone is rather cheap and common, quite incompatible with any piece at all elevated in style; its range is scarcely more than two octaves; and with the exception of the three or four top notes it has a rather weak sound.[5]

[5] *Revue et gazette musicale*, January 2, 1842.

Berlioz includes a player of the flageolet among the members of his fictional orchestra which he describes in his book, *Les Grotesques de la musique*.

> Another, the Apostle of the Flageolet, was full of zeal. We couldn't prevent him from playing in the orchestra, in which he made the most beautiful ornament, even though the flageolet instrument is not a member of the orchestra.
>
> So, he doubled either the flute, oboe or clarinet; he would have doubled even the string bass rather than remain inactive. In response to one of this colleagues, finding it strange that he would allow himself to play in a Beethoven symphony, he said, 'You mechanize [add keys to] my instrument and yet you seem to hate me! Imbeciles! If Beethoven had known me, his works would be filled with flageolet solos and he would have made a fortune. But he did not know me, and died in the hospital.'[6]

[6] Hector Berlioz, *Les Grotesques de la musique* (Paris: Grund, 1969), 53.

Berlioz was somewhat surprised, even shocked, to find that the freedom commonly assumed by players of the Baroque and Classical Period, with respect to the written form of the music, continued into the nineteenth century. He mentions this regarding flutists in his *Treatise*.

Flutists, accustomed to lead the other wind instruments and unwilling to play occasionally below the clarinets and oboes, frequently transpose entire passages to the higher octave ... such abuses should no longer be tolerated.[7]

> 7 Berlioz, *Treatise*, 419.

In his *Memoirs* he speaks of his student days in Paris when he and his friends would attend the opera and comment loudly to the audience around them regarding the names of the players entering the pit, together with 'a few comments on their ability and style of playing.' Here he names a flute player by name who engaged in electing for himself which octave he would perform a passage in.[8]

> 8 Hector Berlioz, *The Memoirs of Hector Berlioz*, ed. David Cairns (London: Gollancz, 1969), 81.

The conductor ought to keep an eye on Guillou, the first flute, who's coming in now. He takes extraordinary liberties with Gluck: the sacred march in Alceste, for instance, where the composer has written for the bottom register of the flutes, precisely because he wants the special effect of their lowest notes. That doesn't suit Guillou, He has to dominate, his part has got to be heard—so he transposes the flute part up an octave, thus destroying the composer's intention and turning an imaginative idea into something feeble and obvious.

In general though, his writing indicates that he found in Paris the highest level of flute playing among the cities he had visited. As he writes once in speaking of German flute players, 'In flutes we surpass them; nowhere do you hear the flute played as it is in Paris.'[9]

> 9 Ibid., 321.

On several occasions, Berlioz writes of specific French flute players whom he admired. In a review of an orchestra concert in the Rue Cadet Hall, conducted by the famous cornetist, Arban, Berlioz mentions the, 'flute solo by M. Demersman, playing with a prodigious ability. Interminable applauding.'[10] And in another place he mentions, 'M. Petiton, the able flutist of the Opéra Comique ...'[11] On one occasion he provided a letter of recommendation for Jean Remusat (1815–1880), a French flutist who was a member of the New Philharmonic Society of London.

> 10 *Journal des Débats*, April 7, 1861.
>
> 11 Ibid., April 13, 1851.

I have learned that there is an opening for a flute professor at the Brussels Conservatory. Allow me to seriously recommend Mr. Remusat. I think that he has true talent for performing and all of the necessary qualities for this job, and that you would be hard pressed to find such an artist of his worth for the position you are seeking to fill. Moreover, he has spirit—a rather rare overwhelming quality for flutists—which should make you want to take a closer look.[12]

[12] Letter to François-Joseph Fétis, London, June 12, 1852, in Pierre Citron, ed., *Berlioz Correspondance Générale* (Paris: Flammarion, 1972), 1494.

During his travels in Germany, Berlioz again finds flutists who take liberties with the music, a practice which he felt was no longer acceptable.

> The artist [in Stuttgart] who plays the part of first flute (M. Kruger Sr.) uses, unfortunately, an ancient instrument that leaves a lot to be desired in the purity of sound generally, and in the ease of production of high notes. M. Kruger also should be on his guard against his penchant that leads him sometimes to play trills and ornaments where the composer was careful not to write them.
> The first flute [in Hechigen is] excellent; except that [he] sometimes has those stray impulses of ornamentation like the one I reproached in Stuttgart.[13]

[13] *Journal des Débats*, August 20, 1843.

He did mention two German flute players he found who impressed him.

> The Hanover orchestra is good … Only praise is to be given to the wind instruments, especially to the first flute, …[14] And 'the first flute (Cantal) and first violin are two first-rate virtuosi …'[15]

[14] 'Hanover-Darmstadt,' *Journal des Débats*, January 9, 1844.

[15] 'Hamburg,' *Journal des Débats*, September 23, 1843.

Berlioz's only comment on flute playing in England refers to the great appeal the instrument had for amateur players.

> Wherever musical sentiment is little developed, love of the flute dominates; look at England.[16]

[16] 'De l'Instrumentation de Robert-le-Diable,' *Gazette Musicale de Paris*, July 12, 1835.

The kind of music he attributes to England can, in fact, be found in enormous quantities in the libraries of the German-speaking countries and in Paris as well. Indeed, Berlioz makes a reference to these amateur flutists of Paris in a letter of 1850, in which he parodies a line from Virgil, *Auri sacra fames* (*Eneide*, III, 37), 'Pleasant appetite for gold,' with one meaning, 'Pleasant appetite for glory.'

> The composers are not falling asleep either and you have no idea of the works that they are sending us. Then come the prodigal children, the pianists and the flutists. *Famae sacra fames!*[17]

[17] Letter to Auguste Morel, Paris, November 4, 1850, in *Correspondance*, 1357.

The Oboe

THE OBOE, FOR BERLIOZ, was an instrument with a wide expressive range, within clearly perceived limits.

> The oboe is above all a melodic instrument; it has a pastoral character, full of tenderness—I might even say, of shyness ...
>
> Artless grace, pure innocence, mellow joy, the pain of a tender soul—all these the oboe can render admirably with its cantabile. A certain degree of excitement is also within its power; but one must guard against increasing it to the cry of passion, the stormy outburst of fury, menace or heroism; for then its small voice, sweet and somewhat tart at the same time, becomes ineffectual and completely grotesque. Even some of the great masters—Mozart among them—did not avoid this error entirely.[18]

As an illustration of Berlioz's detailed knowledge of wind instruments, one finds in a letter to a professor of the Conservatorio in Milan the following correction which should be made in his *Treatise on Instrumentation*.

> There is still an error that I should point out. The trill on the [high] C sharp for the oboe should be marked impossible as it is so absurd.[19]

Among his Parisian colleagues, Berlioz singled out two oboists for praise in his newspaper criticism. The first, 'M. Crass, who sings in such a touching fashion on the oboe ...'[20] and the more famous Brod, 'whose handsome talent on the oboe is so justly famous ...'[21] This last artist Berlioz used as the source for an invented story designed to paint an unfavorable picture of Cherubini, whom Berlioz seemed to resent from his student days in Paris when the older composer was the director of the conservatory.

---

[18] *Treatise*, 164.

[19] Letter to Alberto Mazzucato, Paris, May 19, 1844, in *Correspondance*, 901.

[20] *Journal des Débats*, April 13, 1851.

[21] Ibid., July 21, 1835.

SENSITIVITY AND BREVITY
A FUNERAL ORATION IN THREE SYLLABLES

Cherubini was walking in the foyer of the Conservatory's concert hall during intermission. The musicians around him seemed sad as they had just learned of the death of their colleague Brod, a remarkable virtuoso, the Opera's principal oboe. One of them, approaching the old master, said, 'So, Mr. Cherubini, we have lost poor Brod!'

'Eh? what?'

The musician raised his voice, 'Brod, our comrade Brod …'

'Eh?'

'He is dead!'

'Um, small sound.'

In an early review, Berlioz notices that a high level of oboe playing was difficult to find outside of Paris.

> Another part of the orchestra, which is usually terribly difficult to find in the provinces, is that of the oboes; whether it be because of its great difficulty, or whether for an entirely different cause, the oboe is not honored in the provinces, and artists cultivate it as little as do the amateurs. As for the English horn … it is totally unknown.[22]

In later years, however, he did find a fine player in Lyon.

> The orchestra of the Grand Theatre in Lyon has an exceptionally first-rate oboe player, who also plays the flute well and whose reputation is great. He is Mr. Donjon.[23]

In his travels in Germany, Berlioz found several oboists whom he remembered with praise:

> The first oboe [in Stuttgart is] excellent.
>
> …
>
> The first oboe [in Hechigen is] excellent.[24]
>
> …
>
> In Mannheim I found … a first-rate oboist who plays the cor anglais rather poorly.[25]
>
> …
>
> The Hanover orchestra is good … Only praise is to be given to the wind instruments, especially … to the first oboe (Edouard Rose), one could not play a better pianissimo than he, … The first oboe plays the English horn, but his instrument is very out of tune.[26]

[22] 'De L'Instrumentation de Robert-le-Diable,' in *Gazette Musicale de Paris*, July 12, 1835.

[23] *Les Grotesques de la musique*, 290.

[24] *Journal des Débats*, August 20, 1843.

[25] *Memoirs*, 287.

[26] *Journal des Débats*, January 9, 1844.

In Dresden Berlioz found another fine player, but in this player he again encountered one who continued the old freedom of improvisation. Berlioz could not believe this could happen with the composer conducting his own music. But in our view the elderly oboist was only doing what wind players did in past decades. No doubt he was embarrassed when Berlioz criticized him and no doubt he intended to make no further such additions to the music. But when the concert came we suspect the poor old player could not help himself and resorted to the older tradition. We regard this as a valuable insight into the end of the long period of ensemble improvisation. Berlioz, on the other hand, took it more personally:

> The first oboe has a beautiful sound, but an odd style and a mania for making trills and mordants, which, I must declare, profoundly outraged me. He permitted himself, especially, some frightful ones in the solo of the beginning of the *Scène aux Champs*. I expressed, in a vigorous fashion, my horror of those melodic niceties; he abstained from them maliciously in the following rehearsals, but it was only a trap; and on the day of the concert, the perfidious oboe, quite sure that I was not going to stop the orchestra and call him down, himself personally, before the court and the public, again began his petty villainies, looking at me with a sly air that almost made me fall over backward with indignation and fury.[27]

[27] *Journal des Débats*, September 12, 1843.

Because this is such an interesting incident, we also quote his version of the same occasion as found in his *Memoirs*.[28]

[28] *Memoirs*, 305ff.

> The first oboe has a fine tone but an antiquated style and a mania for inserting trills and grace-notes which outraged my deepest convictions. He indulged in some particularly disgusting embellishments at the beginning of the *Scene in the Country*. I expressed myself on the subject in vigorous terms at the second rehearsal. The sly dog refrained at the two subsequent rehearsals, but it was a feint. At the concert, knowing that I would not stop the orchestra and arraign him personally in the presence of the court, he treacherously resumed his little tricks, eying me with a quizzical air the while. I nearly collapsed with indignation.

Berlioz never forgot this oboist. Years later when making arrangements for a concert in Dresden, he asks sarcastically if the man is still around.

We also will need the first oboe to play the English horn. Is it still the first oboe that played so well the *notes de desagrement* when I was in Dresden eleven years ago?[29]

[29] Letter to Karol Lipinski, Hanover, March 28, 1854, in *Correspondance*, 1714.

Berlioz was fond of the tenor oboe and entrusted some beautiful melodies to it in his orchestral music. He writes of its special character as follows:

> Its tone, less piercing, more veiled and heavy than that of the oboe, does not lend itself so well to the gaiety of rustic melodies. Nor can it express passionate laments; tones of keen grief are scarcely within its range. Its tones are melancholy, dreamy, noble, somewhat veiled—as if played in the distance. It has no equal among the instruments for reviving images and sentiments of the past if the composer intends to touch the hidden chords of tender memories.[30]

[30] *Treatise*, 184.

It is interesting to read in his descriptions of his travels in Germany of the great difficulty he had in finding this instrument. During the late *Hautboisten* and early *Harmoniemusik* period the tenor oboe was a basic wind instrument. When the new clarinet began to push it out of the *Harmoniemusik* ensemble, towards the end of the eighteenth century, it seems to have undergone a rapid fall from usage. It was the demands of Berlioz's music, as much as anything, which brought the instrument back into common use. His complaints regarding the playing of this instrument in Hanover and Mannheim are mentioned above, but in some cities he could not find the instrument at all.

> [In Leipzig] The cor anglais—the instrument, that is—was of such poor quality and in such bad condition and, in consequence, so remarkably out of tune that despite the skill of the player we had to abandon all idea of using it and entrust the solo to the first clarinet.[31]
>
> …
>
> [In Hamburg] it was necessary to do without the English horn.[32]
>
> …
>
> [In Brunswick] There was no cor anglais either; its solos were arranged for the oboe …[33]
>
> …
>
> [In Weimar] there was no cor anglais (I had to transpose the part for clarinet) …[34]

[31] *Memoirs*, 295ff.

[32] 'Hamburg,' *Journal des Débats*, September 23, 1843.

[33] *Memoirs*, 310.

[34] Ibid., 289.

On only one occasion in Germany was he satisfied with a resident orchestral player of this instrument.

> There is in Dresden a very good English horn.[35]

35 'Dresden,' *Journal des Débats*, September 12, 1843.

Given his difficulty in finding a fine player of this instrument, one is not surprised to find two letters of recommendation for a player, Wacker, or Walcker, whom Berlioz heard in Marseille in 1845. Here is a player unknown today, who had recommendations no subsequent player of the history of this instrument could match—recommendations from Berlioz to Liszt and Mendelssohn!

> [In a letter to Liszt] … he plays the English horn in a most superior way and, on that note, there is no English horn currently in Weimar.[36]
>
> …
>
> My Dear Mendelssohn,
>   If you can find a spot in a good German organization for Mr. Walcker, the bearer of this letter, you will not only be doing a service to the court, but also will oblige me greatly. Mr. Walcker plays the oboe and English horn in a most beautiful manner—and beyond that, he is a gifted musician as well—and German. He desires to return to his country. I have most recently appreciated his musical talents in my concerts in Marseille. And, as soon as our good Lord calls to himself one of your oboe players, I should hope that you will think of Mr. Walcker as a replacement.[37]

36 'Marseille,' June 20, 1834, in *Correspondance*, 970.

37 'Marseille,' June 29, 1845, in *Correspondance*, 971.

Berlioz also recalled a fine player in England. In a letter regarding a forthcoming performance of the *Roman Carnival Overture* in London, Berlioz wrote,

> The English horn solo does not call for a special artist—it can be played by the first oboe (who can change instruments). Mr. Barre will play it wonderfully.[38]

38 Letter to George Hogarth, Paris, February 23, 1853, in *Correspondance*, 1567.

Berlioz was also interested in the more distant relatives of the oboe family as he came across them, for example the Asian instrument he heard at the Universal Exhibition.

> Judging from the instruments sent by India to the Universal Exhibition, the music of the East Indians must differ but slightly from that of the Chinese … There was a double-reed wind instrument akin to our oboe,

whose tube, having no holes, produces only a single note. The leader of the musicians who came to Paris some years ago with the nautchgirls of Calcutta used this primitive oboe. He would make an A hum for whole hours, and those who love this particular note got their money's worth.[39]

39 Hector Berlioz, *Evenings with the Orchestra*, trans. Jacques Barzun (New York: Knopf, 1969), 251. Originally published as *Les Soirees de l'orchestra*, 1852.

During his youthful stay in Italy, he was particularly interested in the instrument which he calls the *piffero*. Beginning during the fourteenth century one finds in Italy the appearance of the *pifferi*, a civic ensemble of at least three shawm types. The name was retained during the fifteenth and sixteenth centuries as the ensemble grew into a larger ensemble which included cornetts and trombones. With the gradual decline and disappearance of this great early civic wind band tradition, from the seventeenth century onward, one begins to find the name adopted by small ensembles of wandering beggars. Let us not forget that in the autograph score of the *Messiah*, the 'Pastoral symphony' movement bears in Handel's hand a note suggesting that he heard something like this music played in Italy by a *pifferi* band.

During the nineteenth century it was this peasant *pifferi* ensemble which was heard and commented on by a number of traveling musicians from Northern Europe. Berlioz has left two accounts of his encounter with this instrument.

> There still is, in the Roman states, a musical custom that I am strongly inclined to consider as a remnant of Antiquity. I mean the Piferari. Thus do they name the wandering musicians, who at the approach of Christmas, come down from the mountains in groups of four or five, and they come armed with musettes and with piferi (a kind of oboe) to give pious concerts before the images of the Madonna. Usually they are dressed with ample coats of brown cloth, wearing the pointed hat that the brigands wear, and their very exterior is marked by a certain mystical savagery full of originality. I spent entire hours contemplating them in Rome, head slightly tilted over one shoulder, eyes shining with the liveliest faith, fixing a glance of pious love on the holy Madonna, almost as immobile as the picture they were adoring. The musette, sounded by a great pifero sounding the bass, makes a harmony of two or three notes, over which a double pifero of medium length (would this instrument be the one to which Virgil referred? '... *Ite per alta, Dindyma, ubi assuetis biforem dat tibia cantum*') plays the melody; then above that, two small, very short, piferi quaver the *ris* and cadences and drown the rustic song with a shower of grotesque ornaments. After some gay and merry refrains, repeated a very long time, a slow prayer, grave, with a completely patriarchal unctuousness, brimming with the sincerest expres-

sion, comes to terminate worthily the naive symphony. From close up, the sound is so strong that one can hardly stand it, but at a certain distance, that strange orchestra produces a delicious effect, touching, poetic, to which people, even the least susceptible to such impressions, cannot remain indifferent.[40]

...

    These are mountain people who, on the approach of Christmas, descend into the cities in groups of four or five, to come give pious concerts before the images of the Virgin. A paltry remuneration is allotted to them for that by the owner of the Madonna; and as there is hardly any house which does not have its own, they make, ordinarily, a quite decent collection before returning into their mountains. Long coats of brown cloth, and a conical hat like that worn by brigands, give to their exterior a serious and wild aspect, which their physiognomy is far from belying. They play a kind of crude oboe that they call a *piffero*; hence the name of Pifferari that has been given to them. These instruments are not all of the same dimension, there are some long as our A clarinets, others shorter by a third or half. In the troupes of Pifferari composed of five individuals, in general, here is how the instruments are distributed: the oldest, playing the big piffero, has the bass part; a second one, also of a ripe age, joins to the low sounds of the first, the two shrill notes of the zampogna (musette), so as to form a harmony in three parts; a third, blowing into the piffero of medium length, plays the melody, and the two other young boys of twelve to fifteen, with the help of the short pifferi, of a high and piercing timbre, warbling in the heights all sorts of grotesque embroideries. So the melody is found, in opposition to the ordinary, situated in the middle. The sounds of this singular orchestra have such an intensity, the vibrations of them are so harsh, that, up close, it is almost impossible to stand them; but at a distance, they have a charm that captivates and ends by profoundly moving one. I stopped in the streets of Rome during entire hours to listen to them play two or three hundred times the same tune without interruption. But, for this wild music, another surrounding is requisite than that of the streets and palaces of a city; it is in the mountains, it is in their native habitat that one must hear the Pifferari. I cannot describe the effect that they produce at night in the Abbruzes, when, from the bosom of a black fir forest, the rustic symphony escapes, joyous or melancholic, and comes to echo in the valley, in the ear of the delayed hunter. The profound silence of these solitudes, the strange aspect of the gigantic rocks that circumscribe the scenic place, the picturesque costume of these men, appearing at intervals in the moonlight like phantoms in the clearings of the woods, harmonizes so well with the robust voice of the instruments and the rustic coloration of the songs that they play, all that has such a perfume of antiquity that classical memories, roused, add to the interest of the moment all the prestige of Virgilian poetry, and there are no fatigues, no nervousness nor dangers that do not disappear then to give place to the most delicious reveries.[41]

[40] *Revue européene*, March–May, 1832, 59ff.

[41] *Journal des Débats*, September, 5, 1835.

The Clarinet

IN HIS *Treatise on Instrumentation*, Berlioz offers a description of the clarinet which is quite extraordinary, on first glance, to the modern clarinetists. The different sized clarinets, he writes, are analogous to the horn in so far as one has different sized instruments for use in different keys. While it almost seems he thought of a single instrument in different keys, no clarinetist today would admit that the Bb and Eb clarinet are the same instrument. Berlioz agrees the numerous sizes he knew actually were different in characteristics other than key, but his viewpoint on this question remains considerably different from the accepted practice today. In any case, his description of the character of the clarinet is a moving tribute to this instrument.

> Since there are clarinets in different keys, their appropriate use makes it unnecessary for the performer to play in keys with many sharps or flats … Generally, performers should use only the instruments indicated by the composer. Since each of these instruments has it own peculiar character, it may be assumed that the composer has preferred one or the other instrument for the sake of a definite timbre and not out of mere whim. To persist—as certain virtuosos do—in playing everything on the clarinet in Bb by transposition, is an act of disloyalty toward the composer in most instances …
>
> The character of the tones of the medium register is imbued with loftiness tempered by a noble tenderness, appropriate for the expression of the most poetic feelings and ideas. Only the expression of frivolous gaiety and even of artless joy seems to be denied to the instrument. The character of the clarinets is *epic* rather than idyllic … Its voice is that of heroic love …
>
> There is no other wind instrument which can produce a tone, let it swell, decrease and die away as beautifully as the clarinet. Hence its invaluable ability to render distant sounds, an echo, the reverberation of an echo, or the charm of the twilight. I know no more admirable example of such shading than the dreamy melody of the clarinet, accompanied by the tremolo of the strings, in the Allegro of the 'Freischütz' overture. Is this not the lonely maiden, the blond betrothed of the huntsman, with her eyes raised to heaven uttering her tender plaint, amidst the rustling noise of the deep forest shaken by the storm?—O Weber![42]

[42] *Treatise*, 201ff.

As in the case of the flute, Berlioz seems to have carefully watched the developments in this instrument—especially those by his friend Adolphe Sax.

> The manufacture of these instruments, which remained almost in its infancy for so long a time, has now progressed to a point where excellent results may be expected. Great advances have already been made by M. Adolphe Sax ... The tones of the high register were once dreaded by composers and performers; only rarely and with extreme caution did they dare to use them. By means of a little key close to the mouthpiece of the clarinet, M. Sax has rendered these tones just as pure and mellow, and almost as easy, as those of the medium register. Even the highest Bb which one hardly ever ventured to write, responds on the Sax clarinets without any preparation or effort on the part of the performer. He can play it pianissimo without the slightest risk, and it is at least as soft as that of the flute. To remedy the disadvantages of the wooden mouthpiece (ie., dryness when used infrequently, moisture in the opposite case), M. Sax has given the clarinet a mouthpiece of gilded metal, which increases the brilliance of its tone without being subject to the changes affecting the wooden mouthpiece ...
>
> M. Sax's new bass clarinet is still further improved ... Its tube is very long, and the bell almost touches the ground when the player stands upright. This could have caused a considerable weakening of the tone; but the skillful manufacturer remedied it by attaching a concave metal reflector under the bell. The reflector not only prevents any loss of sound, but also permits the player to emit the tone in any direction and thereby even increases its sonority.[43]

43 Ibid., 226ff.

One clarinetist who remained in Berlioz's memory throughout his life, was a senior performer who, together with his colleagues in the Academy orchestra of 1830, gave a sight-reading performance which caused the composer considerable agony.

> In the day when the Prix de Rome launched me upon my career there was only a clarinet and a half, the old man who had done duty as first clarinet since time immemorial having lost nearly all his teeth and being in consequence unable to sound more than half the notes of his aristocratic instrument ...[44]

44 *Memoirs*, 136.

A few years later, however, he went out of his way to mention an artist he admired in Paris, together with one of his publications.

> One artist of great reputation and merit, Mr. Beer, Solo Clarinet of the Italian Theater … has just had published, by E. Duverger, a *Traite complet de la Clarinette a quatorze clefs*, which we would recommend to all those who are interested in this beautiful instrument.⁴⁵

45 *Journal des Débats*, September, 18, 1836.

On one occasion he was sufficiently impressed with a touring Italian clarinetist to produce a rare letter of introduction.

> Allow me to present to you Mr. Cavallini, the most extraordinary virtuoso that you will hear on the clarinet. He is a technician of surprising ability, to which he has untied grace, charm and a rare distinction of general style. This letter of introduction he has asked me to write to you also offers me the opportunity to convey to you my utmost admiration for his rare talent.⁴⁶

46 Letter to an unknown person, Paris, December, 1841, in *Correspondance*, 762.

In his travels in Germany, Berlioz seems always to have found fine clarinetists.⁴⁷ All in all, he concluded of the German orchestras, 'Their clarinets too are better than ours.'

47 See *Journal des Débats* for August 20, 1843 and January 9, 1844 and his *Memoirs*, 289, 321.

Among those whom he knew was the famous Henri-Joseph Baermann (1783–1847), the clarinetist for whom Weber composed his masterpieces for the instrument. Berlioz mentions Baermann in a letter to Robert Schumann on the occasion of the clarinetist's visit to Paris with his son, Charles (1820–1885), who was also a clarinetist.⁴⁸ There is also an extant letter of 4 April 1840. Berlioz wrote to Baermann to inquire about the possibility of having his *Requiem* performed during a festival in Germany.⁴⁹

48 *Correspondance*, 630.

49 Ibid., 711.

One of the most humorous stories Berlioz tells is about a clarinet soloist in Germany, who was distinctly not in the class of player described above.

A CLARINET CONCERTO

> Doelher had just announced a concert in a large German city when a stranger came to call on him at his home.
>
> 'Sir,' said the man to Doelher, 'my name is W***, *I am a great clarinetist*, and I have come with the intent of having my talent appreciated. But I am not well-known here and you would do me a great service by allowing me to play a solo during the evening that you have organized. Its desired effect would be to attract attention to myself as well as pleasing the public and I would owe to you the fact of having given me my first successful concert.'
>
> 'What would you play at my evening?,' replied the obedient Doelher.
>
> 'A great clarinet concerto.'

'Well then, Sir, I accept your offer. I will put you on the program. Come to the rehearsal, and I am delighted to have been of service to you.'

The evening arrived, the orchestra was assembled, our man appeared and we started rehearsing his concerto. As was customary among virtuosi, he abstained from playing, intent on having the orchestra rehearse their part while he gave the tempo. The principal tutti, largely similar to the peasant march in *Der Freischütz*, seemed rather grotesque to the people present and worried Doelher. 'But,' he said while leaving, 'the solo part will redeem the whole thing.' The man is probably an adept virtuoso and one cannot demand that such a *great clarinetist* be a great composer as well.

The following day at the concert, a little intimidated by the resounding triumph of Doelher, the clarinetist entered the stage.

The orchestra played the tutti, which arrived on the dominant chord, after which began the first solo section. 'Tram, pan, pan, tire lire la re la,' like the *Freischütz* march. At the dominant chord the orchestra stopped and the virtuoso, leaning on his left hip, with his right leg in front of him, put his instrument to his mouth and, holding horizontally both elbows, looked like he was about to play. His cheeks puffed out, he blew, he pushed, he reddened, vain efforts, but nothing came out of his rebellious instrument. He turned it over and eyed it from the bell end as if it were a telescope. Seeing nothing, he tried again, blew with rage—not a sound. Desperate, he ordered the musicians to begin again with the tutti. 'Tram, pan, pan, tire lire la re la,' and during the time that the orchestra played the virtuoso, placing his clarinet between, let us not say his legs, but much higher, the bell to the back, the mouthpiece to the front, started to quickly unscrew the reed and began cleaning the instrument with a cleaning brush …

All of this took a certain amount of time and the merciless orchestra had already finished their tutti and were once again pausing on the chord of the dominant.

'Encore! Encore! Once again!,' cried the man to the musicians. And the musicians obeyed. 'Tram, pan, pan, tire, lire la re la' and for the third time after a few moments the musicians arrived at the unforgiving moment of the solo. But the clarinetist was not ready. 'Da Capo! Encore! Encore!' and the orchestra started up happily, 'Tram, pan, pan, tire lire la re la.'

During this last repetition, the virtuoso, having put back together the various pieces of his cantankerous instrument, and having put it back between … his legs, took a knife out of his pocket and started to scrape at the reed of the clarinet, placed you know where.

Laughter and whispers filled the room. The women looked away, hiding in the back of the boxes, while the men got up to have a better look. One heard exclamations and small smothered cries while the scandalous virtuoso continued to scrape at his reed.

Finally, he feels he has it in shape and the orchestra is back again at the fermata of the tutti for the fourth time. The soloist puts the clarinet in his mouth, spreads and raises his elbows again, and blows, sweats, reddens, stiffens, and nothing comes out! This supreme effort gave way to a sound like lightening, the most piercing and angry squawk you have ever heard. Not even a hundred pieces of satin being ripped all at once, the sound of a flight of vampires, of a ghoul giving birth could come close to the sound of that awful squawk!

The audience held an exclamation of joyous horror, the applause rung out, and the bewildered virtuoso stepped forward and stuttered, 'Ladies and Gentlemen, I do not know what … ac … accident in my cl … cl … clarinet, but I will ha … have it fixed and I would kindly ask that you come to my next mu … musical evening to be held next Monday to hear *the end* of my concerto.'[50]

[50] *Les Grotesques*, 67ff.

The Bassoon

REGARDING BERLIOZ'S REFLECTIONS ON THE BASSOON, one is drawn to his interesting reaction to the high range of the instrument.

> The character of its high tones has something painful and suffering about it, I might even say, something miserable.[51]

51 *Treatise*, 190.

The few comments Berlioz makes about the orchestral bassoons he worked with in Germany are surprising. After the highly technical requirements demanded during the period of Harmoniemusik now it seems a significant decline has taken place. Indeed, Berlioz himself, suggests the level of playing was not as high as it had been during the Classical Period.

> The first bassoon [in Stuttgart], M. Neukirchner, is a first rate virtuoso who, perhaps, attaches too much importance to making a parade of great difficulties; he plays, moreover, on such a bad bassoon that doubtful intonation wounds the ear every instant and spoils the effect of even the best interpreted phrases by the performer.
> ...
> The two bassoons [in Hechigen] leave a little to be desired.[52]
> ...
> The Hanover orchestra is good ... The two bassoons (there are only two) play in tune, an extremely rare thing.

52 *Journal des Débats*, August 20, 1843.

The Saxophone

BERLIOZ'S COMMENTARY ON THE SAXOPHONE is especially valuable and interesting because he was in exactly the right place and time to observe the birth of this new family of instruments. The reader may be surprised at the description of the new instrument which Berlioz gives here in its initial introduction to the public. It was in fact the *tenor* saxophone which first appeared, reflecting Sax's original idea of creating a family of instruments to strengthen the otherwise weak tenor-baritone portion of the orchestral tessitura. The reader will also find descriptions of the sound and character of the first saxophones in the descriptions of Berlioz as well almost unrecognizable. The dark and vocal instrument Berlioz heard was changed by clarinet players in New York City, ca. 1905, who changed the mouthpiece into a cylindrical bore for ease in doubling on it for jazz. Thereafter the original sound was forever gone.

Here is how Berlioz introduced the new instrument to the world in 1842.

> The *saxophone*, so-called from the name of the inventor, is a brass instrument, quite similar to the ophicleide in its form, and furnished with nineteen keys. It is played, not with an embouchure like the other brass instruments, but with a mouthpiece similar to that of the bass clarinet. So the saxophone would be the head of a new family, that of brass instruments using a reed. Its range is three octaves, starting from low Bb below the treble staff (key of F); its fingering is almost the same as that of the flute, or of the second part of the clarinet. As to the sonority, it is of such a nature that I do not know a low instrument currently in use that can, in this respect, be compared to it. It is full-toned, soft, vibrant, of enormous force, and capable of being played sweetly. It is very superior, to my mind, to the low notes of the ophicleides, for intonation, for the stability of the sound, whose character moreover is completely new and does not resemble any of the timbres that are heard in the current orchestra, except, perhaps, a little, that of the low E and F of the bass clarinet. Thanks to the reed with which it is provided, the saxophone can swell and diminish sound; it produces in the upper range, notes of a penetrating vibration that even could be happily applied to melodic expression. Doubtless, it will never be appropriate for rapid runs, for complicated arpeggios; but low instruments are certainly not destined

for light maneuvers; so it is necessary, instead of complaining, to rejoice in the impossibility of abusing the saxophone and destroying its majestic character by giving it musical futilities to perform.[53]

[53] 'M. Ad. Sax,' in *Journal des Débats*, June 12, 1842.

Another early reference is found in his *Treatise on Instrumentation*, where he tries to capture something of the subjective nature of the new instrument. It is important to remember that when he was describing the character of this instrument, he was describing an instrument the reader probably had not yet actually heard.

> These newly gained orchestral voices have rare and valuable qualities. In the high range they are soft yet penetrating; in the low range they are full and rich, and in the middle range they are very expressive. On the whole it is a timbre quite its own, vaguely similar to that of the cello, the clarinet and the English horn with a half-metallic admixture which gives it an altogether peculiar expression …
>
> Agile, suited just as well for rapid passages as for soft melodies and for religious and dreamy effects, saxophones can be used in any kind of music; but they are particularly suited to slow and tender compositions …
>
> Ingenious composers are going to achieve wonderful, still unpredictable effects by joining the saxophones with the clarinet family or by means of other combinations.[54]

[54] *Treatise*, 399.

Another interesting description was written at the time of the Universal Exhibition of 1855, in which Adolphe Sax was one of only four manufacturers who received a gold medal.

> The saxophones are soft and non-violent sounding instruments, played with a simple reed mouthpiece like the clarinet. These new voices contribute a rare and precious sound to an orchestra. Soft and penetrating in the high range, full and mellow in the low range, their medium range is something expressive and profound. In sum, it is the *sui generis* tone, likened vaguely to the sounds of the cello, the clarinet and the English horn, clothed in a half-brass tint giving it a particular accent all its own. The body of the instrument is a parabolic brass cone, with a system of keys. Agile, unique in its excerpts of a certain rapidity, almost as much in the gracious cadenzas and religious dreamy effects of harmony, the saxophone can be listed as an instrument with great advantages for all types of music, and especially for all slow and soft types.
>
> The tone of high notes in low-pitched saxophones is painful and arduous, while those of the low notes are on the contrary grandiose and calm, if not pontifical. All, especially the bass and baritone saxophone, have the ability to enlarge and diminish the sound in the low ranges, something we have not heard until now, something all their own and

almost organ-like in expression. The tone of the soprano saxophone is much more penetrating that that of a Bb clarinet and in C without having the piercing and often bitter sound of the small clarinet in Eb. One can say as much for the soprano. Skillful composers will, later on, take advantage of the wonderful part that the saxophone plays in association with the family of clarinets as well as in other combinations that will be discovered and exploited. This instrument is played with great ease; the fingering is similar to that of the flute and oboe. The clarinetists, already familiar with the mouthpiece, will become masters of the instrument in no time at all.[55]

[55] *Journal des Débats*, January 12, 1856.

Two of these early descriptions of the saxophone are especially interesting as Berlioz also provides the names of some of the very first performers on this new instrument. Here again we find the wonderful subjective prose of Berlioz.

The voice of the saxophone, whose family contains seven individuals of differing sizes, is midway between the voice of the brass instruments and that of woodwind instruments; it partakes also, but with much more power, of the sonority of the bowed instruments. Its principal merit, as I see it, is in the varied beauty of its *accent*; now low and calm, now impassioned, now dreaming, or melancholic, or vague, like the weakened echo of an echo, like the indistinct moaning of the breeze in the woods, and even better, like the mysterious vibrations of a bell, long after it has been struck. No other existing musical instrument, to my knowledge, possesses that curious sonority placed on the *boundary of silence*.

The *decrescendo* and the *piano* of the singers in the Imperial Russian Choir, those marvelous choristers alone, whom the good Lord certainly must envy of Emperor Nicholas, can give a precise idea of those delicious half-tones, those twilight sounds of the saxophone, which, applied with talent in the playing of some poetic inspiration, would plunge the hearer into an ecstasy that I can conceive of, and that I shall not try to describe. But, as yet, nothing has been composed for this new voice, and the young M. Verroust, one of the excellent bassoonists of the Opera, is, I believe, the only one who is making at this moment any attempt to master it. In this area, everything remains to be created in the teaching and the practice. As to the perfecting of the instrument itself, it is complete, and except for some working out of details, the task of the inventor, M. Sax, in this regard, is finished.[56]

[56] 'Exposition de l'Industrie,' in *Journal des Débats*, August 21, 1849.

...

M. Soualle, who, recently returned from London, has created a great sensation by making heard for the first time in Paris, with all its advantages, the saxophone, the *chef-d'oeuvre* of Sax. This instrument has expressive, incomparable qualities; the precision and the beauty of the sounds that it produces, when one well knows its mechanism, are such that it can, in slow pieces, challenge the most able singers. It weeps, it sighs, it dreams; it possesses the *crescendo*, it can weaken its voice gradually to the echo of an echo of an echo, down to total dusk. Within a few years, when the use of the saxophone will be spread among the players, composers will be able, by means of this admirable organ, to produce effects of which one has no idea at this moment.[57]

[57] *Journal des Débats*, April 13, 1851.

Berlioz, who criticized the Conservatoire for its lack of breadth in its course offerings, was delighted to call the attention of the public to the fact that the saxophone had been officially accepted into the curriculum.

Already the study of that precious instrument which [Sax has] invented has been admitted into the musical Gymnase; a special class of saxophone has been created in that establishment.[58]

[58] Ibid., February 14, 1847.

It was only a short time before these new students began to achieve extraordinary levels of success.

Sax, for his part, over impotent obstacles, pursues the success of his instrumental innovations, and eventuality has confirmed our predictions. Everywhere, effectively, Sax's instruments are operating a revolution in the military bands where they have been introduced. At the competition of the Music School, after only eight months of study, the saxophone, that instrument treated as a myth, as a chimera, whose very existence they were even going to deny, has won a First Prize, two Second Prizes, and two Runner-up Honors unanimously; the other instruments of Sax, saxotrombes and saxhorns, have also won several prizes and have obtained mention, all the more honorable as their teaching in the Gymnase classes has taken place for only five or six months.[59]

[59] Ibid., October 12, 1847.

The Trumpet

BERLIOZ LIVED AT A TIME when there was a greater diversity of instruments of the trumpet family in general use than at any time in the history of the instrument. In his *Treatise on Instrumentation*, Berlioz gives the reader his general current perspective on the three main classes of the instrument, the trumpet, the cornet, and the bugle.

> The tone of the trumpet is noble and brilliant. It is suitable in expressing martial splendor, cries of fury and vengeance as well as songs of triumph; it can render vigorous, violent and lofty feelings as well as most tragic accents.
>
> In spite of its proud and distinguished timbre, the trumpet has been degraded as few other instruments. Up to the time of Beethoven and Weber, all composers—not even excepting Mozart—limited its use to the low sphere of mere filling in voices or to a few commonplace rhythmic formulas, as vapid as they are ridiculous, and usually contrary to the character of the piece in which they occur. This trivial practice has at last been abandoned.[60]
>
> ...
>
> In France the cornet is very much in fashion at present, especially in certain musical circles where elevation and purity of style are not considered essential qualities. It has become the indispensable solo instrument in quadrilles, galops, variations and other second-rate compositions.
>
> Gay melodies played on this instrument will always run the risk of losing some of their nobility, if they possess any. If they lack it, their triviality is greatly increased. A commonplace phrase which might appear tolerable when played by the violins or wood-winds would become trite and vulgar if rendered by the blaring, obtrusive and coarse tone of the cornet.
>
> ...
>
> The tone of the bugle is not very pleasant, it has no distinction, and it is hard to play on it in tune ...
>
> Bugles appear to me to hold no higher rank in the hierarchy of brass instruments than the fifes do among the woodwind instruments ...
>
> In cavalry bands and even in some Italian orchestras one finds bugles with seven keys.

[60] These three, the *Treatise*, 285–336.

During his travels in Germany, Berlioz became aware of the advantages of the new piston trumpet and henceforth became one of those arguing for the acceptance of the new instrument in France.

> Prejudice for some time combated the use of cylindrical-valved trumpets so common today in Germany, but with less force, however, than has been brought to combat the new horns. The question of the stopped tones, which no composer uses for trumpets, naturally is left aside. They limit themselves to saying that the sound of the trumpet would lose, because of the cylinder mechanism, much of its brilliance, which is not the case, at least to my ear. Yet if a keener ear than mine is needed to distinguish a difference between the two instruments, they will agree, I hope, that the resulting inconvenience of that difference for the cylindrical-valved trumpet is not comparable to the advantage that this mechanism gives it to be able to run, without difficulty and without the least inequality of sound, a whole chromatic scale of two and a half octaves in extent. So I can only applaud the almost total abandonment into which the valveless trumpets today have fallen in Germany. We do not yet have in France any chromatic (or cylindrical-valved) trumpets; the incredible popularity of the piston-valved cornet has had victorious competition up to this day, but unjustly so, in my opinion, the timbre of the cornet being far from having the nobility and the brilliance of that of the trumpet. It is not, in any case, the instruments which we lack; Adolphe Sax presently makes cylindrical-valved trumpets, big and little, in all the possible pitches, common and uncommon, which excellent sonority and perfection are inarguable.[61]

[61] *Journal des Débats*, October 8, 1843.

Among his contributions as a newspaper critic, one finds many reviews of new books and educational materials reflecting a very wide field of interest on the part of Berlioz. The following reviews of new method books for the trumpet and cornet also reveal the depth of his own knowledge of these instruments.

> Since the creation of the trumpet class [at the Conservatoire], M. Dauverné, an able artist from the Opéra and the Société Concerts, was named Professor. It is to his teaching and to his examples that we owe the good players on this instrument that Paris possesses today in such great numbers. The *Method* that he has just published obtained a very favorable review in the Musical Section of the Institute. We could not do more to highlight the merit of this work than to reproduce here the terms of the academic report. Here they are:

The *Trumpet Method* of M. Dauverné has the double merit of being a complete treatise for the use of people devoted to the study of that instrument, and to present at the same time an interest and a usefulness which will make it searched out by composers. The properties, character, and resources of the trumpet are explained in this method with the greatest clarity, and concern not only the ordinary trumpet, its range as well as the particular range of each of its slides, but also all the chromatic trumpets, with pistons and cylinders. The numerous exercises composed by the author are very well written and consist of graduated lessons, of studies of diverse types arranged for two, three, and four trumpets. A historical *precis* precedes the Method and indicates all the transformations and modifications that the trumpet has undergone from Antiquity up to our times. This type of introduction bears witness to a great deal of research and knowledge. In the appendix that follows the introduction, the author transcribed several pieces composed in the last century for three, four, and even up to seven trumpets; these diverse works, curiously, attest to the surprising ability of the trumpeters of that epoch. This section of music validates the Method of M. Dauverné, the most complete work which has been written on this subject.

I shall add to this praise, so well merited, that the didactic and historical part of the work was edited in excellent terms, a rare thing, and that many facts contained in this volume can interest society and savants without any musical preoccupation. I shall direct one single reproach to M. Dauverné: he has not given the complete range of the instrument.

The trumpet, like all brass tubes, produces a first very low sound, followed by another still quite low, at an octave higher than the first. The author of this *Method* only admits the second note, that it presents as the first, by adopting as the second note, the note at the fifth, a fifth which is really the third note … I know very well that this fundamental pitch, which only speaks clearly on high-pitched trumpets, in G and in Bb only, really is not of any usefulness. But I am sorry that M. Dauverné did not indicate it because of the incertitude that that lacuna will leave in the minds of composers, who, for the most part, are ignorant of the phenomena of resonance of metallic tubes, and who only employ, consequently, brass instruments in an empirical fashion, without wondering about the causes that establish, between the great numerous and diverse members of that family, here the inarguable affinities, there the extremely sharp differences. This observation apart, I can only praise the *Method* of M. Dauverné, and I must recommend it to orchestral musicians desirous of playing that instrument a little better than cavalry soldiers, as well as to young composers who want to put to use with skill and knowledge one of the most characteristic voices of the orchestra.[62]

62 *Journal des Débats*, February 3, 1857.

…

Fine! There are names that represent something; and when virtuosos such as Alard Forestier take the trouble to state how people should play their instrument, one must believe them, because they are sure of what they say. Forestier is, really, one of the small number of instrumentalists who know how to sing and to do the difficult, resulting from the sound, the mechanism, and the style. He has written, on the three-valved cornet, a very beautiful and very good work that we recommend, not only to players, but even more perhaps, to composers, the majority of the latter writing for brass instruments, cornets, and trombones especially, almost by chance and without even knowing the range. Forestier has been a part of the Opéra orchestra for several months, where his solos in the ballets are causing a sensation.[63]

63 *Journal des Débats*, November 23, 1844.

As with each instrument, Berlioz was always observant of the leading performers and often mentions them in his writing and correspondence. For example, in a review of Meyerbeer's *l'Etoile du Nord*, Berlioz singles out the principal trumpet of the Opéra, 'Ricquier has done the trumpet aria in such a way as to make the whole theater applaud.'[64]

64 Ibid., February 21, 1854.

The most famous player in Paris was of course the great Jean-Baptiste Arban (1825–1889), Professor of saxhorn at the École Militaire in 1857, founder of the cornet class at the Conservatoire in 1868, and author of the book on trumpet playing which is still a fundamental course of study for the instrument. Berlioz recommended him to Liszt in a letter of 3 September 1853, and on one occasion contributed an original poem in his honor, referring to Boreas, the ancient God of the Winds.

Arban himself, that soul from Baden, has returned to Paris. He now is occupied with great difficulty in introducing into his Cadet Street Orchestra normal tuning, which the musicians, vexed at being obliged to buy new instruments, are calling *police tuning*.

Recently a newspaper was publishing a caricature of the great cornetist, ornamented with some light verse that he, Arban, took from me three or four years ago in Baden for a similar publication, and which he asks me to inflict upon you. Here they are:

Like Boreas puffing his cheeks
They praise you as being a great blower;
And quite often, of your cornet
They say: It certainly is a 'wind' instrument!
That's not true, and I beg to differ;
It's a larynx, if you please;
Wind blows and doesn't sing,
Arban sings and doesn't blow![65]

65 *Le Monde Illustré*, November 19, 1860.

In other reviews, as in the notice of a new overture by his friend, Georges Kastner, and of a concert in the Rue Cadet Hall, Berlioz offers more sincere praise and gives us a vivid picture of Arban's playing and its effect on the audience.

> M. Kastner has composed a complete and carefully developed overture. It contains a solo for *bugle à cylindres*, which M. Arban played beautifully.[66]
>
> ...
>
> A very beautiful orchestra, where are to be found first class artists ... directed with verve, I would even say with fire, by Arban. [The repertoire included] a cornet solo played by Arban, who mocks the impossible, whose lungs are forge bellows, who catches his breath only in order not to frighten his listeners; his success caused foot stamping by the audience.[67]

As much as Berlioz admired the cornet playing of Arban, he worried about the popularity of this instrument overshadowing the traditional trumpet. He makes a specific reference to this with respect to the areas outside of Paris.

> Trumpets are almost as rare in Lyon as they are in Marseilles, and we had great difficulty finding two. The valve cornet's charms, and the success that they have for the virtuoso in balls, become more and more irresistible for the provincial musicians. If we are not careful, the trumpet, in the big cities of France will soon, like the oboe, become a myth ... and in twenty years people will believe in it as much as they do the unicorns' horn.[68]

Berlioz mentions this again in a letter of 1857.

> You will have a difficult time finding the number of trumpets necessary to perform the *Olympie* march. You will find the poor replacement of wheezy cornets incapable of giving the high G and for which you will have to transpose the parts in F or the cornets in A. This would be a shame and all of the high notes would be missed or transposed an octave lower and would make no sense. Unless, since I have been in the provinces, a revolution has occurred, you know that I had such trouble finding two poor trumpets.[69]

[66] *Journal des Débats*, December 6, 1844.

[67] Ibid., April 7, 1861.

[68] *Revue et Gazette Musicale*, October 15, 1848.

[69] Letter to George Hainl, Paris, January 16, 1857, in *Correspondance*, 2201.

Before leaving Berlioz's comments on the trumpet in France, we must not forget his very valuable review of a new military application called *Le Téléphonie* (the first coinage of that word, by the way), for it is a rare extant description of this extraordinary system.

From the most ancient times, the trumpet was used as the principal means of field communication in the military. Because the effectiveness of this system of communication depended on the ability of the common soldier to recognize the trumpet signal in question, the signals themselves had to be fairly brief and few in number. During Berlioz's lifetime a violinist and composer named, Jean-François Sudre (1787–1862), developed a kind of Morse code for the trumpet which would theoretically permit extensive and detailed communication between field commanders. Sudre campaigned for years to have the military try his new system and finally a field demonstration was requested by the military authorities in Paris. Nothing so interesting, of course, could escape Berlioz's attention. Also of some interest here is the prediction by Berlioz of the coming of the age of the airplane.

LA TÉLÉPHONIE

M. Sudre is offering to us at this moment a new and sad example of the fate of all the inventors in our inattentive, forgetful, and jealous society. For twenty years he has been fighting, swimming against the current, speaking, writing, experimenting, proving that a discovery of the highest importance for armed forces of the earth and sea, and even also for the rapid propagation of pacific ideas, is in his possession. He is demonstrating that this discovery is his, that he alone made it, that he then perfected and simplified it to the point of making its use extremely easy, and for twenty years they have sent him about his business, they scorn him in a thousand ways, they make him promises not kept, in his regard they commit unspeakable abuses of confidence, and meanwhile, the poor man is using, in order to exist, his last resources and those of his friends. *La téléphonie*, or acoustical wireless, is the art of transmitting afar orders and news by means of a very small number of sounds combined in diverse manners. M. Sudre had at first employed for his sound signals the five principal notes of the bugle (do–sol–do–me–sol); now his is limiting himself to three sounds (sol–do–sol). With these three notes he can communicate 3,159 orders. Naval tactics can only give 1,815 (in clear weather), with the aid of 34 colors, flags, or pennants. Two minutes suffice [with this new bugle system] to send three orders nearly 2,000 leagues, approximately. These sound signals consequently can be transmitted at night as well as during the day, in a calm atmosphere, or in the middle of mist and rain. The use of the *téléphonie* costs nothing, since in the smallest army corps there are men whose duty consists of playing the clarion.

In very little time the *téléphonie* method can be taught in a sure manner to the monitors charged with the transmission of orders and of the interpreting of those which are transmitted to them; the inventor proved it many times. To the objection that they raised of the inability of the clarion to carry sound signals to great distances, M. Sudre answered with the following proposition: 'Give me eight cannons, and by their tones, I shall say what you would like to dictate to me, to a monitor possessing the secret of my method, and placed at the extreme limit of the distance where the noise of a size 12 ordinance gun can reach.' The experiment attempted in the presence of M. the Duke of Montpensier and several superior offices, and M. Sudre being assured that the eight artillerymen that were placed at this dispositions could fire at precise moments where he so commanded, he transmitted with a very great rapidity and a scrupulous fidelity, at an enormous distance the five following orders, improvised by M. the Duke of Montpensier:

> 'Rally the sharp-shooters!'
> 'The enemy is abandoning his position!'
> 'How much time can you stay in the position where you are?'
> 'Send us a company of light infantrymen!'
> 'Come to headquarters!'

The prince and all those in attendance were struck by such a conclusive proof, and warmly congratulated M. Sudre on the excellence and the obvious utility of his ingenious invention.

All the commissions and under-commissions, named thirty different times to assure that the proof was exact and the exactitude proved, having always obtained the same result, the Minister of War, the Minister of the Marine, the Academy of Beaux-Arts, a considerable number of officers and artists were obliged to agree that the solution to the problem was complete, the utility of that method evident, and its use as sure as it was easy.

After having used on his works both the small fortune that he possessed and twenty years of his life, M. Sudre, who moreover has always refused to communicate his secret to foreign powers, who would have paid him very well for it, M. Sudre, I say, had an evident right to an honorable recompense. One commission, named by a Minister of War finally concluded, several years ago, in an *eighth report* on the *téléphonie* method, that in exchange for the ceding of the inventor's secret to the government, a sum of *50,000 francs* be allotted to him as a national recompense. This offer being accepted without observations by M. Sudre, he, believing the affair ended, communicated without reservation the key of his method the the members of the commission. And yet the *téléphonie* method has not yet been adopted officially, and the fifty thousand francs have not been given over, and the poor inventor, in order to live, is driven to the last expediencies. If he is not indeed driven mad, he will die of hunger, and it is a true scandal whose causes the Assembly of the Representatives will shortly be called upon to examine.

But this is the fatal law to which the unfortunate, bent under the weight of a new idea, have, in all times and in all places, been subjected. Two years have not passed when they wrote before, here, very seriously to prove the impossibility of the use of the electric telegraph and the absurdity of the attempts made for its application. Yet, today human thought circulates lightening fast from one end of Europe to the other, and in the northern half of America, by means of this simple wire, so ridiculed, whose conduction power [they said] would be paralyzed by the simple contact with a magpie. Napoleon did not recognize the future of steam, and Fulton, in his eyes, was only a fool, whose claims and experiments obsessed him. Shortly, we will have the repetition of the same spectacle for a discovery even more important, that of the directing of lighter-than-air craft by means of a combination of propellers and inclined planes. Obviously, the latter, once demonstrated and put into usage, the relations of the diverse peoples who make up the large human family, will be entirely changed; an immense revolution will be accomplished whose fortunate consequences are incalculable. This is precisely why the audacious mechanic who wishes to give man wings capable of defying the winds and swooping over the storm, will experience a stronger and more obstinate resistance. He will be ruined, he will die in harness; he expects to, he is prepared for it. But navigation of the aerial ocean will nonetheless be opened to us sooner or later, and our descendants will be astonished then, because a corner of the veil had already been lifted, that their fathers, doubting for centuries the solution to the problem, should have been so seemingly determined to prowl the terrestrial crust like the most infirm animals.

Time is a great teacher, true, but man is a very stupid scholar.[70]

70 *Journal des Débats*, November 17, 1849.

Another young composer in Paris at the time of Sudre's demonstrations was Wagner, and the similarity between's Sudre's concept and the *leitmotiv* idea is inescapable.

In the end, it was Time itself which prevented the application of this system. By the time there was another major European battle, telegraph had become available and, of course, it was far superior to any form of trumpet language. Sudre's system ultimately became a purely rhythmic code for teaching the deaf, dumb, and blind.

For the most part, Berlioz found in Germany a level of orchestral trumpet playing which was unknown in Paris. As he comments in a letter to a fellow critic in Paris,

> However, you can easily find here great trumpet players who have a great sound and can reach the high notes with no problem. Cylinder trumpets are also easy to find and are excellent.[71]

[71] Letter to Joseph d'Ortigue, Leipzig, February 28, 1843, in *Correspondance*, 816.

He mentions this general level of playing again in his *Memoirs*.

> We … have no conception how far superior the Germans are to us in brass instruments, especially trumpets.[72]

[72] *Memoirs*, 321.

In his written commentary Berlioz points to a number of outstanding orchestral trumpeters he encountered in Germany:

> The Weimar orchestra is a good one … I especially noticed a superb valve trumpet (Sachse).[73]
>
> …
>
> The Hanover orchestra is good …; the valveless trumpets quite good; there is an excellent piston-valved trumpet; the artist who plays that instrument is named, like his rival in Weimar, Sachse [they were in fact brothers]—I do not know to which of these two to give the palm.[74]
>
> …
>
> The Dresden trumpets also have cylinder valves; to their advantage they can take the place of our piston-valved cornets, which they are not acquainted with there.[75]
>
> …
>
> In Mannheim I found … an intrepid pair of trumpets.[76]

[73] Ibid., 289.

[74] *Journal des Débats*, January 9, 1844.

[75] Ibid., September 12, 1843.

[76] *Memoirs*, 287.

Only in Hechingen, a small court, did Berlioz find German orchestral trumpeters who were distinctly weak.

> As for the trumpets [in Hechigen], they leave a little to be desired when they play.[77]

[77] Ibid., August 20, 1843.

In his *Memoirs* he uses stronger language, 'their incapacity is total.' In fact, for a performance he gave there of his *Harold in Italy*, he tells us,

I suppressed all the trumpet passages which were clearly beyond the players' grasp.[78]

[78] *Memoirs*, 281.

Berlioz mentions the German trumpet players again in their performance during the celebration in Bonn for the unveiling of the Beethoven monument.

When the statue appeared, applause, hurrahs, trumpet fanfares, volleys from cannons and bells, all this admiring fracas, which is the voice of glory in civilized nations, broke out again and saluted the image of the illustrious composer.[79]

[79] *Journal des Débats*, September 3, 1845.

For a performance in London of his *Roman Carnival Overture*, Berlioz makes a rather specific request:

You also know that in order to perform this piece we need two very loud valve cornets (Koenig and another one, for example), plus a Basque drum [tambourine], a triangle, and a pair of cymbals.[80]

[80] Letter to George Hogarth, Paris, February 23, 1853 in *Correspondance*, 1567.

In his final reference to the trumpet, in a newspaper review of 1862, Berlioz brings some matters to the attention of the conductor.

The trumpets were not in tune with the rest of the orchestra and their high notes of a range which was too high and made our sensitive ears suffer a true torture. We point this out to Mr. Pasdeloup.[81]

[81] *Journal des Débats*, January 28, 1862.

The Horn

FROM OUR PERSPECTIVE TODAY it would be easy to think that once the effective valve became available, horn players would immediately, and gratefully, abandon the hand stopping and begin using the valves in the modern fashion. But, oddly enough, in some places it took more than a half-century for horn players to figure out the possibility of simply 'fingering' the notes. As these players understood the valve, its invention was remarkable enough as a device to eliminate carrying around all those crooks—one could simply depress a valve and in effect create a new natural horn.

At first Berlioz seems to have had, to some degree, this perspective. He believed it was important to continue playing the instrument as a natural horn, in those cases where the composer had such an instrument in mind. To do otherwise would be the dangerous abuse he mentions in the following description of the instrument.

> The horn is a noble and melancholy instrument—notwithstanding the frequently quoted hunting fanfares. In fact, the gaiety of these flourishes arises rather from the melodies themselves than from the timbre of the horn. Hunting fanfares lose much of their gaiety if they are not played on real hunting horns—instruments of little musical value, whose strident and obtrusive tone differs greatly from the chaste and reserved voice of the French horn. However, by forcing the flow of air in the tube of the horn in a particular manner, its tone can be made to resemble that of the hunting horn. This is called making the tone *brassy* …
>
> Since the introduction [of valved horns] into orchestras, many composers have shown a certain hostility toward these new instruments because some horn players have used them in cases where an ordinary horn is indicated … This is, of course, a dangerous abuse; but it can easily be checked by the conductor.[82]

[82] *Treatise*, 259ff.

In a newspaper article of 1843 Berlioz addressed this issue again, now with the suggestion that a special new notational symbol be introduced by which a composer could *request* stopping, together with the question of the difference in timbre between the old and new style horns.

Several composers show hostility to the valved horn, because they believe that its timbre is no longer the same as that of the valveless horn. I experimented several times by listening alternatively to the open tones of a valveless horn and to those of a chromatic, or cylinder-valved horn; I swear that it was absolutely impossible for me to discover the slightest difference of timbre or sonority between the two. Moreover, they have made an objection, apparently well-founded, to the new horn, but which, however, it is easy to destroy. Since the introduction of that instrument (perfected, according to me) into the orchestra, certain hornists, using cylindrical-valved horns to play parts of the ordinary horn, find it easier to produce on open tones, with this mechanism, stopped notes, intentionally written by the composer. Actually, this is a very grave abuse, but it must be imputed to the performers, and not to the instrument. Far from it, since the valved horn, in the hands of an able artist, can produce not only all the stopped sounds of the ordinary horn, but also the entire range without using a single open tone. It is necessary to conclude from all this that the hornists must know how to use the hand in the bell, as if the valve mechanism did not exist, and that composers, henceforth, must indicate in their scores, by means of some kind of sign, which horn notes in the parts must be stopped, the performer not to produce open tones except for those bearing no notation.[83]

[83] *Journal des Débats*, October 8, 1843. In his *Memoirs* (p. 318) Berlioz changed the first word to 'a number of.'

As with the case of all the other wind instruments, Berlioz was aware of all important developments made of the Paris manufacturers. The following note is to a manufacturer, on Rue Serpente!, who was also a horn player in the Italian Theater and one of the people Berlioz consulted before writing the series of articles which became the *Treatise on Instrumentation*.

I thank you, Sir, for the information that you were so kind to give me concerning the cor à pistons. I would be remiss in not commenting on the improvements that you have made in the manufacture of this instrument.[84]

[84] Letter to A. A. Raoux, Paris, January 11, 1842, in *Correspondance*, 763.

Among his reviews, one finds two French hornists who were known to Berlioz by name as fine players, such as M. Rousselot of Paris.[85] Another, Baneux, Berlioz would later recommend to Liszt for the orchestra in Weimar.[86] Earlier, in an article, Berlioz introduces this player, who had been a student of Dauprat at the Conservatoire.

[85] *Journal des Débats*, August 9, 1839.
[86] In a letter of September 3, 1853.

We must note that among the newly arrived, M. Baneux, an excellent hornist, who, after having played a quite difficult service for a number of years for the Opéra-Comique, finally, tired of war, left the theater of the 'ariette nationale' in order to go give concerts in Italy. Good horns are very rare there, so M. Baneux has been received everywhere with the most flattering welcome. He is an excellent acquisition, for which we congratulate the Gymnase-Musical.[87]

[87] *Le Rénovateur*, October 12, 1835, p. 171.

On one occasion, Berlioz attended a recital at the Conservatoire which included a performance by Gallay, a horn player whose name is still well-known to horn students today through his educational studies.

Mr. Gallay then came to play for us a potpourri on themes from Bellini for horn solo. The talent of this virtuoso has been known and appreciated for some time. The opinion of the artists and amateurs is unanimous that Gallay has everything that a horn player of the first rank should have: excellent embouchure, stable intonation, in tune, purity of sound, and good taste in ornamentation.

We, however, would have much rather heard him play pieces truly composed by him, rather than this collection of arias whose principal flaw is that they have been overplayed at the moment. Singers, opera singers, and instrumentalists of all sorts no longer live but for the themes of Bellini. In the salons, in the great and small concerts, even in the streets—thanks to military bands, we hear only the Duet from the *Puritains*, or that of the *Capuletti*, or a melody from the *Pirate*, a cavatina from *Straniera*, etc. Nevertheless the horn solo of Mr. Gallay was nonetheless vigorously applauded, and justly so.[88]

[88] *Revue et Gazette Musicale*, February 14, 1836.

One horn player whom Berlioz heard from time to time, and could never take seriously, was Eugene Vivier.

Vivier has given his consent for a second concert—tonight he has doubled the price of the seats in the Italian Theater. He has an atrocious program and the house will be full.[89]

[89] Letter to Theodore Ritter, Paris, May 23, 1856, in *Correspondance*, 2130.

Vivier seems to have had a reputation not only as a hornist, but as an ingenious practical joker. His skill at playing chords on the horn can be measured by a conflict he had with a Bonn innkeeper who heard him playing the horn one night and tried to charge him for the three extra guests staying in his room.[90]

On his tour of Germany, Berlioz found that the modern valve horn was too brilliant in the upper range, unlike the old natural horn.

[90] Elwart, *Histoire de la Sociétés des Concerts*, quoted in *Memoirs*, 277, fn. 6.

> I only reproach the horns [of Frankfurt] for the very common fault in Germany of frequently rendering brassy the sound of forcing, above all, the high notes. That means of production denatures the timbre of the horn; it may on certain occasions, it is true, have an excellent effect, but it cannot, I think, be adopted methodically in the school of study of that instrument, and the slightly veiled, yet pure and noble sound of the horns in France seems to me infinitely preferable.[91]

In Stuttgart he found the same objection.

> One distinguishes among the horns [in Stuttgart] M. Schuncke; he, also, like his colleagues in Frankfurt, makes the sound of the high notes a little too brassy. The cylindrical-valved (or chromatic) horns are used exclusively in Stuttgart.

In Hechigen Berlioz found the two available horns, 'leave a little to be desired'[92] and in Hanover, 'the horns are not first rate, but they will do.'[93]

In Northern Germany, Berlioz found the transition to the valve type horn not yet completed.

> We noted among the horns M. Levy, a virtuoso who enjoys a beautiful reputation in Saxony. He, as well as his colleagues, used the horn with cylinder valves, which the court of Leipzig, almost alone among the courts in North Germany, has not yet accepted.[94]

In the Berlin Opera, this transition had only recently been made.

> The horns are splendid, and all of the rotary-valve variety—much to the regret of Meyerbeer, who thinks as I did until recently about the new mechanism.[95]

Finally, in a reference to a passage in his *Roméo et Juliette*, Berlioz warns another conductor,

> Now, I will point out that the quartet of horns have a very dangerous passage that you must always have rehearsed before the full orchestral rehearsal. The horn part in Ab is very difficult and sometimes the musician—due to fatigue or inability to do otherwise, plays this solo an octave lower. This must be avoided with care. The entrance of the Horn in Ab is also very dangerous and you must not allow the horns to slow down the movement.[96]

---

91 *Journal des Débats*, August 13, 1843. In his *Memoirs* (p. 271) he rewords the above passage to read, 'This kind of tone-production debases the natural quality of the horn.'

92 *Journal des Débats*, August 20, 1843.

93 Ibid., January 9, 1844.

94 Ibid., September 12, 1843.

95 *Memoirs*, 318.

96 Letter to Karl Eckert, Paris, October 28, 1856, in *Correspondance*, 2182.

The Trombone

In his *Treatise on Instrumentation* Berlioz earned a place in the history of orchestration by being the first composer to be concerned not with just technical matters but with the *character* of the various instruments. It was such an obvious consideration, especially beginning with the nineteenth century when feeling was becoming the recognized heart of music, yet he stands alone. Even today no writer has matched the dramatic description he offers of the trombone.

> In my opinion the trombone is the true head of that family of wind instruments which I have named the *epic* one. It possesses nobility and grandeur to the highest degree; it has all the serious and powerful tones of sublime musical poetry, from religious, calm and imposing accents to savage, orgiastic outbursts. Directed by the will of a master, the trombones can chant like a choir of priests, threaten, utter gloomy sighs, a mournful lament or a bright hymn of glory, they can break forth into awe-inspiring cries and awaken the dead or doom the living with their fearful voices …
>
> The character of the timbre of the trombones varies with the degree of loudness. In fortissimo it is menacing and terrifying …
>
> The pianissimo of the trombones, employed in minor chords is gloomy, mournful—I might almost say, horrible. Especially if the chords are short and interrupted by rests, one can imagine strange monsters uttering groans of repressed rage from a gruesome darkness …
>
> In my opinion no one has used this particular expression so dramatically as Spontini in his incomparable funeral march in 'La Vestale,' and Beethoven in the immortal duet of Leonore and the jailer in the second act of 'Fidelio …'
>
> Gluck, Beethoven, Mozart, Weber, Spontini and several other composers have fully comprehended the high value of the trombones. They have ingeniously employed the different characteristics of this noble instrument to depict human passions as well as to reproduce the sounds of nature. They have faithfully preserved its power, its dignity and its poetry. But to force it—as the majority of contemporary composers does—to howl in a Credo crude phrases more fitting for a saloon than for a church; to play as if to celebrate Alexander's entry into Babylon, when there is actually nothing more than a dancer's pirouette; to strum the tonic and dominant of a song in which a guitar could furnish an adequate accompaniment; to join its Olympian voice with the trashy melody of a vaudeville duet or with the frivolous noise of a quadrille; to prepare in the tutti of a concerto the triumphant entry of an oboe

or flute—all this means degrading a magnificent individuality, making a slave or a buffoon out of a hero, marring the sound of the orchestra, paralyzing all rational progress in instrumentation; it means destroying the past, present and future of art, committing a wanton act of vandalism and disclosing a lack of feeling for musical expression which comes close to stupidity.[97]

[97] *Treatise*, 305, 328, 329.

In one place, Berlioz points out an instance where a composer failed to use the trombone in music appropriate to its character.

> The prisoners' chorus in Gaveaux' opera, *Que ce beau ciel, cette verdure*, etc., is written about the same theme but, alas, compared with that of Beethoven it seems very gloomy and flat. Let us also remark that the French composer, who is very careful about using his trombones in the remainder of his score, lets them enter here, exactly as if they belonged to the family of instruments possessed of a timbre sweet, calm, and suave. Whoever can explain this strange fancy?[98]

[98] Hector Berlioz, *Beethoven by Berlioz*, trans. Ralph De Sola (Boston: Crescendo, 1975), 56. Originally published as *Voyage musical en Allemagne et en Italie*, 1844.

As in the case of each wind instrument, Berlioz seemed to have a remarkable and very precise knowledge of the practical characteristics of the trombone, as we can see in a letter relative to a future concert in Brunswick.

> I am so eager to have you hear the *Fantastique*, which you do not know yet, that I am taking great care with the rehearsals. Choose the members of the orchestra well and I ask you above all to pick good wind instrument players and four GOOD timpani players. Please find out whether or not you can get two trombones in Bb, because if the second and third trombones from the theater are in F, as is often the case in Germany, it will be impossible for them to play the low Bb and A pedal notes which are in the *Marche au supplice* and which produce a terrific effect that no other instrument can do in their place. We need tenor trombones in Bb or bass trombones in Eb, but these are extremely rare.[99]

[99] Letter to Robert Griepenkerl, Prague, April 1, 1846, in *Correspondance*, 1031.

It should also be mentioned that Berlioz knew of, and mentioned in a letter of 1 May 1854, a journal named *Die Posaune*.

The one aspect of trombone playing in Paris which seemed to puzzle Berlioz, was the fact that the bass trombone had not been promoted.

> The only cause of [the bass trombone's] infrequent use is the great fatigue experienced even by the most robust players …

> The tone of the bass trombone is majestic, awe-inspiring and formidable … Unfortunately, it is entirely lacking in Paris; it is not taught at the Conservatoire, and thus far no trombone player has been willing to study it.[100]

[100] *Treatise*, 299.

In making the point again, Berlioz proposes a substitute.

> We have a very much admired, and very admirable, opera that begins with a pedal note on Eb in the third trombone. The note exists on the bass trombone in use in Germany, but not on the tenor trombone that is in usage in Paris for the performance of the low part. Fortunately, the ophicheide sounds it, and the composer, with a little inattention, can delude himself, and believe he is hearing what he has written.[101]

[101] *Journal des Débats*, October 2, 1839.

He was delighted when he found at the Universal Exhibition in 1856 yet another invention by Sax which contributed to the lower range of the instrument.

> Mr. Sax has now completed the low range of the trombones. These instruments have always possessed, but it is not well-known, four low notes at the bottom of their scale, called pedal tones, a name most certainly given them due to the similarity to the pedals of certain organs. These notes are isolated by a weakness of an augmented fourth that separates them from the range produced by using the slide of the trombone. Mr. Sax removed this weakness and added five half-tones that were missing to the trombone's first low octave, giving it a wide range of three and a half octaves. The [new] system has only one piston incorporated into the body of the instrument and that the player moves with the thumb of the left hand, conserving all of the freedom of the right arm to move the slide. All orchestras should have at least one of these beautiful instruments.[102]

[102] Ibid., January 12, 1856.

While there were trombonists in Paris whom Berlioz admired very much, one, named Rome he recommended in a letter to Liszt of 3 September 1853. On the other hand we see a nice example of the sense of humor of Berlioz in a fictional player of a fictional orchestra who was quite a character! Probably this characterization epitomizes many authors of a great many method books for all instruments of this period which one can find in Paris libraries today.

> [Another] had a passion for the trombone. The trombone, according to him, would dethrone, sooner or later, all the other instruments. He was the prophet Isaiah. St. John would have played in the desert, in order to

prove the trombone's immense superiority. He bragged about having played, in haste, on a train, in a steam boat, and even while swimming in a lake twenty meters deep. His Method contains, presumably together with the author's exercises to teach trombone playing while swimming on lakes, as well joyful music for festivities and weddings. At the end of one of these masterpieces is written, 'When this piece is sung during a wedding, drop a stack of dishes at the measure marked "X"—it has an excellent effect.'[103]

103 *Les Grotesques*, 55.

Berlioz seems to have found a very high level of trombone playing in the German orchestras, although he apparently was not satisfied with the solo playing in his *Symphonie funèbre*. This is no surprise to me as this solo for trombone looks very easy on paper but because of the slow tempo becomes very difficult in performance.

You can tell [Swedish artist, Antoine Guillaume] Dieppo that I have not yet found his match and that the trombones which have tried to play the Oraison gave me a pain in the chest, not to mention the ears.[104]

104 Letter to Joseph d'Ortigue, Leipzig, February 28, 1843, in *Correspondance*, 816.

One trombonist in Germany, whom Berlioz considered a rare artist was Nabich. His description of his playing, heard over a ten-year span of time, suggests he would be a great artist today as well.

But what is even more impressive, is to hear M. Nabich sing on the trombone. One would never believe, before having the proof, that it would be possible to sweeten, as he does, the voice of this terrible instrument. M. Nabish is moreover such a master of the immense difficulties that the use of the slide presents, his embouchure so exact, his attack so precise, that the enormous difficulties do not stop him at all; he trills with the most complete ease and precision, and his diatonic scales tossed full-throated in the fastest movements, have something thunder striking because of their volume of sound and their impetuosity. M. Nabich, recently attached to the ducal orchestra of Weimar, is certainly one of the most precious acquisitions that Liszt may have made in order to increase and perfect the resources of that orchestra, which he directs lovingly.[105]

105 *Journal des Débats*, April 13, 1851.

…

M. Nabich is a first class trombonist, who plays his redoubtable instrument with passion. He has tamed it, made of it his slave; he constrains it, when he chooses, to sing, murmur, to forget its bellowing character. M. Nabich, moreover, is a virtuoso of style, and his phrasing is always in good taste. He plays on the slide trombone some passages that would be difficult even on the valve trombone. Unfortunately his rare talent, his persevering studies, his love and his faith will not be able to make the trombone cease to be the trombone, that is to say, a powerful orchestral instrument, not appropriate for intimate music nor for salon concerts.[106]

[106] Ibid., April 7, 1861.

In Stuttgart, Berlioz heard a trombonist who really interested him, among other reasons for his ability to play chords.

> The trombones [in Stuttgart] are of a beautiful intensity; the first (M. Schrade), who, four years ago, was part of the orchestra of the Vivienne concerts in Paris, is a remarkable talent. He knows his instrument intimately, plays works of the greatest difficulty, coaxes from the tenor trombone a magnificent sound: I could even say *sounds*, since he knows the means of a still-unexplained procedure to produce three and four notes at the same time, like that young hornist with whom all the musical press in Paris was recently preoccupied. Schrade, on a pedal point in a Fantasy that he performed in public at Stuttgart, sounded simultaneously, and to the general surprise, the four notes of the chord of the dominant seventh of the note Bb, disposed thus (from top to bottom): Eb, A, C, F. It is left to the acousticians to explain this new phenomena of the resonance of sonorous tubes; it is for the rest of us musicians to study them carefully and to use them to our advantage if the occasion presents itself.[107]

[107] *Memoirs*, 277.

During his tour of Germany Berlioz found many of the wind players in the smaller cities to be rather weak. In Hechigen everything seems to have been quite poor and with the trombone Berlioz was again disappointed. There was only one, who, 'leaves something to be desired when [he] plays.'[108]

[108] *Journal des Débats*, August 20, 1843.

In describing a performance of his own *Harold in Italy* in Hechigen, Berlioz mentions this player once more, now with some sarcasm.

> The solitary trombone was left to his own devices; but as he wisely confined himself to the notes with which he was thoroughly familiar, such as Bb, D, and F, and was careful to avoid all others, his success in the role was almost entirely a silent one.[109]

[109] *Memoirs*, 281.

In Berlin Berlioz finds the bass trombone again, and again wonders why the instrument should be missing in Paris.

> Berlin is the only German city I visited where you find the true bass trombone in Bb. We have not yet got any; Parisian musicians refuse to play an instrument that is so tiring to the chest. Prussian lungs are evi-

dently more robust than ours. The Berlin Opera has two bass trombones. Their combined volume of tone is so great as to obliterate the alto and tenor trombones playing the two upper parts. The aggressive tone of the instrument is indeed calculated to upset the balance of the three trombone parts as written by composers nowadays. There is no ophicleide at the Berlin Opera, and in works of French origin, which nearly all contain a part for it, they replace it not with a bass tuba but with a second bass trombone. The effect of having two of these formidable instruments, one above the other (the ophicleide part being frequently written an octave below the third trombone), is disastrous. You hear nothing but the bottom line; even the trumpets are all but drowned. When I came to give my concerts I found that the bass trombone was much too prominent—although in the symphonies I was using only one—and I had to ask the player to sit so that the bell of the instrument was laid against the surface of the desk, which acted as a sort of mute, while the alto and tenor trombonists stood to play. Only in this way could all three parts be heard. Having made repeated observations of the kind in Berlin, I now believe that the best solution in the opera house is after all the solution adopted at the Paris Opéra, and that is to use three tenor trombones. The tone of the small, alto trombone is thin and its high notes are poor; I would vote to exclude it too from theater orchestras. The bass trombone I would use only when the trombones were in four parts and there were three tenors capable of standing up to it.

If my words are not golden, at least you will grant they are rich in brass.[110]

[110] Ibid., 319ff.

The Tuba and Bass Winds

BERLIOZ LIVED DURING AN EXTRAORDINARY PERIOD of experimentation in the search for an effective bass member of the wind choir, a period of a few decades which begins with the serpent and ends with the modern tuba. Even by 1843, when he published his *Treatise on Instrumentation*, it was still a crowded field.

[The Alto Ophicleide]
Alto ophicleides are used in some military bands for filling out the harmony … their tone is generally unpleasant and rather commonplace.[111]

[111] *Treatise*, 138.

[Bass Ophicleide]
The sound of these low tones is rough; but in certain cases, under a mass of brass instruments, it works miracles. The highest tones are of a ferocious character, which has not yet been utilized appropriately. The medium range, especially if the player is not skilled, recalls too closely the tone of the serpent and cornett; … Nothing is more clumsy—I could almost say, more monstrous—nothing less appropriate in combination with the rest of the orchestra than those more or less rapid passages played as solos in the medium range of the ophicleide in certain modern operas. They are like an escaped bull jumping around in a drawing-room.[112]

[112] Ibid, 337.

[The Double-Bass Ophicleide]
The double-bass ophicleides, or monster ophicleides, are very little known. They might be useful in very large orchestras; but up to the present nobody in Paris has been willing to play them because of the volume of breath required. This surpasses the lung power of even the strongest man.[113]

[113] Ibid., 338.

[Russian Bassoon]
In my opinion it might be dropped from the family of wind instruments without the least injury to art … Russian bassoons are found in military bands. It is to be hoped that they will disappear forever as soon as the bass tuba becomes generally adopted.[114]

[114] Ibid., 348.

[The Bombardon]
This instrument, whose tones are very powerful, can execute only passages of moderate speed. Rapid runs and trills are unplayable on it.[115]

[115] Ibid.

[The Bass Tuba]

This is a kind of bombardon, whose mechanism has been improved by Herr Wieprecht, director of all music bands in the Royal Prussian guard regiments ... Its tone, incomparably more noble than that of the ophicleides, bombardons and serpents, has something of the vibrant timbre of the trombones. It is less agile, but more powerful than the ophicleides, and its range extends lower than that of any other instrument in the orchestra. Its tube, like that of the bombardon, produces the tones of the F major chord ...

Of course, this instrument is as unsuited to trills and rapid passages as the bombardon. It can play certain broad and slowly moving melodies.[116]

[Saxtuba]

Saxtubas are instruments with cup-formed mouthpieces and a mechanism of three cylinders. They have tremendous sonority and their sound carries very far; hence, they are extremely effective in open-air bands.[117]

Of these choices, the ophicleide was the most acceptable available instrument in Paris. In a letter regarding preparations for a concert in Frankfurt, Berlioz, in a list of instruments needed, seems to make no preference in requesting, '1 ophicleide or Tuba.'[118] On the other hand, the following year, in a similar list of instruments needed for a concert in Dresden, he seems to prefer an ophicleide.

For *Faust*, we will need ... one true ophicleide (if not, a tuba).[119]

During his guest appearances with German orchestras, Berlioz found this wide variety of instruments being employed. In two cities he found an ophicleide:

The Darmstadt orchestra is ... exceptional in possessing a first-rate ophicleide.[120]

...

[In Hamburg] I found a vigorous ophicleide, ...[121]

In two cities Berlioz had to make do with the Russian Bassoon.

[In Dresden] There are no ophicleides; the low part is held down by the Russian bassoons and serpents ...[122]

...

---

[116] Ibid., 339.

[117] Ibid., 401.

[118] Letter to Gustav Schmidt, Paris, July 15, 1853, in *Correspondance*, 1618.

[119] Letter to Karol Lipinski, Hanover, March 28, 1854, in *Correspondance*, 1714.

[120] *Memoirs*, 348.

[121] *Journal des Débats*, September 23, 1843.

[122] Ibid., September 12, 1843.

As to the ophicleide, there was none of any kind in Brunswick. I was offered as substitutes a bass tuba (a magnificent low instrument of which I shall be speaking in connection with the military bands of Berlin)—but the young man who played it did not seem to have thoroughly grasped its mechanism, being even uncertain of the true range—and after that a Russian bassoon, which the player persisted in calling a contrabassoon. I had great difficulty in undeceiving him as to the name and nature of his instrument, which sounds as it is written and, like the ophicleide, is played with a mouthpiece, whereas the contrabassoon, a transposing reed instrument, is simply a large bassoon which reproduces most of the bassoon's compass an octave lower. Anyway, the Russian bassoon was chosen to do the best it could in place of the missing ophicleide.[123]

[123] *Memoirs*, 310.

In another two cities an additional trombone was the only available bass wind.

[In Leipzig] The ophicleide, or rather the abject brass object masquerading under that name, bore no resemblance to the French variety, having practically no tone. It was therefore declared null and void and replaced, after a fashion, by a fourth trombone.[124]

[124] Ibid., 297.

...

In Mannheim ... there is no ophicleide; Lachner had attempted to devise a substitute for this instrument, which is used in all modern scores, by having a valve trombone made with a compass extending to bottom C or B. In my opinion it would have been simpler to send for an ophicleide, and much better from the musical point of view, as the two instruments have little in common.[125]

[125] Ibid., 287.

In Weimar he found a bombardon.

There was no ophicleide, a tolerably powerful bombardon being substituted.[126]

[126] Ibid., 289.

No doubt Berlioz was most pleased in the cities where he found the new tuba.

The Hanover orchestra is good ... There is no ophicleide; one can turn to good account some bass tubas from the military band.[127]

[127] *Journal des Débats*, January 9, 1844.

...

The bass tuba has completely dethroned the ophicleide in Prussia, so much so, as if, which I doubt, it had never reigned there. It is a large brass instrument, derived from the bombardon, and provided with a mechanism of five cylinders which give it, in the bass, a range that only exists on the organ; it descends to the low bass A, actually a fifth lower than the low E of the four-stringed contrabass.

These extreme notes in the lower range are a little vague, it is true; but doubled in the octave higher by another bass tuba part, they acquire a roundness and a strength of unbelievable vibration. The sound of the medium and the high range of the instrument is moreover very noble, it is not dull, like that of the ophicleide, but vibrant and very fitting to the timbre of the trombones and trumpets, of which it is the true contrabass and with which it unites supremely well. The actual range of the bass tuba chromatically includes four octaves from A to A, and even a little more. Wieprecht was the one who invented and propagated it in Prussia. A. Sax makes some now in Paris.[128]

[128] Ibid., November 8, 1843.

Percussion Instruments

BERLIOZ, WITH HIS EAR FOR SUBTLE ORCHESTRAL COLORS, was particularly frustrated with the simple and limited percussion instruments of the orchestras and bands of his day.

> Percussion instruments are really in their infancy, and the theory of resonance of sonorous materials that are struck, if one omits the metallic strings of the piano, has hardly been studied. This study, at least, has produced nothing up to this day. The percussion machines that we use in orchestras are, with the exception of the timpani, whose sonority, even, is so rarely good, and whose tonality is so imprecise and whose range is so limited, the instruments, I say, small drums, bass drum, cymbals and triangle, despite the advantage that one can get from them sometimes, are the remnants of Middle-Ages barbarism; they establish between our orchestras and Oriental chivari groups, a real bond, and for us a quite humiliating one.[129]

He mentions the 'Middle-Ages barbarism,' again in his *Memoirs*, when he describes going with his teacher, Le Sueur, in 1822, to the Chapel Royal where he heard a,

> traditional fanfare in five-time performed on a fife and an enormous drum—a grotesque noise worthy of the barbarity of the Middle Ages which begot it.[130]

The above passage was written with the broad public in mind, but in a private letter he mentions this same incident in quite a different light. A noble had written Berlioz with some question about a timpani passage in the *King Lear Overture*.

> Concerning the timpani passage in the Overture to *King Lear*, here is my response:
> Still in 1830, it was customary in the French Court under Charles X to announce the entrance of the king in his apartments, after Sunday Mass, by using an enormous drum which was beat in a bizarre rhythm of five beats, performed in the tradition of times past. That gave me the idea to accompany in this manner the entrance of Lear into his chambers for the scene where he splits up the state.[131]

[129] 'Exposition de l'Industrie,' in *Journal des Débats*, August 21, 1849.

[130] *Memoirs*, 51.

[131] Letter to Baron Wilhelm von Donop, Paris, October 2, 1858, in *Correspondance*, 2320.

In his contemplation of the possibilities for percussion, he imagines entirely new and rather extraordinary possibilities.

> Yet, the timpani, and it is truly irritating, are no longer even admitted into military bands. But if they were still to be found there, they would be of mediocre importance, in comparison with the unknown instrument that remains to be found, and whose effect I envision thus: imagine a great number of cymbals of different dimensions, each producing, instead of their frail and confused quivering, a tuned sound and of a beautiful timbre, although loud, and essentially metallic, like that of ordinary cymbals; there would result, from their simultaneous striking, a sudden harmony, quite similar, with an energy of vibrations incomparably greater, to a chord struck on several harps and pianos, in a small, local enclosure. Now, let us imagine an instrument capable of producing, not only one note or chord, but several chords struck in this way with reverberation, and the problem will be solved. Whether this be a collection of steel bars, of metallic plates, of any other totally different sonorous material *struck* so that this special sonority may be obtained, I do not know, but I believe in the possibility of such a result, and I imagine that one will find later the entire family of great percussive instruments, that will be, to those which we now possess, like Pan's flute to the organ, the timpani to the piano.[132]
>
> ...
>
> It would be worthy of that ingenious and indefatigable artist [Sax] to work now to fill the enormous *lacuna* left in the orchestra by the absence of a family of percussion instruments. We have in this genre only poor instruments (very useful undoubtedly on occasion, but of an inferior order, however), such as the timpani, the cymbals, the bass drum and the triangle. These sonorous devices produce, all of them except the timpani, noises and not truly musical sounds. Moreover, they each only sound one pitch, and in this respect, we are hardly more advanced than savages. Rich, varied, and sonorously precise percussion instruments, like the piano, but much more powerful, absolutely are missing for us. Blades, metallic stems, gut cords, bells of all forms and sizes, glasses, in all, a batch of sonorous bodies are appropriate to make excellent ones. It is a question of discovering the system, and certainly, sooner or later, they will discover it. It is really strange, that considering the unbelievable multiplication of wind instruments for a hundred years and more, and the marvelous development that the transformation of the clavecin into the piano has been worth to us, that one cannot perceive the slightest attempt to create in the orchestra something similar to which I am requesting. Art has not taken a single step in that direction since the first day.[133]

With respect to the timpani, Berlioz immediately recognized the importance of an invention to improve the tuning process.

---

[132] 'On the Reorganization of Military Bands,' in *Journal des Débats*, April 1, 1845.

[133] Ibid., October 12, 1847.

Regarding the tuning of the timpani, I should make mention of an important discovery for which the composers are indebted to M. Brod. That artist, whose handsome talent on the oboe is so justly famous, is, moreover, an able mechanic. He searched for a means to give the tuning of the timpani a swiftness and a precision that one feels the need for every day; he has succeeded by means of circles placed inside the metallic shell, and which a pedal moves from bottom to top in order to place them against the lower side of the skin. These concentric circles number six or seven; the smallest, the middle one, which thus reduces the diameter of the timpani by almost half, gives the sound of the instrument a clarity that the most violent tension of the skin alone could produce, and that one could only attain by means of turning the screw that is still used today, as slow as it is laborious. An instantaneous movement, like that needed for use on the piano pedals, suffices to change with the greatest precision the pitch of each timpani, something that is almost impossible with the ordinary apparatus, when the timpanist, obliged to get another pitch in the course of a piece, hunts, *all the while counting his rests*, to give to his instrument a different pitch, often quite far from that which the orchestra is sounding at that moment. Let us hope that the precious discovery by M. Brod will not be lost, and that in fifteen or twenty years the conductors of the lyric theaters will place the composers and the public in a position to profit by it.[134]

[134] Ibid., July 21, 1835.

We were surprised to read Berlioz arguing for the possibility of a timpanist playing three instruments. The use of multi-timipani by a single player was not unknown in the eighteenth century and Druschetzky wrote compositions for five and even six instruments making a scale possible. No doubt because Paris was not connected with the court *Harmoniemusik* tradition,[135] Berlioz was unaware of all the exciting things going on in Vienna and Budapest.

[135] Paris, on the other hand, was the center for publication of *Harmonie*-like works for the military.

For many years composers complained about the impossibility of using the timpani in chords in which neither of their two tones appeared, because of the lack of a third tone. They had never asked themselves whether one timpanist might not be able to manipulate three instruments. At last, one fine day they ventured to introduce this bold innovation after the timpanist of the Paris Opera had shown that this was not difficult at all … It took seventy years to reach this point![136]

[136] *Treatise*, 371.

In the same way, his comments elsewhere about timpanists suggest that Berlioz found this was not yet a highly developed art in Western European orchestras (even though the timpani had been played for centuries in the East). In a letter to England relative to a forthcoming concert there, he was worried about rather simple techniques.

> These timpanists are used for a piano effect in four parts at the end of the *Adagio* [of *Harold in Italy*] and must know how to play *soft rolls*.[137]

[137] Letter to George Hogarth, Paris, May 4, 1853, in *Correspondance*, 1596.

Indeed, one letter, written near the end of his life, suggests that perhaps it had been Berlioz's experience as a conductor himself to find percussionists in general rather undependable.

> You will, I think, begin your rehearsals [of *La Fuite en Egypte*] with the orchestra. On this note, I would recommend that you choose with great care good musicians for the percussion instrument parts. Without that, everything will be put in disarray by the rhythmic errors which the cymbal, bass drum, tambourine, etc., players never avoid making. And bad musicians, time and time again, only know how to make ridiculous noises. This is very dangerous.[138]

[138] Letter to an unknown person, May 3, 1859, in *Correspondance*, 2372.

Berlioz was especially sensitive to the over use of the bass drum and cymbal by composers of his time, as the reader will see below, under his comments relative to the use of percussion in opera. One of his chief dislikes was the custom of one player playing both the bass drum and cymbal, a custom one still finds today.

> Among the percussion instruments with indefinite sound the bass drum is certainly the one which has done the greatest mischief and has been most misused in modern music. None of the great masters of the last century thought of introducing the bass drum into the orchestra. Spontini was the first to use it in the triumphal march in 'La Vestale' and later in several pieces of his 'Fernand Cortez'; there it was in its proper place. But it is really the height of folly to use this instrument in all ensembles, in every finale, in the most meaningless choruses, in dance tunes and even in cavatinas—as has been done during the past fifteen years; to call the matter by its right name—it is really sheer brutality …
>
> It is needless to add that in these cases the bass drum is almost never used without the cymbals—as if these two instruments were inseparable by nature. In some orchestras they are even played by the same musician … This economical procedure is intolerable; the cymbals lose their sonority and produce a noise similar to the sound of a falling bag full of old iron and broken glass. The resulting music is utterly trivial and

devoid of any brilliance. It is perhaps suitable for the accompaniment of dancing monkeys, jugglers, mountebanks, swallowers of swords and snakes in public squares and at dirty street corners.

…

The conductor must resist the parsimonious custom … of having the cymbals and the bass drum played by the same musician. The sound of these cymbals attached to the bass drum … is only a vulgar noise fit for dance bands.[139]

[139] *Treatise*, 391, 419.

In a list of extra instruments needed for a performance in London, Berlioz asks for a cymbal player, adding, 'as he can not play the bass drum at the same time.'[140]

Apart from the kind of cymbal associated with the bass drum, Berlioz in his correspondence often speaks of cymbals in different pitches. These are presumed to be the ancient small cymbals, such as those used in dancing. A typical reference is found in a letter to Franz Liszt.

[140] Letter to Frederick Gye, Paris, May, 1853, in *Correspondance*, 1597. Unfortunately this tradition still exists in Europe. I have guest conducted bands where the cymbal was permanently screwed onto the bass drum.

I have also included, even though you did not say anything about them, two pairs of small cymbals in B♭ and F which are necessary for the Scherzo. They cost 100 sous for each pair.[141]

[141] Letter to Liszt, Paris, July, 1852, in *Correspondance*, 1505.

Not only was Berlioz concerned with the specific instruments used, but he also reveals a surprising understanding, for the time, of the details of performance technique. Regarding the small cymbals in the *Roméo et Juliette*, and a rare reference to the suspended cymbal, he writes,

To play these two pair of small cymbals, you should not slam them together, but rather hit the edges together like this [small diagram of two cymbals touching each other at their edges], and lightly—otherwise the sound is detestable. You will need two good musicians who will need to be placed close to the conductor. If not, if they are some distance away, they will always be later and later as the piece goes on. There is also in the middle of this piece a note hit on one of the large pair of cymbals, using a sponge-headed bass drum stick. The artist, once he has hit the cymbal, must then pick up the little cymbals. It is a real gymnastic stunt that you will have to explain to them by following the instructions in French in the score.[142]

[142] Letter to Karl Eckert, Paris, October 28, 1856, in *Correspondance*, 2182.

The following year, for a performance of *Benvenuto Cellini* in London, Berlioz requests cymbals somewhat larger for the dancers.

In addition, we also need at the theater two guitars, two tambourines, one small anvil, and several pairs of cymbals of medium size [*cymbales de moyenne grandeur*] for the dancers.[143]

[143] Letter to Frederick Gye, Paris, May, 1853, in *Correspondance*, 1597.

Of the concert gong, Berlioz observes,

The gong or tamtam is used only in compositions of a mournful character or in dramatic scenes of the utmost horror.[144]

[144] *Treatise*, 395.

Berlioz's comment in his *Treatise on Instrumentation* on the sound of the single tambour is somewhat surprising. On the other hand, his comment here perhaps explains why he always requested at least six for performances of his *Symphonie funèbre*.

The small drums proper are used almost exclusively in large bands. Their effect increases and becomes more noble in proportion to the number of drums employed. A single drum—particularly if used in an ordinary orchestra—has always appeared to me to sound low and vulgar.[145]

[145] Ibid., 397.

It should also be mentioned that Berlioz maintains in his *Treatise on Instrumentation* that it was Mozart who first named the orchestral bells, 'Glockenspiel.'[146] The name, if this is true, comes from the famous Salzburg bells which are called by that name.

[146] Ibid., 388.

In one of his letters, Berlioz makes it clear that his understanding of the percussion instruments, especially the unusual, colorful ones, was not limited to a question of instrumentation, but extended to a very modern understanding of their musical potential.

I kept the Basque drum [tambourine] because I had a talented artist to play it who did some solos that were delicately performed with an excellent, faraway effect better than anything we could have heard in Paris. Beyond that, the pianissimo of the timpani, in this concert hall, were barely audible, the contrast of the rhythms lost by leaving the timpani by itself. No, that was exactly what I wanted; for the tambourine is like the violin—you must know how to play it, not just hold it.

On his travels in Germany, Berlioz commented on the quality of the instruments and players he found. This remained true for the percussion area and he found in Hechigen a timpanist to be one who, 'leaves a little to be desired when he plays.'[147] For a performance of the *Harold in Italy* in this town, Berlioz suggests that even the local aristocrat was aware of the weakness of this player.

[147] *Journal des Débats*, August 20, 1843.

> The Prince stood beside the timpanist to count his rests for him and see that he came in in the right place.[148]

[148] *Memoirs*, 281.

In Hanover, Berlioz had problems with both the players and their equipment. Broken cymbals was apparently a problem he found in several German cities.

> The timpanist is mediocre; the musician having the part of the bass drum is not a musician; the cymbal player is not sure, and the cymbals are broken to the point that there only remain no more than a third of each.[149]

[149] *Journal des Débats*, January 9, 1844.

In recounting his experiences in Berlin, Berlioz mentions finally finding cymbals in good repair, in the opera orchestra. He also mentions, however, that the timpanist in this orchestra was not the equal of the one he knew in the Paris Opéra.

> The timpanist is a good musician but his wrists lack suppleness; his rolls are not sufficiently rapid. In addition, the instruments he plays are too small; their tone is feeble, and he is familiar with only one sort of stick, an ineffective kind half-way between our leather-headed sticks and the sponge-headed variety. In this respect the Germans as a whole are far behind the French. Even as regards technique, with the exception of Wieprecht, the director of military bands in Berlin who plays the drums with the force of a thunder-clap, I heard no player to compare in point of precision, rapidity of roll and delicacy of nuance with Poussard, the admirable timpanist at the Paris Opéra. Should I also mention the cymbals? Yes, if only to tell you that a whole and unblemished pair, neither cracked nor chipped, is extremely rare; I did not find one in Weimar, Leipzig, Dresden, Hamburg or Berlin. This always made me furious, and I have kept an orchestra waiting for half an hour and refused to start the rehearsal until they brought me two brand new cymbals, suitable vibrant and Turkish, to show the kapellmeister whether I was wrong to object so strongly to the ludicrous fragments of broken plate offered to me under that name. There is no denying that certain parts of the orchestra are still maintained at a shockingly low standard in Germany. They do not seem to realize what can be done with them and what is done in other places; the actual instruments are poor and the players have no conception of their full possibilities. This is true of timpani, cymbals and even bass drum, as well as of cor anglais, ophicleide and

harp. But the real responsibility lies with the composers and their style of writing. By never demanding anything of significance from these instruments, they make it almost impossible for their successors who write in a different style to achieve anything with them.[150]

[150] *Memoirs*, 320.

Berlioz also mentions the difficulty of finding a sufficient number of timpani for a performance in Berlin of his *Requiem*.

Fortunately I had forewarned Meyerbeer, and he had already begun his search for the necessary forces before I arrived. The four little brass orchestras were easy to come by; we could have had thirty if we had wanted them; but finding the drums and the men to play them was a problem. Eventually, both were mustered with the help of the excellent Wieprecht.[151]

[151] Ibid., 336.

Part 2
On Wind Instrument Manufacture

On Wind Instrument Manufacture

BERLIOZ'S INTIMATE KNOWLEDGE of the instruments of the orchestra did not spring entirely from his needs as a composer, however brilliantly that knowledge is demonstrated in his scoring. It was also fostered by the fact that he was fascinated by, and liked, the instruments themselves, as he mentions in his *Memoirs*.

> I enjoy the company of musical instruments. If I were rich, I would always have a grand piano, two or three Erard harps, some of Sax's trumpets and a collection of Stradivarius violins and cellos in the room with me as I worked.[1]

[1] *Memoirs*, 71

It is no surprise therefore to find among the wide range of topics which Berlioz covered as a contributor to several newspapers his reviews of the periodic industrial exhibitions which included displays of musical instruments. Apart from his own artistic interests, this entire subject of wind instrument manufacture must have been interesting to him because of the extraordinary developments which took place during the nineteenth century. And beyond this, one of his friends was Adolphe Sax, the most important and innovative wind instrument maker of the century.

The earliest of these exhibitions which he reported on was an 'Exhibition of Industry Products,' in Paris in 1839. He reminds the listener of the tremendous developments in woodwind manufacture during the second and third decades of the century, in particular the improvement of the flute, an instrument many composers had complained about.

> Among the orchestral instruments, the only ones that were marked out for, and that received, ingenious improvements in our epoch are the woodwind instruments. The flute, clarinet and the bassoon, especially, had conserved serious faults of tuning or of sonority, which the ability of virtuosos only imperfectly succeeded in disguising. Boehm's discovery for flutes, which consists of a new way of boring the holes for the player's fingers, and which unfortunately also completely changes the adopted fingerings, has put onto the right track important improvements for bassoons and clarinets. We have already had occasion to speak

of this beautiful invention; soon, thanks to it, the instruments whose scales were the most defective will be of irreproachable intonation and of a perfectly equal sonority in all registers.[2]

[2] *Journal des Débats*, May 28, 1839.

In the same review, he mentions some of the new and unusual wind instruments which makers brought forward for display. The numbers of entirely new wind instruments which appeared in Paris between 1825 and 1850 even exceeded, in number, any comparable period during the sixteenth century.

> One can often hear in *Guido* and *Gingora* M. Leclerc's mellophone, which has something of the flute, the horn, the clarinet, and the basset horn all in one: we cannot explain the interior mechanism of it, M. Leclerc having kept the secret of it to himself up to the present time.
> M. Paris's harmoniphone, or clavier oboe, is destined to replace in provincial orchestras the oboes and English horns whose study is very bad and very little cultivated outside of Paris. In this respect, it is one of the most useful inventions.[3]

[3] Ibid.

Ten years later Berlioz reviewed another industrial exhibition, with what must have been an even larger collection of wind instruments. For Berlioz's sensitive ears the sound of it all, of hundreds of people trying out the instruments, was almost too much even for him.

> As for the new improvements that the Exhibition of 1849 has brought forth in broad daylight, … I certainly did not learn that they invented something for the organ, nor for the melodium, harmonium, psalmodium, antiphonium, cacophonium, and other bastards of the organ, which mew, sigh, yap and wail around their father, so as to make the Exhibition Hall, where these noisy little brats are collected, inaccessible to musicians. When to these cries there comes at the same time the noise to be added to the chopping of two or three pianos delivering themselves over to their *fantasies* in different keys, you really have something that gives to the musician gifted with some aural sensitivity an attack of *delirium tremens*, or an attack of death-dealing cholera. Talk to me about Pleyel's exhibition space, and about Erard's; there no one is improvising. These gentlemen do not need to make the public appreciate their products; everybody knows their excellence. They are enclosed in a superb silence whose charm visitors appreciate as much as majestic eloquence. If I had a piano to buy, I would go to Erard's or Pleyel's for the single reason that neither one of them is having his instruments heard at the Exhibition.

Sax is in the same situation, very fortunately. Can one imagine, really, a small army of virtuosos, blowing, all at the same time, into the big and little brothers of the baritone sax-horn, into the sons of the bass saxophone, into the mothers and grandmothers of the Eb clarinet, without counting the wild children of the tuba, the impolite race of trombones, with or without valves, and the raucous family of simple horns and valved horns? That *concert asiatique* would render in vain all architectural precautions to assure the solidity of the buildings of the exhibition; we would see beams snap, walls crack, curtains torn every which way, and roofs cave in with a thousand disasters. But, no, these brass and wood stentors remain silent under their glass tents, and the strollers can circulate in all security. The manufacturers next to Sax's, the prudent friends of that ingenious artist, imitate his silence …

One of them, M. Barteh, has adapted to the simple horn a slide similar to that on English trumpets, and which might have been useful before the invention of valves and cylinders. Also one notes among the works of one exhibitor, brass instruments, along with all their pitches, or interchangeable bodies. This innovation has as its only result that of making the instrument heavier or more fragile, without improving its timbre and without making the blowing easier. There is also a fanfare trumpet that compressed air activates. Had not this idea been suggested by the project of a gigantic organ driven by steam, whose theory M. Sax allowed us to consider several years ago?

Among woodwind manufacturers, M. Godfroy is noted for his flute specialty. From the celebrated M. Boehm, he has just bought a new patent of an invention for a flute in metal that they say is excellent.[4]

4 'Exposition de l'Industrie,' in *Journal des Débats*, August 21, 1849.

In 1851, Berlioz himself served on the jury of an exhibition held in the Crystal Palace in London. For days he and the jury of ten had to judge on the basis of listening each and every instrument, keyboard, strings, and winds. He complains to his sister,

> I take advantage of this moment of rest they are giving us today to send you some of my news. I have been in London for a month and a half and am very busy with the crazy job of examining the musical instruments displayed at the Exposition. There are days when I am filled with discouragement and when I am on the brink of returning to Paris. No one can imagine such an awful job like this one I am burdened with. They have me actually *hear* each wind and brass instrument. My head is splitting from having to listen to these hundreds of vile machines, each more defective than the next, with but three or four exceptions.[5]

5 Letter to his sister, Adele, London, June, 1851, in *Correspondance*, 1417.

6 *Journal des Débats*, December 30, 1851.

In one of his newspaper articles[6] Berlioz gives a long and interesting discussion of how the jury voted and the international politics involved. In another journalistic recapitulation of this experience, he complains of inadequate financial support from his own government, for these long days of adjudicating.

> The members of the jury who defended at London the interests of the French producers ... went to London with their faith in a promise of recompense of expenses incurred by the stay which M. the Minister of Commerce had given to them. Two weeks before the end of their work, the payment of this indemnity was suspended for several among them, without a single line having been written to them to warn them about it; they learned about the suppression of appointments in the offices of M. Saltandrouze, by chance and not officially. They abandoned them there without due process, like unfaithful valets. So that, not being able, at the height of their debates, to betray flatly the interest of the members by abandoning their post, these members of the jury had to stay in London during all the rest of the session, at their own expense. *The minister had no more money, the credit was exhausted*. Oh! How worthy of France is such a procedure! How much love of their country and respect for its institutions this is calculated to inspire in artists, savants, industrialists! And what confidence strangers are going to have in our commerce on seeing the Minister of this same commerce declare bankruptcy so flatly! Now M. de Casablanca, on whom the claims caused by the debt that his predecessor had contracted rebounds, responds to the betrayed members of the French jury that *if there remains, at the end of the operations relative to the Exposition, anything left over of the disposable funds,* he will share some of it with them. Marvelous, this caps it; the jury members now have the appearance of soliciting a favor. They are somewhat beggars, they are extending their hands. And if there is not anything *left over* to give them, they will discharge them with these words: 'Go away, good people, go away, we can do nothing for you.'[7]

7 Ibid., November 27, 1851.

In 1855 a great exhibition was held in Paris and on this occasion Berlioz pays tribute to the Paris instrument makers for their half-century of extraordinary work.

> I only have left to discuss the Medal of Honor of M. Triébert. This manufacturer showed a great number of excellent oboes, wonderful English horns, to which he has adapted the system employed by Boehm for flutes, and which doubtless, will soon be adopted generally for all pierced instruments. Due to this, is the extremely good intonation of those of M. Triébert, and the complete freedom of their mechanism. M. Triébert, moreover, thanks to a very ingenious machine he has invented, makes reeds of a superior quality; and we all know that the reed does even more for or against good sonority in the oboe than strings do for the violin.

Although the flute and clarinet manufacturers of Paris did not obtain any First Class Distinction, I believe I must say here that they succeeded in their specialty to a very remarkable degree of ability. The clarinets still leave something to be desired for the intonation of only two notes; they are, nevertheless, the best that may be found. As to the flutes of Paris, constructed according to Boehm's system, but of wood and not of silver like those of German manufacture, one must agree that they are exquisite and really irreproachable. The bassoon is still out of tune, very much out of tune ... It is an instrument of great utility that the composers would never consent to do without in orchestras; try then, you manufacturing gentlemen, to improve it. In Paris they also make excellent horns, with or without valves, good trumpets and excellent trombones. We have even heard a new kind of steel cymbal, of a sonority incomparably more distinguished, less strident, less harsh to the ear than those of the Turkish cymbals. In general, the percussion instruments have remained stationary: they are still quite crude affairs ...

To sum up, the means of action available today to music are as numerous as they are varied, and if it has not managed to accomplish the prodigies that we believe her capable of through the ingenious use of its vast resources, it is because real protection has not yet been accorded to it, it is because people have not fully recognized the importance of certain questions of teaching, it is because music with us is supported rather than loved and respected, finally, it is because we are in this regard in a twilight state of civilization. However that may be, the instrument manufacturers in Paris are today the finest in the world, it would be difficult to contest that; they are progressing; let us therefore recognize that they certainly deserve great merit from the musical society.[8]

8 Ibid., January 15, 1856.

Berlioz was again a member of the jury and again complains of the fatigue.

I will be there at that hour, that is if the Exposition Jury has not reduced me to a slave by that time. We have heard 387 pianos, at least 400 brass instruments, without counting the slew of flutes, the bunches [*fagots*] of oboes and others commonly called bassoons, and bellowing troops of melodiums, of harmoniums—we are exposed now to the wind of the organs and of the calomnie. We will have suffered like martyrs during two months and that is all that came of it.[9]

9 Letter to Camille-Marie Stamaty, Paris, September, 1855, in *Correspondance*, 2029 bis.

Berlioz published at this time a somewhat bitter satire of his experience of an adjudicator, in the form of a report from an imaginary adjudicator from a country in the South Pacific.

To: Her Majesty Aimaia Pomare, Queen of Taiti, Simeo, Oushine, Raiatea, Bora-Bora, Toubouai-Manou and other islands from which the works recently received the silver medal from the Universal Exhibition.

Majesty, Gracious Queen,

    Exhibition soon over. Our friends the judges and I are happy.

    A lot of suffering, a lot of sweating to hear and judge musical instruments, pianos, organs, flutes, trumpets, drums, guitars and tom-toms. Great anger from the judges against the nations that produce pianos, organs, flutes, trumpets, drums, guitars and tom-toms.

    Men of the nations all want to be first and ask that their friend be last; offer us to drink kava, to accept fruits and pigs. Us, judges very angry and still without fruits nor pigs say they were the best producers of pianos, organs, flutes, trumpets, drums, guitars and tom-toms. Then after we studied, examined, listen all, we the true judges, obliged to go and get other judges who have not studied, examined or listened all the instruments of music and ask them if we find the best. They say no. So again we leave angry, very angry, and want to leave France and the Exhibition.[10]

---

[10] *Journal des Débats*, October 19, 1855.

Adolphe Sax

A SEPARATE SECTION IS WARRANTED for the greatest musical instrument maker of the nineteenth century, Adolphe Sax. This great inventor, constantly struggling against the legal, and not so legal, opposition of his jealous competitors, had no more vocal champion than Hector Berlioz. Berlioz's newspaper articles, many of which have never before been translated, trace this relationship over nearly twenty years. Berlioz's writing on the saxophone itself, we have presented above.

The first article Berlioz wrote on Sax, the man, was an introduction to the Paris musical society written in the year Sax moved to Paris.

> The art of instrumentation, stationary for a long time, has made in the last twenty years veritable progress, thanks to the movement imparted by some great masters. People have oddly abused their inventions, it is true, and the excess of imitators often made excellent spirits miss the time when that musical power was yet unknown. But, what is not abused? ... and what force does not offer any dangers? ... Can one say because of that that it is necessary to regret the invention of power, detonating metals, that of steam machinery, and the domination that man has succeeded in exercising over the electric flow? Philosophically, the thesis of the advantages of ignorance can be sustained; but it is none the less evident today in the nature of the human spirit to hunt the unknown, to record each important discovery and to conserve it at any cost.
>
> So we abuse in vain now musical instruments, use them senselessly, without reserve nor art; the nature of beautiful effects that they can produce being known, the public and the artists are fatally led to desire them, even to demand them in every new production. This art of instrumentation would necessarily, in developing, lead and determine the progress of instrument-making. One can judge the immense step that it made it take by comparing, for example, the pianos of Erard and Pape to the *clavecins* of the last century; the flutes one used in the time of Devienne to the current flute of Boehm; the old clarinets to those made today by M. Adophe Sax, and the shapeless and horrible *serpent* of our cathedrals to the magnificent, serious instrument that this young and able artist has just invented.
>
> Stringed instruments are far from having followed the same route; today we have hardly any string-makers that one might compare with the Amati, the Stradavari, etc.; no doubt that results from the very

nature of their art, which was thrust from the beginning to a high degree of perfection. The making of wind instruments, on the contrary, had remained almost in its infancy; it is today on a path that cannot fail to lead to magnificent results. Mr. Adophe Sax, of Brussels, whose works we have just examined, doubtless will have contributed powerfully to the revolution that is in the making. He is a man of penetrating mind, lucid, obstinate, persevering despite any obstacle, of great cleverness, always ready to replace, in their specialty, workers incapable of understanding and incorporating his plans; at one and the same time, a calculating man, an acoustician, and if needed, a foundry-man, machine-turner, a chiseler. He knows how to think and act; he invents and he executes. Before speaking of his new instrument, let us speak of the improvements that he has just brought to the family of clarinets.

By lengthening somewhat the tube of the soprano clarinet towards the bell, he made it gain a half-tone in the lower register; consequently, it can now sound the Eb. The Bb of the middle register, bad on the old clarinet, is one of the best notes on the new one. The trills from Bb to B natural or to C in the middle, from A to Bb in the bass, from E to F sharp, the arpeggios in octaves of F to F, and a number of other unplayable passages, have become easy and of good effect. People know that the notes of the high register were a horror to composers and to players, who did not dare make a use of them except rarely and with extreme precautions. Thanks to a little key placed near the mouthpiece of the clarinet, Mr. Sax made these sounds as pure, as soft, and also as easy, as those in the middle. Thus the high Bb, that they did not ever dare to write, now comes out without needing either preparation or effort on the part of the player; one can attack it *pianissimo* without the slightest danger, and it is at least as sweet as that of the flute. In order to remedy the inconveniences that dryness of one part and humidity of another necessarily caused in the use of mouthpieces, depending on whether the instrument has gone several days without being played, or on the contrary, had been used too long a time, Mr. Sax gave to the clarinet a gilt metal mouthpiece that augments the brilliance of sound and does not undergo any of the variations common to wooden mouthpieces. The clarinet has better range, uniformity, ease, and intonation than the old one, without changing the fingering, except to make it easier, in a few cases.

The new bass clarinet of Mr. Sax resembles the old in name only. In the latter, the holes are suppressed and replaced by keys that are adapted to points corresponding to the nodes of the vibrations; it has twenty-two keys. Above all, what distinguishes it is a perfect intonation and a temperament identical in all the nuances of the chromatic scale. Its augmented diameter produces a greater volume of sound without the playing of the octaves and of fifths being paralyzed, nor even hindered; again, this advantage results from a key-hole pierced near the mouthpiece of the instrument. Its range is three octaves and a sixth; but it is not to the immensity of this scale that one must attach the most value; obviously the bass clarinet is not destined to figure in the high registers, the beauty of its low sounds alone gives it such a great value. Since the tube is very long, the player standing, the bell of the instrument almost touches the ground; hence, a very annoying stifling of the sonority, if the able manufacturer hadn't thought to remedy it by means of a concave metallic reflector that, placed beneath the bell, prevents the sound from being lost, directs it wherever one wishes, and augments the volume considerably.

Composers will owe a great deal to Mr. Sax when his new instruments have come into general usage. May he persevere; encouragement from the friends of art will not be lacking.[11]

[11] 'M. Ad. Sax,' in *Journal des Débats*, June 12, 1842.

The above article was the one which also first introduced the saxophone to the public, which has been quoted above. The following year, Berlioz mentions the inventor's work in the field of brass instruments.

The able manufacturer Adolphe Sax currently established in Paris, has demonstrated superabundantly the superiority of [the cylindrical valve] over that of piston valves, almost completely abandoned presently in all Germany, while that of cylindrical valves for horns, trumpets, tubas, bass tuba are coming into general usage. The Germans call those to which that mechanism is applied *instruments a soupape* (Ventil horn, Ventil trompetten).[12]

[12] Ibid., August 20, 1843.

Two months later, Berlioz writes for the first time about the unbelievable struggles which Sax was undergoing in attempting to establish himself in Paris.

Would you believe that this young and ingenious artist has a thousand difficulties in making himself understood and in maintaining himself in Paris? People renew persecutions worthy of the Middle Ages against him, and which bring back to mind the doings of the enemies of Benvenuto Cellini, the Florentine sculptor. They lure away his workmen, they steal his plans, they accuse him of madness, they direct lawsuits at him; with a little more audacity, the would assassinate him. Such is the hatred that inventors always provoke among those of their rivals who invent nothing. Fortunately the protection and the friendship with which M. le Général de Rumigny has constantly honored the capable manufacturer have helped him to sustain that miserable fight up to the present; but will it always suffice? ... It is up to the Minister of War to put such a useful man, of such a rare specialty, into the position of which he is worthy because of his talent, his perseverance, and his efforts ... A commission of three hundred trumpets and of one hundred bass tubas, addressed to Adolphe Sax by the minister, would save him.[13]

[13] Ibid., October 8, 1843.

By 1844 Sax was beginning to enjoy success in Paris, as well as abroad. Berlioz mentions, in support of his friend, Sax's success in a visit to England.

> Sax is returning from England, where his new instruments have been appreciated as they deserve, not only by the artists, but by the first amateur of the three kingdoms of the Royal Arts Society, Prince Albert, who has received the ingenious artist with the most flattering cordiality.

This continued success and acceptance was celebrated in a party given for Sax by his workers in 1846. Berlioz joins in the enthusiasm.

> Everything was in an uproar in the Neuve-Saint-Georges Street last week: sky rockets were fired off above the roofs of the houses, colored fireworks, bursting, shattered the air; then, after all this pyrotechnical fracas, came the songs and instrumental fanfares. These were Sax's numerous workmen who were celebrating Sainte-Cecile Day and were having a party for their employer. They gave him, besides this occasion, a present suitable to make him remember how many obstacles he had to conquer and the persecutions he had to endure in order to win out with his ingenious discoveries. They gave him a bronze statue of Galileo in the Inquisition prisons, repeating, with that patience which strength and reason, sure of itself makes possible, *Et pur si muove* (and yet it does move). Well yes! … *si muove*; these good people chose the epigraph very well, and the cause of their master is going to triumph hugely. Despite all the intrigues, the cabals, the protests, even the infamies of which they made themselves guilty in order to hinder him and to ruin him, his work is recognized as excellent and precious by all who are intelligent and who are men of good faith. Sax's instruments are spreading by the thousands, not only in our military bands, but even in the foreign armies of the old continent, in England, and in the New World. Three hundred harmonious Cyclops, wresting with brass, polishing ebony and ivory, melting pewter and silver, hardly suffice, in his immense Paris and Melun workshops, for the task which incessant orders coming from all parts of the world impose upon them these days. *Et pur si muove!* and in six years a beautiful revolution will have been accomplished in our military bands, and Sax's fortune will be made.[14]

14 *Journal des Débats*, November 29, 1846.

In February 1847, Berlioz writes a very interesting article describing Sax's thoughts about expanding the string instrument family.

Without mentioning Sax's gigantic steam organ, dedicated to presentation of public-event music, and which would be to contemporary organs as the great bell of Notre-Dame is to small bells, let us cite his instrumental program for a complete modern orchestra, a program that an able composer could turn into such a brilliant account. A. Sax proposes, in order to give to a very large symphonic orchestra all resources and all possible sonority, to bring to diverse families of wind instruments, a numerous family of strings, bowed, composed of very high pitched violins, sopranos, altos, tenors, baritones, basses, and contrabasses of diverse sizes and different pitches. That is to say that while assuming the contemporary, non-transposing violin in C, there would be other violins, higher and lower, with pitches differing from the above-mentioned, always remaining, however, tuned in fifths, that would become transposing violins in F, in G, in Bb in B, like the wind instruments, and, while augmenting the range of the scale, the lower especially, would give, by the intercrossing of open strings, a much greater sonority to the instrumental mass. It is only to be feared that inattentive composers, employing all the diverse instruments at the same time, might destroy the character appropriate to each pitch, and might so render, in certain cases, very annoying, the qualities of sonority of the new orchestra of stringed instruments. For example, in the current state of the orchestra, the sound of Bb minor is dull and lugubrious; obviously, if, for a piece that must have this character, the composer uses violins appropriate to make it, by the intervention of open chords, less lugubrious and less dull, that change will not be to the advantage of the effect which is intended to be produced. But a similar inconvenience is inherent in all the branches of the art, no matter what they may be; everywhere abuse, or unintelligent and misplaced usage, may be found side by side with the ingenious use of the resources at the disposal of the art. These inventions will make composition more difficult, more arduous, but also, the effect produced more powerful and more beautiful when the composer knows how to turn to a good advantage the diverse means which I mention, and which M. Sax is working to furnish him with.[15]

15 Ibid., February 14, 1847.

In the same article, Berlioz reminds the readers that the inventor must work while constantly being harassed by lawsuits.

Sax is not yet free of the lawsuits directed at him by his manufacturer rivals. Using as a pretext that he is a bachelor and Belgian, while they are French and fathers of families, they would like to make him withdraw the patents that he has acquired for the perfecting of wind instruments. These are two very good reasons, no doubt, but it is doubtful that they will prevail before the judges if the plaintiffs have no others to give. The works of Sax are excellent for art in general and for military music in particular. Thanks to the talent and to the perseverance of this artist, thanks to the questions that he has raised, to the discussions that he has initiated, to the measures that he has provoked, our military bands are obviously on the path of progress on several accounts. The regimental groups are a little more numerous than they were before; soon military musicians, more able, armed with better instruments, will be both better paid and more highly esteemed ... And while they harass him by claiming his inventions, he continues to elaborate other plans, to ripen other projects, which, at a time less far distant than we perhaps think, will see realization.[16]

16 Ibid.

Two years later Berlioz reviews some of the new brass instruments which Sax has invented and points to the recognition which the inventor has begun to enjoy throughout Europe and even in North America.

M. Sax, despite the obstacles of every kind that they never stop raising, continues to advance and achieve the perfecting of numerous families of wind instruments that he has adopted and those which owe the light of day to him. Principally, such are the families of the sax-horn, the saxotromba, and the saxophone. The first includes six members: the soprano, the alto, the tenor, the baritone, the bass, and the contrabass. The sax-horn possesses a timbre that is loud and sweet at the same time. The saxotromba has less voluminous sounds; it comes from the sax-horn and several other well-known instruments, such as the horn, the trumpet, and the trombone. M. Sax has standardized and brought back to a single fingering the fingerings of these diverse instruments, those old as well as those of which he is the inventor, so that in knowing how to play any one of them, one knows how to play all the others. If one plays, for example, the valve cornet, one also can play the valve horn, the valve trombone, trumpet, bugle, all the sax-horns, and all the saxotrombas. But, just because the fingering and the mouthpieces of these beautiful instruments is easy, it does not follow that one may play them so as to bring out all their advantages, make them agreeable or powerful in solos and in ensembles, in a word, so as to prevent them from losing any of their value without persevering and well-directed studies. And that is one of the most annoying prejudices that one must indicate in our musical state. A violinist, a cellist, a pianist, will work ten hours a day for eight or nine years before acquiring an ordinary talent, sometimes even without acquiring it, and yet one expects a soldier, on the other hand, who hardly knows how to read his notes, not to play detestably on the sax-horn or trombone six months after one has put one of these instruments in his hands! Hence, doubtful intonation, the instability and bad quality of the sound, vulgar phrasing, and consequently, a bad impression of the instrument. Give to a scratcher an admirable Stradivarius violin, he will grate on your ears, if you have any; Sax's most marvelous brass instrument, under the same conditions, cannot fail to do the same. It is necessary to know from Mssrs. Forestier, Dieppo, and Caussinus, how much time they labored before playing the cornet, the trombone and the ophicleide as well as they play them. The same question could be posed to Mssrs. Distin, who, armed with five Sax instruments, have acquired such a great reputation in France, in Germany, and in England, and who are chasing about with so much success in North America. One remembers, even in Paris, where everything is quickly forgotten, the marvelous purity of the sounds that these able artists drew from the brass instruments, the sax-horn especially, their intonation, their softness and singular charm, which lent them the sweetest and tenderest melodies … Whoever would have thought, eight years ago, that French instruments, played by Englishmen, would tour the world so to the sound of applause? Yet those were only instruments more or less close relatives of the trumpet. One can expect quite different results from the young family of saxophones, when true virtuosos, such as those that I have just named, will cause to be heard, the way that they should be heard, this new and magnificent instrument. Effects that composers may draw from it in the orchestra, especially for musical drama, are incalculable.[17]

[17] Ibid., August 21, 1849.

We may be sure that Berlioz took great pride in the success which his friend, Sax, was now enjoying so widely. We may also grant him the right to take some small credit for helping in support of the inventor.

We have been among the first to recognize the importance and felicity of the attempts of [Sax] and to predict the revolution that he was going to bring into the making of instruments … The revolution that we were announcing has been accomplished today and the most ardent detractors of M. Sax have been reduced to making use of his instruments, or imitating them.[18]

[18] Ibid., January 17, 1851.

In April 1851, Berlioz wrote a letter of introduction for Sax to take to London. Berlioz wrote part of this letter in rather hesitant English (here in italics), but the reader will understand what he was trying to say.

I present to you my friend Sax, who is coming to London to display his magnificent instruments. *Be kind for him as you are, and any thing more, for every one; as you are for me. I will be in London* in a few weeks. I am part of the commission sent by the Minister of Commerce to do a report on the Exposition.[19]

[19] Letter to Morris Barnett, Paris, April 25, 1851, in *Correspondance*, 1405.

In an article the following November, Berlioz informs the Parisian readers of Sax's singular success in the exhibition of instruments in London.

> The success of Sax at the [London] Universal Exposition was great. The crowd thronged every day around his display in the Crystal Palace, to listen avidly to these new instruments with such soft and energetic voices. As to the opinion of the musical jury regarding him, at the end of a few days, it was fixed: English, German, American, Swiss, and French jury members all were promptly in agreement. 'Sax,' they said, 'is the first in the manufacture of all the instruments that he has shown; and, moreover, he is an incomparable inventor.' The first place medal consequently was conferred unanimously and without discussion. Independently of the new members that he introduced into the instrumental family, some rebellious timbres that he conquered and purified, he has obtained in the ensemble of the manufacture of instruments in brass a degree of perfection which people did not believe it possible to attain. Before Sax, that industry was in its infancy; in a few years of intelligent efforts, he has lifted it to the highest degree of perfection.[20]

20 *Journal des Débats*, November 27, 1851.

In this same article Berlioz reveals that Sax not only has invented the new family of saxhorns, but has now authored his own Method book for them.

> M. Sax has just published a *Method* for saxhorns of all dimensions, that is to say for the entire family of that instrument which he fathered. People often confuse the sax-horn with the saxophone, another invention of the able manufacturer, and still more precious, in my opinion. The sax-horn is a brass instrument with a mouthpiece and pistons, like trumpets and cornets. It has a brassy, energetic sound, which adept players manage to sweeten, nevertheless, whose effect is excellent in military music. The saxophone, to the contrary, although also of brass, is an instrument with a single reed, with a keyed mechanism, and is played with a clarinet mouthpiece. Its timbre, sweet, tender, expressive in the highest degree in the high and middle registers, takes on a majesty somehow pontifical in the low register. From the grouping of the soprano, alto, tenor, bass, and contra-bass saxophones will be born admirable effects, entirely new, to which the composers, doubtless, will not be long in having recourse to as a resource, and whose importance in dramatic music, especially, will become considerable.
>   For the saxophones, as for the sax-horns, whatever may be the instrument which one uses, be it low, middle, or high, the fingering is the same. And, this practice is not one of the least advantages that Sax's system presents. Thus, the player who plays the sax-horn or the high saxophone can without difficulty play the lower instruments of the same family after very little time on an exercise destined only to acquire

the habit of new proportions. Sax's *Method for Sax-horn*, published by Sax, contains a multitude of excellent exercises, very well conceived and logically graded. It will give eminent service to teaching in the military bands of the cavalry and of the infantry, where the use of that instrument today is very nearly general.

By 1854, Berlioz could happily report that Sax had finally begun to enjoy freedom from the legal harassment of his competitors.

> Sax has just brought back his victory from l'Alma. He won in the final instance all his lawsuits; his imitators are condemned to pay him considerable damages and interest. They are fleeing in all directions, tossing in their footprints thousands of counterfeit saxophones, tubas, and sax-horns.[21]

21 Ibid., October 11, 1854.

In his review of the results of the Universal Exhibition in Paris, in 1855, Berlioz surveys the broad success of Sax's work.

> The immense superiority of Mr. A. Sax over his competitors lies in the production of brass instruments, his improvement of many weaknesses, and the newly created families all contribute to his public notoriety. We only speak here of the instruments which, due to their recent introduction into the artistic world, are the least well-known …
>
> Mr. Sax has also produced families of sax-horns, saxo-trombas and saxo-tubas, necked-brass instruments with conical mouthpieces with a three, four or five cylinder mechanism. Their sound is round, pure, full, even, resounding and perfectly homogeneous throughout the entire range of its scale. They are typically found in almost all French military bands. The extremely high pitched sax-horns and the so-called band basses (*contre-basses d'harmonie*) are soon to be found in all large orchestras or symphonies.[22]

22 Ibid., January 12, 1856.

In 1859, both Berlioz and Sax became patients of a homeopathic doctor, Jan Hendrick Vriès, who had achieved some extraordinary cures for patients whom traditional doctors had been unable to help. Berlioz details these relationships in the following letters.

> Our friend Sax for the last four years has had an awful time with his upper lip, and little by little, a horrible tumor formed—a cancerous mushroom—infected and full of pus. Velpeau, Ricort, and all of the other princes of science declared that he was lost, that the only hope was to cut off his left cheek, but without any assurance that the disease had

not spread elsewhere. Sax refused this horrible operation—we introduced him to Dr. Vriès, who after inspecting the tumor said, 'There is still time—I will save him.'[23]

...

Our friend Sax for the past four years has had pain in his upper lip and this pain has become an awful bulb, somewhat like a mushroom, that you cannot look at without horror. All of the doctors of Paris declared him dead. They proposed amputating his left cheek, but without any assurance of success. The cancer, according to them, could very well come back after such an awful operation, and spread to his neck, or the nap of his neck.

Sax refused this mutilation. He wrote his will and put his affairs in order and waited to die of gangrene in the next 24 hours.

We took him to an Indian doctor who looked at him and said that there was still time and that he could save him. And, by using his medicine, he stopped all pain. He went by 3 or 4 times each day to gauze the cancer and the bump slowly dried and after two months fell off and Sax is, today, a cured man. And all of his friends, who thought he was a condemned man, kissed him as a condemned man coming back alive from the gallows. One of my neighbors on the Rue Pigalle had a cancerous bump on his elbow and Dr. Vriès started to cure him—the day before yesterday, I met this man's valet who told me that the bump had dried and fallen off and that he was resting to regain his strength.

Ah! Our poor sister would be full of life today if only the Indian doctor had been in France at the time when her cancer was eating away at her!!!

I don't dare to tell you to come and consult him for your daughter, because it does not deal with cancer. However, his science is not restricted only to curing these awful ills. He heals me and I think you should take Josephine to see him.

I stop writing to start crying again. Ah, to die, to die, rest, silence![24]

...

I have been sick for the past six weeks. I am starting to feel better, thanks to the help of the famous Black doctor [from an anonymous pamphlet which appeared in Paris in 1859, 'The Black Doctor by a White Doctor,' announcing that traditional medicine had proved that the secret herbs used against cancer were nothing but aloe leaves soaked in rum, and his pills, potassium and sugar.], the savior of our friend Sax. You know that Sax had skin cancer of the upper lip and was pronounced terminal by all the medical community in Paris. And here he is radically cured—his awful bump on his lip has fallen off, and has not come back. Next Thursday Sax's friends, and in great number, will give Dr. Vriès a dinner at the Hotel du Louvre which promises to be very gay and even musical.[25]

---

[23] Letter to his Brother-in-law, Camille Pal, Paris, January 7, 1859, in *Correspondance*, 2342.

[24] Letter to his Sister, Adele, Paris, January 10, 1859, in *Correspondance*, 2345.

[25] Letter to Auguste Morel, Paris, February 13, 1859, in *Correspondance*, 2354.

The banquet Berlioz mentions in the last letter was given on 17 February 1859. It was attended by a very select gathering of people, which included not only Berlioz, but the composers Meyerbeer, Vieuxtemps, and Ambroise Thomas, together with the famous French historian, Kastner, and the critic Joseph-Louis d'Ortigue.

A review gives the musical program, but does not mention the *Hymne pour la consecration du nouveau tabernacle*, which Berlioz wrote at this time in honor of Dr. Vriès and which may have been performed on this occasion. This review, however, does reveal that it was Berlioz who made the toast to the conductor of the band which performed.

> The friends of Adolphe Sax, and there are a good number of them, had a debt to pay; an homage to offer to the famous doctor who, by sparing him any painful operation, gave him back to us perfectly safe and sound at the end of a few months. With the care of MM. J. Mathieu, E. Mareuse, and Léon Kreutzer, a banquet had been prepared in the magnificent rooms of the Louvre Hotel, and more than one hundred twenty guests were united there last Thursday.
>
> It was a family celebration in which literature and the arts had their representatives; musical art especially counted there, illustrations of all kinds, and because of a special favor, the admirable band of the Guides, under the direction of its excellent conductor, M. Mohr, had been authorized to go to Paris to play during the banquet the best pieces of its repertoire: the 'March' from the *Prophet*, and the fourth *March with Torches*, of Meyerbeer; the Overture to *Zampa*, of Hérold; a *Fantasy on Quentin Durward* of Gaevaert; the *Carnaval romain Overture* of Berlioz; a *Fantasy on Moses*, of Rossini; a duet from the *Magician*, of Halévy; the *Overture to Oberon*, of Weber; a *Fantasy on Giralda*, of Adam; another on the *Black Domino*, of Auber; the *Overture of Caïd*, of Thomas; and a *Waltz* of Lanner. Bravos and acclamations of enthusiasm greeted the most part of these works, which lost nothing of their grandeur, of their finesse, nor of their charm in passing through the voices of sax-horns and of saxophones.
>
> Towards the end of the banquet, M. J. Mathieu rose first, and in a few words was able to interpret the sentiments that animated the entire assembly; fraternal friendship for Adolphe Sax, recognition and admiration for Doctor Vriès, his savior. M. the Baron Taylor came next, and in an improvisation doubly Oriental in his lively colorfulness, as well as in its fortunate brevity, greeted the marvelous doctor, having arrived expressly from the country which sent us before only its poetry and its diamonds, to bring us something more precious yet, to give back health,

life to an artist who needed all his strength to achieve his brilliant mission. M. Berlioz spoke also a few words in the honor of M. Mohr and of his harmonious ensemble.[26]

[26] *Revue et Gazette Musicale de Paris*, February 20, 1859.

The complete text of Berlioz's remarks is not known, but one newspaper reported that his remarks ended with the toast, 'To M. Mohr, a lively man, we drink to Mohr.'[27]

[27] *La France musicale*, May 22, 1859.

It is difficult to find information on Mohr, although various notices in the Parisian newspapers regarding his performances seem to confirm that he was held in high regard. For example, another issue of the *Revue et Gazette musicale* (2 October 1859), in reporting on a massed band concert given by some 1,200 players in the Palace of Industry, notes,

> These festivals offer proof through which the superiority of our military bands over all others in Europe becomes more and more evident. The bands of our Imperial Guards are of the first rank and among the names of their skillful conductors that of M. Mohr occurs most often.

We should also observe the one of the compositions performed during the banquet described above, was a band arrangement of Berlioz's *Roman Carnival Overture*. As there is a manuscript fragment of such a band arrangement in the State Library, Berlin (Ms.1550), which carries Mohr's name, we may suppose it was his version which was performed on this occasion before the composer.

There is an interesting report in an American journal (*Dwight's Journal of Music*, 14 January 1854) of an earlier performance of this arrangement under Mohr's baton. This report is appropriate to mention here as it names the band as the 'Société de la Grande Harmonie,' and mentions that this organization was founded by none other than Sax. The program is given as: *Overture, Carnaval romain*, Berlioz; *Fantaisie sur Giralda*, Adam; *La Marche aux flambeaux*, Meyerbeer; *Overture to Zampa*, Hérold; *Air varié*, Mohr; and the *Benediction des poignards*, Meyerbeer; together with some vocal solos with piano and a work for piano and cello.

The Meyerbeer *Marche*, better known in English and German as a *Fackeltanz* was one of four such original works for band, although all were scored by Wieprecht. The report in *Dwight's Journal of Music* includes a description of how these

Torch Dances were used in the actual court wedding ceremonies, which we quote on behalf of those conductor's who have always wondered about their background.

> The composition of this kind of morceau belongs to a ceremony of the middle ages, and is still observed in the German Courts. On the day of the betrothing of a prince or princess royal, it is the custom for each of the betrothed, with torch in hand, to make the tour of the salon several times, and to pass before the sovereign; the prince giving his hand to a lady, and the princess hers to a gentleman of the Court. All the guests follow the betrothed, who change partners each time until all present have walked round the room with them. The march is always written in 3–4 time. It is a slow movement in the style of a polonaise, and scored for a military band.

Berlioz's final published tribute to Sax celebrates the inventor's arrival at last to a position of unquestioned acceptance by Parisian society.

> And finally, there he is, our courageous, our unvanquished friend Sax, there he is, almost free of lawsuits: he has won them all, after eighteen years of litigation! He keeps only a half-dozen small ones to stay in practice. All his rivals, all his imitators, or almost all, are down, and he leaves them there. He has had them condemned to pay him some half-millions, and they pay it. Gold showers upon him; one would take him for a tenor. I do not feel that I would be capable of his determination, I confess it. In his place, instead of always moving with that same slowness of the watch-hand, up to the moment of triumph, reduced to despair by my despoilers, I would have used my last hundred francs to buy a pair of dueling pistols to blow their brains out.
>
> Everything comes to him who can wait. Ah! if we could live two hundred years, a double-century, those of us men of ideas (because we have ideas, even sometimes *idées-fixes*), and if, on the contrary, *the others* would die in thirty or forty years and pass on as imbecilic as they arrived, with what ease we would overcome the obstacles, the lawsuits, the imitators, the gainsayers, the bad conductors, the stupid professors, the bad amateurs, the insulters …[28]

---

28 *Le Monde illustré*, November 24, 1860.

Part 3

On Bands

On Bands

THE LOCAL MILITIA BAND IN LA CÔTE-SAINT-ANDRÉ would have not only been the first band Berlioz heard, but also the first music he would have heard. These small militia bands, formed throughout Europe, including England, where they were called Volunteers, came into being at the beginning of the century as a by-product of the Napoleonic Wars. It was a way for the local population to put on uniforms on Saturdays and make believe they were not missing out on the greatest events of their lifetimes.

La Côte-St.-André hired a new militia band conductor in 1817, named Imbert. His contract required him to rehearse the band twice a week and to make himself available for teaching private lessons in the village. One of his students was the young Berlioz.

An extant inventory of instruments[1] owned by the militia band in April 1821 (seven months before Berlioz left for Paris), gives us some idea of its size:

[1] *Memoirs*, 537.

2 clarinets in F
7 clarinets in C
2 piccolos
1 bassoon
3 horns
1 'old-style' horn
1 'old-style' trumpet
1 valved trumpet
1 trombone
bass drum
cymbals
triangle

For the rest of his life, Berlioz followed the development of bands with interest, especially in France. His writings contain his observations on their instrumentation, performance techniques, their repertoire, their conductors, and, sometimes, just his reactions to listening to them.

I stayed listening to the Austrian Emperor's hymn, which was being played, far away in the Kiosk of the Konversationshaus [in Baden], by the Prussian military band; and the strains of which were carried to me in fragments from the depths of the valley, by the south wind. How touching is that melody of good old Haydn![2]

[2] 'Address to the Academy of Fine Arts of the Institute,' September 11, 1861, in Berlioz, *Mozart, Weber and Wagner*, 88.

In another place he mentions hearing this same Hymn by Haydn in Prague, a performance in which he noticed the quality of the band as well.

On the subject of military bands, I listened to the band of the regiment at that time garrisoned in Prague playing, between noon and four o'clock on a public holiday, a hymn composed by Haydn for the Austrian Emperor. This tune, with all its touching dignity and majesty, is so simple that I was scarcely in a position to judge the quality of the performers. An orchestra which could not play satisfactorily such a piece would be, in my opinion, made up of musicians who don't know how to play even a scale. Only, these musicians played in tune, which is an extraordinarily rare thing among military bands.[3]

[3] *Revue et Gazette Musicale*, August 27, 1848.

In his *Treatise on Instrumentation*, Berlioz makes a few observations on the sound of the band and its instruments, based on years of experience listening to them. It seems clear that he heard a certain nobility in the nineteenth-century band's principal melodic voice, the clarinet.

If the mass of brass instruments in grand military symphonies suggests the idea of warriors covered with glittering armor, marching to glory or to death, so do numerous clarinets playing in unison seem to represent loving women who, with proud glances and deep affection, exalted by the sound of arms, sing during the battle, crowning the victors or dying with the vanquished. I have never been able to hear military music from afar without being profoundly moved by that feminine quality of tone present in the clarinets; it has always left me with impressions similar to those received when reading ancient epic poems.[4]

[4] *Treatise*, 209ff.

It is interesting that Berlioz made such a strong distinction between the clarinet and the oboe in this regard.

The theme of a march, however vigorous, beautiful and noble it may be, loses its nobility, vigor and beauty when played by oboes. It may possibly preserve its character if given to the flutes; played by clarinets, it almost invariably retains it full power.[5]

[5] Ibid., 164.

In his treatise there are three paragraphs which address the very top heavy sound of the early nineteenth-century band, with its variety of small flutes and small clarinets, and with Berlioz's suggestions for balancing the sound somewhat.

> The small clarinet in high F, formerly much used in military music, has been displaced almost completely by the clarinet in Eb. This is justified by the fact that the latter is less like screaming, and is quite adequate for the keys ordinarily used in compositions for band. Clarinets lose proportionally in purity, sweetness and nobility as their key is raised higher and higher above that of Bb.
>
> ...
>
> It is a great pity, and of great detriment to wind instrument bands, that bassoons should be entirely excluded from them, whereas the rough and harsh sound of these orchestras could be considerably softened by an appropriate number of large and small bassoons ... The contrabassoon is very valuable in large bands, but only few players care to use it. Occasionally it is replaced by the ophicleide, whose tone, however, has not the same depth, since it is in unison with the ordinary bassoon, and not in the octave below ... I think, therefore, that in the majority of cases it is better to do without the contrabassoon part than to replace it in such fashion.
>
> ...
>
> The effect of a great number of bass tubas in a large military band is beyond imagination. They sound like a combination of trombones and the organ.[6]

[6] Ibid., 198, 206, 339.

Regarding the repertoire he heard, there is no question that Berlioz found little enjoyment in the noisy fanfares of the trumpets. More than once he complains along the following lines:

> The flourishes played on clarion, consisting exclusively of the three notes of the common chord, are necessarily of a boring uniformity bordering on vulgarity ...
>
> At best, [the clarion and fife] can serve the purpose of leading recruits to the parade, although in my opinion our soldiers—young or old—ought never to listen to such music; for there is no reason why they should become accustomed to the vulgar.[7]

[7] Ibid., 336.

This being the case, in his review of a fanfare played on a very formal social occasion, Berlioz writes a clever sentence—one capable of several understandings, according to the inclination of the listener.

> When it comes to fanfares, military bands, such as those Mr. Schiltz has recently had us hear with such success at the National Guard Ball, are in their natural element ...[8]

[8] *Journal des Débats*, June 28, 1837.

In this same review, although we may suppose Berlioz had little interest in the dance tunes commonly played by bands of this period, he recommends one as being a better example of this kind of music—although the entire reference may just be for political reasons vis-a-vis the dedication. It was the husband of this lady to whom Berlioz would dedicate his *Symphonie funèbre*.

> Speaking of the [National Guard] Ball, I can not conclude without mentioning the military quadrille, dedicated to MMe Duchess d'Orléans, by M. Tolbecque, a piece full of verve, which was also played with success at the Court, in the city, and at the opera; we recommend it to the enthusiasts.

On the other hand, Berlioz also mentions a few band compositions which seem to have impressed him as repertoire of genuine worth.

> They write me from Brussels that ... Snel, the savant Chapel-master of Sainte-Gudule, has produced at the carnival of Courtrai, a great new spectacle of his composition, for choruses and wind band with a triumphal success. That is true glory![9]
>
> ...
>
> I must mention ... the remarkable symphonic ensemble works that M. Bellon, on the invitation of M. Sax, has composed for fourteen brass instruments. The pieces, written with the aim of showing the progress that has been made recently on the sax-horn and the saxophone by our musicians, moreover produced an excellent effect on the audience that M. Sax had gathered to hear them. One can recognize the ingenious and spicy manner of treating a melodic subject, and the art of modulating and linking chords, the dominant qualities of the talent of Reicha, who was the teacher of M. Bellon.[10]

[9] *Journal des Débats*, November 23, 1844.

[10] Ibid., June 29, 1850.

In Berlin he heard a funeral march by Wieprecht, which he thought was beautiful.[11] And then there is the very interesting reference to a 'huge' battle symphony for two bands, a work recalling the Battle of Leipzig. Unfortunately Berlioz was not available to hear an even larger composition by Wieprecht on this theme, a *Tone Poem* for three bands performed in 1863.

[11] This work by Wieprecht is available at www.whitwellbooks.com.

> The clarinets [in Potsdam] sounded especially valiant playing a huge symphony-battle composed for two bands by the Ambassador of England, the Count of Westmoreland. This very remarkable piece did the greatest honor to the author of *Torneo*, of the *Magnificant*, and of so many other dramatic and religious compositions, which have placed the Count of Westmoreland (better known by musicians under the name, Lord Burghersh) at the head of the amateur composers of Europe.

Berlioz knew and actually conducted a wind ensemble work little known today, the *Nonett* for winds by Félicien David. Following are three extant notes regarding the acquisition and return of the score and parts relative to a performance on 6 April 1845.

> Félicien David, before leaving, authorized me to have his *nonetto* for wind instruments performed at my next concert. I was told today that his work was in your possession. Would you please let me have it and send it along with the separate parts you may have, along with the score. I will hasten to return them to you after the concert.[12]
>
> ...
>
> Please do not forget to give the parts of the *Nonetto* of David to Mr. Roquemont at his copy office at the Opera as soon as possible. I am most obliged.[13]
>
> ...
>
> Most of the separate parts of the *Nonetto* of David have been copied by one of the players, Mr. Urbain, if I am not mistaken. I believe I only had to have an ophicleide and horn part transposed. All that I have is therefore at your disposal, and the copying costs were so little they are not worth mentioning. I thought that all of this had been sent you by my copyist, Mr. Roquemont. Since this is not the case, I am going to write him about this. I think that you will not miss an opportunity to publish it and that Escudiers will offer you an acceptable price that is fitting for such a beautiful work. Richaut is also anxious to acquire it. I thank you for the letter from David which pleased me greatly.[14]

Another reference to a wind chamber work is very interesting. In a letter written in his official position as *Biobliothecaire du Conservatoire*, Berlioz mentions what may be wind quintets by Reicha, owned by Louis François Dauprat (1781–1861), hornist and professor at the Conservatoire. These may be Quintets unknown today, as the familiar 24 Quintets were all published and known in Paris long before this date.

[12] Letter to Louis Jourdan, Paris, March 15, 1845, in *Correspondance*, 950.

[13] Letter to D. Urbain, Paris, March, 1845, in ibid., 951.

[14] Letter to Louis Jourdan, Paris, April 21, 1845, in *Correspondance*, Nr. 959.

> I have the honor to inform you that the Conservatory Library is in the most satisfactory state in which to view a most precious and rich collection, up to now thought lost or misplaced and now found. In addition, they have added a few recently acquired pieces. Mr. Dauprat has some quintets from Reicha, hand written by himself and which until now have never been printed in separate parts.[15]

[15] Letter to Theodore Lassabathie, Paris, December 6, 1855, in ibid., 2058.

We find this an interesting reference to the Reicha quintets and indeed in the National Library in Paris one can find 24 quintets in a manuscript copy which belonged to Dauprat. On the other hand, the quintets had long been published when Berlioz wrote this letter which makes his statement, 'which until now have never been printed in separate parts' particularly interesting. In 1825, an English encyclopedist, John Sainsbury, who knew and had visited Reicha, was fully acquainted with the momentary fame of the quintets and knew which hall in Paris they were performed in, mentioned that they were scored for English horn and not oboe. In view of the fact that Berlioz was particularly fond of the English horn one has to wonder if Dauprat had some quintets which are not known to us today and that this is the reason he made a point of this in his letter.

Berlioz knew several band directors by name, as for example Valentine Bender, conductor since 1832 of the Musique des Guides, Brussels,[16] Mohr, of the Guides in Paris, discussed below, and, 'Mr. Cressonnois, one of our most talented military band conductors.'[17]

[16] *Memoirs*, 265.

[17] *Journal des Débats*, January 28, 1862.

He seems to have often heard local military bands in the cities where he visited. Such a reference appears in a letter to his sister.

> You have no doubt seen in the newspapers that … [my Requiem] has recently been performed in St Petersburg with great success … They united singers from the Imperial Chapel (the best singers in the world) and those from a regiment of the guard (excellent), plus the orchestras of St. Petersburg.[18]

[18] Letter to his sister, Nanci, Paris, August, 1841, in *Correspondance*, 751 bis.

In a review of the premiere of Halévy's *La Dame de Pique*, Berlioz reveals he even knew of the odd chapter in the history of the Russian bands, the bands of serfs in which each player learned only one pitch, much like the bell choir we hear today.

This ensemble is usually known as the Russian Horn Band and they made a brief sensation touring in London after the first of the nineteenth century.

> The orchestra's imitation of Russian musicians playing only one note each is sharp and accurate.
> The Parisian ninnies will now believe more than ever that Russian music is only played in this way. In fact one of these bands of single-note musicians still exists, organized by an obstinate German musician some thirty years ago as a matter of curiosity than anything else. We would be happy today to have in our military bands instrumentalists such as those who are [actually] in the Russian Imperial Guard. Some of our soldier musicians would be even more happy to have but one note to play.[19]

[19] *Journal des Débats*, January 1, 1851.

Bands in the German-Speaking Countries

IN HIS ACCOUNTS IN THE *Journal des Débats* of his 1843–1844 travels to Germany, Berlioz singles out two bands for mention for their high quality. These were the bands he heard in Darmstadt and Dresden.

> In Darmstadt there is a military band of thirty musicians; I certainly envied the Grand Duke for having it. All of them play in tune, and with style, and possess a sense of rhythm, which gives interest even to the drum parts.[20]

> …

> [In Dresden] The military band is very good, even the drummers are musicians; but the reed instruments that I heard did not seem irreproachable to me; they leave a lot to be desired for intonation, and the conductor of these regiments certainly ought to order from our incomparable manufacturer, Adolphe Sax, some of his clarinets.
>
> There are no ophicleides; the low part is held down by the Russian bassoons and serpents.[21]

One can see here again his recommendation that the conductor should turn to Sax for better instruments. This is yet another example of Berlioz's thorough knowledge of the 'state of the art' in the development of the instruments available to bands. He makes the same kind of observation with regard to a band he heard in Stuttgart.

> I was surprised not to see [the cylindrical valve] adopted for the trumpets in military bands, actually quite good, of Stuttgart; they are still using two-piston valved trumpets, very imperfect instruments and very far, in sonority and quality of timbre, from the cylindrical-valved trumpets used at present everywhere else. I am not speaking of Paris; we shall come to use them in ten years or so.[22]

In a letter to his sister, Berlioz mentions another German military band, one in Frankfurt, who joined in the celebration of his visit to the city.

[20] *Journal des Débats*, January 9, 1844.

[21] Ibid., September 12, 1843. In his *Memoirs*, p. 306, Berlioz adds 'tubas' following the word 'serpents.'

[22] *Journal des Débats*, August 20, 1843.

> I gave two concerts at the Frankfurt theater, all with a fabulous success. In Frankfurt they gave me a great dinner with crowns, verse, speeches, toasts, etc. The Prussian military band came to play the overture of my *Franc-Juges* underneath the windows of the hotel. This, finally, did me in.[23]

23 Letter to his Sister, Adele, Paris, September 7, 1853, in *Correspondance*, 1627.

There were two band directors in Germany whom Berlioz held in high personal respect. One was a fixture in Baden, the resort Berlioz frequented in his later years, 'M. Kennemann, the intelligent and devoted bandmaster of Baden.'[24]

24 'Address to the Academy of Fine Arts of the Institute,' September 11, 1861, quoted in *Mozart, Weber and Wagner*, 93.

The other was, of course, Wilhelm Wieprecht of Berlin, the man who played so fundamental a role in the development of the modern band. Berlioz must have been very excited by the number of players available, their discipline, and their organization.

> As to the military bands [in Berlin], it would be difficult not to hear at least some of them, since, during every hour of the day, on foot or on horseback, they wander the streets of Berlin. These small isolated troops cannot, however, give any idea of the majesty of the large ensembles that the Director-Instructor of the Military Bands of Potsdam (Wieprecht) can form when he wishes. Imagine that he has under his command six hundred musicians and more, all good readers, well versed on the mechanism of their instrument, playing in tune, and favored by nature with indefatigable lungs and lips of iron. Hence, the extreme facility with which the trumpets, horns, and cornets give the high notes which our artists cannot reach. These are regiments of musicians, not musicians of regiments. M. le Prince of Prussia, anticipating the desire that I had to hear and study at leisure his musical troops, had the gracious kindness to invite me to a matinee, organized for me at his residence, and to give Wieprecht orders consequently.
>
> The audience was few in number; there were only twelve or fifteen at the most. I was astonished not to see the band; no sound betrayed its presence, when a slow phrase in F minor, well-known to me, came to make me turn my head towards the biggest room of the palace, where a vast curtain hid them from our sight. His Royal Highness had had the courtesy to have the concert begun with the Overture to *Francs Juges*, which I had never heard so arranged for wind instruments. There were three hundred twenty men strong, conducted by Wieprecht, and they performed the difficult piece with a marvelous precision and that furious verve that you show for it, those of you in the Conservatoire, on great days of enthusiasm and spirit.
>
> The solo of the brass instruments, in the Introduction, was especially striking, performed by fifteen large bass trombones, eighteen or twenty tenor and alto trombones, twelve bass tubas, and a swarm of trumpets …
>
> The clarinets seemed to me as good as the brass instruments …

Next came a brilliant and chivalrous piece for brass instruments alone, written for the festivals of the court by Meyerbeer, under the title, *la Danse aux Flambeaux*, and in which is found a long trill on D, which eighteen cylinder-trumpets held, while fingering them as rapidly as clarinets might have been able to do, during sixteen measures.

The concert concluded with a funeral march, very well written and of a beautiful character, composed by Wieprecht. They had had only one rehearsal!![25]

[25] *Journal des Débats*, November 8, 1843.

In reflecting on these experiences in Germany when writing his *Memoir*, Berlioz recalled,

I must … also describe the choral society and the military bands—two quite different institutions, both of first-rate importance, and both of such splendor beside anything we possess in the same line that one's national pride cannot but feel thoroughly chastened by the comparison.[26]

[26] *Memoirs*, 322.

The only two Austrian bands which Berlioz mentions on his 1843–1844 tour were also stationed in Germany. One he knew only by reputation and was disappointed not to be able to hear and use in a performance of his *Symphonie funèbre*.[27]

[27] *Memoirs*, 600.

Having arrived at Mainz, I found out about the Austrian military band that was here the preceding year, and which had, according to Strauss (the Strauss of Paris) performed several of my overtures, with a verve, a power, and a prodigious effect. The regiment had left, [so] no more band music (it was really a great band), no more concerts possible![28]

[28] *Journal des Débats*, August 13, 1843.

Berlioz mentions this band in his *Memoirs*,[29] but improves its aesthetic image by changing 'prodigious effect' to read 'immense success.'

[29] *Memoirs*, 266ff.

One Austrian band he actually heard, in Baden, performed in the so-called, 'Conversation Salon.' The present writer, when recently serving as the president of the jury for an international piano competition in Italy, visited an intact nineteenth-century hotel which still had a room with a sign reading, 'Salon for Music and Conversation.'

Two military bands alternate with the Conversation Orchestra for the daily musical service. The Austrian band is excellent and enjoys such a popularity that in the evenings when it is heard, the crowd obstructs the surroundings of the pavilion where it projects its rich harmony, and it is very difficult to find seats if one does not get there an hour in advance, and if one is not in the good graces of the Salon de Conversation ushers who, in such cases, carry on a little trade of the most comical kind. This is for the ordinary musical fare of the public at Baden.[30]

---

[30] *Journal des Débats*, September 24, 1857.

Bands in France

DURING THE NINETEENTH CENTURY, France was a leader in the development of the modern European civic band movement. By the end of the century one survey found 1,711 band societies in France, and which does not include brass bands.[31] However, judging by one of his newspaper articles, Berlioz was not impressed with the general aesthetic level of most of these bands.

31 *L'Orphéon* (Paris: Librairie Charles Delagrave, 1908).

> The provincial amateurs and artists love too much to parade in the front row. They are not happy to blend their individuality into the mass of the ensemble. Further, to call a spade a spade, they have far too much presumption and far too little perseverance to give the necessary care to the rehearsals.[32]

32 *Revue et Gazette Musicale*, June 11, 1837.

Nevertheless, there was one of these civic band societies which caught his attention and which Berlioz describes several times in his earliest newspaper articles on bands.

> Mr. Aubery du Boulley has founded in the departments of l'Eure, Eure and Loire, and l'Orne, a vast Philharmonic Society, which includes the cities of Evreux, Nonancourt, Damville, Barnay, Beaumont-le-Roger, Couches, Breteuil, Verneuil, Tillieres, Grosbois, Chartres, Dreux, Brezolles, Alencon, Montagne, Gace and Longny. Using all of his influence as a property owner, at Grosbois, where he lives, and on the people who depend, more or less, on him, he teaches the music and without hesitating in the face of considerable expenses, supplies the majority of his students with the expensive instruments they need. He started with his brother's instruction, then his sons, his gardener and the other workmen, some village inhabitants, and ended up with an excellent brass band composed of three bugles, six trumpets, one cornet à piston, one trumpet à piston, an alto ophicleide, three bass ophicleides, two buccins, and three trombones.
>
> But he didn't stop there. The above mentioned towns and villages supplied him with new students who, joined together later, today make up an ensemble of 200 players. We don't know what is the most admirable in this man, his rare unselfishness or his unshakeable steadfastness. It is clear that this man loves music, as Mr. Aubery du Boulley does not possess more than a modest existence, yet spends all of his time and money on music. It has been all work, and studies, and a difficult task to find his students, bring them together and then teach them. The large

ensemble gets together twice a year. Before each of these gatherings the untiring professor goes to all of the villages and towns where his students live, spends two weeks with each one of them to rehearse carefully and does not leave them until they have been well rehearsed and are perfectly in shape to do him honor on the day of the great assembly. The musical discipline has spread among his population to the extent that the departments he goes to are fighting to be named as the location where his band will meet. This favor will only be granted if free lodgings are provided for all of the musicians. The most recent of these events took place in Breteuil in July. There were 200 musicians and at 11:00 AM assembled at the church, which was surrounded with a mass of listeners, who came from as far as 40 miles away. Mr. Aubery conducted [the band] and the pieces he conducted especially for this occasion were played to perfection. No feeling of rivalry was present at this brotherly meeting, only the unique feeling of solidarity to do justice to the enterprise motivated the members. In the evening, as the group was proceeding to the reception area, they played several quadrilles during which 500 people danced to the sounds of this grand orchestra, surrounded by 15,000 spectators. On Monday, at 6:00 AM, called by the drums and trumpets, the little musical army met at the Place de Breteuil and after a farewell number played by the entire group they went their separate ways home.[33]

33 *Journal des Débats*, September 19, 1836.

...

Musical propaganda is not slowing in the provinces either; M. Aubery du Boulley, the indefatigable amateur, who causes battalions of musicians to rise from the earth as if by enchantment, has conducted again his Philharmonic Congress. They say there were not fewer than four hundred wind instruments ... That is a military band that would have been worthy to precede the Imperial Guard on the return from the Austerlitz campaign.[34]

34 Ibid., January 31, 1837.

Berlioz repeated this story of Aubery du Boulley and his band the following year in a different journal. There he adds one new sentence describing these civic players.

There is no doubt that these instrumentalists do not have the quality of those at the Opéra or the Conservatoire, and the music they play is not of the same level, however, they work rather well together to form a united ensemble of wind instruments that generally give a rather satisfactory and sometimes grandiose result.[35]

35 *Revue et Gazette Musicale*, June 11, 1837.

A large part of the success of many of these civic societies was the establishment of attached music schools to train young people as future band members. Therefore Berlioz was delighted when he heard of plans to form a military school of music.

> Military music is perhaps, of all the art forms, the least appreciated in our provinces. We are far from the Germans in this field, but less so than in all the others. I must omit Paris from this judgment; the theater artists almost all belonging to a military band in the capital, giving them an enormous superiority over all others with which we might compare them. But we will soon see great progress in the area of wind instruments. One artist of great reputation and merit, Mr. Beer, Solo Clarinet of the Italian Theater, has just been placed at the head of one special Military Music School. This is a good idea, coming from the war minister, and the army will not delay in reaping the fruits of its success. Only those soldiers who show the greatest musical aptitude, and who agree to leave the ordinary military service to learn how to play the wind instruments, will be sent for three years to a school directed by Mr. Beer. There, they will be exposed to a fruitful education quite different than the one they would have been subject to had they remained in the provincial barracks, run by masters of often mediocre talent. After a time, they will enter the army hierarchy where they will constitute a group of able instrumentalists and within a period of time France will possess a considerable group of excellent and competent military concert bands.[36]

[36] *Journal des Débats*, September 18, 1836.

Berlioz was also one of the first to see that if French military bands were to rise to the level of the German bands the first step must be the acquisition of better instruments.

> Our military bands certainly do not yet have cylindrical-valved trumpets, or a bass tuba (the most beautiful of the low instruments). A considerable manufacture of these instruments will become inevitable to put the French military bands on the same level with those possessed by Prussia and Austria.[37]

[37] Ibid., October 8, 1843.

In his *Memoirs* Berlioz makes this recommendation more specific.

> If French Military music is to achieve the standard of Prussian and Austrian, we will have to manufacture these instruments. A government order to Adolphe Sax for three hundred trumpets and a hundred bass tubas would be the salvation of him.[38]

[38] *Memoirs*, 319.

In 1842 the French government finally decided to make a major study of the instrumentation of military bands, and appointed a committee for this purpose. While the committee was making its study, many interested parties, especially instrument makers whose entire future was at stake, made recommendations, both to the committee and to the press. Berlioz at this time contributed a major newspaper analysis of his own.

> In Paris at the moment, people are very much occupied by a proposition, the simple announcement of which has caused, among artists, wind instrument manufacturers, and those in the offices of the War Ministry, an extraordinary uproar. It deals with the examination of our Corps of Military Music, and of reorganizing them according to a new plan, if there are sufficient grounds to do so. Hence, nervousness, terror, threats, protests of extraordinary intensity, arising from the crowd of interests *harmed* or compromised by this measure, which, if adopted, puts at odds industrial rivals—the bitterest of all—and pits the moving force of new ideas against the force of inertia derived from routine and prejudices. These violent battles are always a subject of astonishment for upright minds, situated outside the fact that it would be the most natural thing in the world to adopt, whether it be an invention whose usefulness is demonstrated and which augments the sum of human forces, or whether it be a simple perfecting of what already exists. But the history of the efforts of modern genius, especially, in each of its attempts, whatever may have been the aim, is there to show the existence of the inexorable law, and primordial, so to speak, which imposes on him such rigorous testings and makes his development so *painful*. And, to cite a fact that relates to the subject which concerns us, weren't years of debate necessary in order that the bolt action rifle be permitted to replace flintlock guns, and didn't the latter of yesteryear have even yet more difficulty replacing the wick and punk musket?
>
> In music, every day the modern mind comes up against theories born in the epochs of the infancy of the art, and which time, reason, experience, backed by a crushing mass of contrary facts, have not been able to destroy completely. In conflicts of this nature, *power* can only be resigned, for some time, to doing its part in *resistance*, and to persevere then with an indefatigable energy, without abandoning one's basic stance.
>
> As soon as it was seriously entertained to study the current organization of the Corps of Military Music of France, M. the Minister of War gave this labor to a special commission, under the Presidency of M. the Général of Rumigny, who doubtless will need the firmness and rectitude of mind for which he is known, to lead the affair to a good conclusion.

Some important modifications were judged necessary by the majority of competent and disinterested men. They must bear principally on the nature of wind instruments currently in use, on the diverse systems by which they are manufactured, and on the manner of grouping them. Hence, the opposition of the musicians, obliged to undertake new studies, and of manufacturers, whose stores are filled with old products, now of little usefulness, and who are not sure of being successful in the production of new ones.

Military bands, it cannot be repeated too often, find themselves placed in completely exceptional circumstances. They certainly are not destined to be heard in concert halls, nor in theaters; they must resound out-of-doors.

Yet, they know that, for the immense majority of sonorous means which the art has at its disposal, an enclosed place with reflectors is absolutely necessary, without which even a colossal number of players would produce no effect. A thousand musicians singing or playing stringed instruments, for example, on an open plain, would barely be heard at a small distance and would have absolutely no effect on the audience placed near them; while only four can have, in a room, an excessive effect. That is why it is generally true to say that outdoors music does not exist. What one hears sometimes in big squares, enclosed on all sides, or planted with large trees serving as reflectors, does not invalidate what I am saying. Out-of-doors, in flat countryside, is where armies maneuver. So, there is needed, for bands destined to be heard, a very specific organization, which permits them to combat as advantageously as possible, the unfavorable happenstances in which they find themselves placed.

In this case, instruments whose sound is of short-range carrying power, however beautiful the timbre may be and however useful everywhere else, must not take part. Included in this number are bassoons, horns, ordinary flutes, and clarinets in the lower register. The great fault of French military music results from the disproportionate force accorded by them up to now to the two extremes of the range of sound. The basses, confined to a great number of ophicleides playing, more or less in tune, in unison, and the piccolos doubling in the high octave the Eb clarinet, are heard almost exclusively, while the entire interior of the band and the immense interval that separates the lowest sounds from the highest sounds seems almost empty. Absolutely no intermediate harmony, hence absolutely no connection between the extremities, this music seems written for the basses and the upper parts alone. The number of middle parts, however, is very great, since there are up to five clarinet parts, at least four horn parts, and two bassoon parts. But, with the exception of the first clarinets in Bb, playing an octave lower than the Eb clarinets, all the others are lost, and the parts of the second, third, and fourth clarinets, playing necessarily in the middle and chalumeau registers, produce, when one listens for them at close range, a sort of confused humming, at the least useless, and absolutely imperceptible at any distance away. The same is true for the bassoons, whose number is moreover always very restricted, and the horns, whose sound is of very short projection, and which have only a small number of notes that resound somewhat.

Instruments of long-range carrying power, those that project sound afar, even in half-strength nuances, are trumpets, cornets, bugles, tubas, ophicleides, clarinets in the high range, and piccolos. Oboes, it is true, have a quite piercing sonority when they are in sufficient numbers, and it probably could be augmented even more. The *pifferi*, a kind of large oboe which the peasants of Abbruzes use, resound at enormous distances, and everyone knows about the violence of sonority of the Scottish bagpipe; but besides the fact that this second timbre, added to that of the clarinets in our military bands, would be a luxury, when we are occupied above all by the necessary, its character, one must agree, is rural rather than martial, and it elicits much better memories of pastoral joys than of warrior enthusiasm. In any case, it is not necessary, and becomes useful only through its fusion with other timbres, like the bassoons and horns, in large orchestras of a hundred musicians and more.

It seems to me, therefore, that if a reform in the organization of the corps of military music were adopted, it ought to have as its objectives:

1. The suppression of instruments useless out-of-doors, such as bassoons, oboes and horns, and the second, third, and fourth clarinets in Bb;
2. The exclusive use of instruments of long-range carrying power, yet brilliant and sweet, when they are good and well played;
3. The admission of the entire family of bugles with valves (saxhorns), high, middle, and low;
4. The augmentation of the number of trumpets with valves in different pitches, of cornets with valves, and of slide and valve trombones;
5. The gradual substitution, because one cannot do it all at once, of low tubas for most of the ophicleides; and perhaps, the introduction of a certain number of *quintes* flutes, which have fallen into disuse today, but which can be heard very well and correct a little, by doubling them at the octave and unison, the harshness of the *neuvieme* piccolos, commonly called in Eb.

The reform ought to be directed also towards instruments of bad quality that are placed in the hands of students, and a single one of which, out of tune or incomplete, suffices to detune an otherwise satisfactory ensemble.

I have spoken several times already of the magnificence of the military bands of Prussia: their superiority over ours is incontestable: nevertheless, we could take it away from them in short order, thanks to the excellence of the cylindrical brass instruments manufactured today in Paris by Adolphe Sax. This ingenious manufacturer, whose inventions and improvements brought to instruments already well-known are of considerable value, is perhaps the first cause of the attempt at reform that is occurring at this moment. The success that has crowned his attempts has had a good bit of publicity, and each day his work is being completed. His new instruments, especially bugles with valves, which he calls sax-horns, are of unusually good intonation and sonority; the brilliance of his chromatic trumpets is incomparable; he brought the tuba from Berlin, modifying its mechanism advantageously, and giving somewhat more low pitch to its range. The tuba is in F, he constructed his in Eb by giving it spare tubing that permit it to be put into D, into Db, and into C. This instrument, which is only a gigantic trumpet with valves, has always seemed to us to be much superior to the ophicleides. This is the reason: just like the keyed bugle, the most out-of-tune of brass instruments, the ophicleide has its body pierced with enormous holes, whose closing is effected by a large key covered with one of the most dissimilar materials to that of the instrument itself; the thick leather that is used for that, putting it over the opening to which the key corresponds, produces naturally the effect of a mute. Besides this, the tube of the instrument undergoes at every instant new modifications that make its tone quality unequal, because of the greater or fewer number of keys that remain open, and the quite considerable space that remains below each opening, preventing the interior surface from being smooth and continuous, must render still more unsure the intonation of its sounds. This is the reason for the excessive rarity of artists who play in tune on the instrument, such a rarity that one can hardly find three in Paris, at the head of which must be placed M. Caussinus, a professor in the *Gymnase musical*. The sound of Sax's tuba is not only more stable than that of the ophicleide, but a louder and more beautiful; its brassy vibrations harmonize completely with those of the trombones, and do not have the dull sound of the best played ophicleide; in a word, it is to the trumpet what the string bass is to the violin. It would be necessary at least, I believe, to keep some ophicleides for the playing of certain passages that require more agility than the tuba really possesses.

The make-up of the military band recently proposed to the Commission by M. Sax comes very close to that which I would suggest, and fits completely with the ideas that I have just proposed. Here is his:

6 trumpets with valves
2 small sax-horns (bugles with valves in Eb)
4 large sax-horns in Bb
4 large tenor sax-horns in low Eb
2 large baritone sax-horns with three valves in low Bb
2 large bass sax-horns with four valves in low Bb
4 tubas in Eb with three valves (contrabasses of the band)
2 cornets with valves
2 trombones with valves
2 ordinary tenor slide trombones
2 ophicleides in Bb
1 piccolo in Db (named Eb)
1 Eb clarinet
6 soprano clarinets in Bb, playing in unison, and rarely in two parts
2 pairs of cymbals and a triangle
1 side drum, 1 tenor drum, 1 bass drum; or 45 instruments.

In a score so set up, there is a balance of musical forces and a connection between the diverse parts of the instrumental mass. Obviously the holes that I have indicated in the harmonic scale of our present military bands, are filled. The brass contrabasses join the basses, these to the baritones, the baritones to the tenors, the tenors to the contraltos, and the contraltos to the sopranos. The timbres, being similar, mesh together perfectly, and the closeness of the diverse members of the family of bugles, whose sonority is completely homogeneous, permit the composer the use of phrases running the gamut of extraordinary length: the different bugles, high, medium, and low, perform then successively the fragments of the passage or of the melody that best fits their respective ranges, handing them off, one to another, without one being able to identify, between the melodic fragments, the slightest break in continuity, and the totality of the pattern seems to be played by one sole and single instrument of an immense range. People have seen many times, in the symphonies of Beethoven, the use that this great master was able to make of such interlacing, given to violins, violas, and cellos, whose timbres, however, are far from having the sameness that is to be noted between those of the large and small bugles. Only, I find insufficient the single piccolo that M. Sax adds to the high clarinets, and this is where there would be lacking, to my mind, a certain number of *quintes* flutes, of which I spoke above. I am saying again that I am certainly not a partisan of the system which would tend to exclude from military bands all the woodwinds. Far from that, their timbre, that of the clarinets above all, possesses, even in loudness, a characteristic of penetrating sweetness, a certain proud tenderness, which one senses without being able to explain it, a secret analogy with the bellicose accents of the brass voices.

Such a band of forty-five able musicians, armed with the instruments of Sax, or of another maker who makes those as good, would only leave to be desired one thing that no one would worry over, and towards which, up to the present, no research, that I know of, has been directed. I mean the percussion instruments. Among those that we possess, the timpani alone give stable, perceivable sounds, the others only make noise serving to accentuate the rhythm with greater or lesser energy. Yet, the timpani, and it is truly irritating, are no longer even admitted into military bands. But if they were still to be found there, they would be of mediocre importance, in comparison with the unknown instrument that remains to be found, and whose effect I envision thus: imagine a great number of cymbals of different dimensions, each producing, instead of their frail and confused quivering, a tuned sound and of a beautiful timbre, although loud, and essentially metallic, like that of ordinary cymbals; there would result, from their simultaneous striking, a sudden harmony, quite similar, with an energy of vibrations incomparably greater, to a chord struck on several harps and pianos, in a small, local enclosure. Now, let us imagine an instrument capable of producing, not only one note or chord, but several chords struck in this way with reverberation, and the problem will be solved. Whether this be a collection of steel bars, of metallic plates, of any other totally different sonorous material *struck* so that this special sonority may be obtained, I do not know, but I believe in the possibility of such a result, and I imagine that one will find later the entire family of great percussive instruments, that will be, to those which we now possess, like Pan's flute to the organ, the timpani to the piano.

Didn't Sax also dream about a steam organ of antediluvian dimensions, destined to sing of joys and sorrows from the top of towers to a whole populace? Only, the plan of his titanic instrument exists in his head, he only lacks the millions to execute it; while, in mine, the plan only exists only as an idea. But this is not my domain; in matters of instruments and voices, composers are less apt to create than to destroy …

To return to the discussion aroused by the *memoire* of Sax on the subject of the projected reform, and to conclude, it only remains for me to approve of the adoption that he proposes of the complete families of cylindrical brass instruments, as the basis and fundamental principle of military bands, admitting some other instruments only to vary the timbres, but on the condition that none of these instruments be dull sounding, nor of a lackluster or simple sonority. All his bugles, cornets, tubas, all his trumpets, all his valve trombones having the *same fingering*, there would result also the advantage for the musician of being able to change instruments without being constrained to do new studies. To become acquainted with the embouchure, if it is of a different size, that is the entire task, several days suffice, often even several hours, for that. It goes without saying that he fights with all his strength against the use of those abominable clarions, or simple bugles, that play at most only five notes and that march at the head of our infantry regiments, tooting the most stupid fanfares that one can imagine, in the most out-of-tune unison that a human ear can stand. This is pure barbarity: one only can conceive such playing at the head of a regiment of *Cossacks*. It is strange that we must mention its existence in this country.

If the reform whose necessity I have indicated, and which we have vowed to bring about, is adopted, it is clear that the heads of music who are composers will have a great deal to do to form a repertoire according to the new instrumentation's organization. In this case, one ought to profit by the occasion to have written some commissioned pieces and some fanfares in a style better than those in use up to the present. Everything in art is as constrained as in science, and there is no necessity to conserve in the bugle calls and the simplest military marches the ridiculous and low style of clowns.

The news of the examination that they are undertaking at this moment on the question that we have just touched on is causing a great agitation, especially among the manufacturers of wind instruments. Not only those in Paris have gotten together, but even deputations from the provincial makers joined them to consult on the means of parrying the danger with which they believe they are threatened. It is true, I said so at the beginning, that if the reform is adopted in the direction indicated, they will have trouble producing their old products, and this will be a loss for them; but it is equally true, in this case, that an undetermined number of new instruments having necessarily to be manufactured for the needs of the army, this circumstance can be very favorable for their business.

The monopoly of bugles, trombones, trumpets, and tubas has been promised to no one, new instruments will be examined: if those of Sax are the best, they should be adopted; but if it happens to the contrary, that his emulators win over him, these will be selected: nothing is more evident. Moreover, this question is completely secondary: it is not a question of the interests of the manufacturers, but rather those of art and the army. The agitation of the shop foremen where wind instruments are made is understandable, but it must not, and cannot, have more influence on the decision to be made by the Commission than, doubtless, the joy of some brass metal sellers, assured, if the reorganization occurs, of a sudden increase in their profits. With such considerations, we arrive, by the following the chain of interest, up to the working miners who extract the mineral.[39]

39 'On the Reorganization of Military Bands,' in *Journal des Débats*, April 1, 1845.

The committee, suffering from too much input and too little personal experience, finally decided to pick two opposing recommendations for instrumentation and hold an outdoor, public demonstration—a battle of the bands. One plan, submitted by Carafa, an establishment figure and head of the current military school of music, was little more than an expanded *Harmoniemusik*. The other plan, by Sax, was much stronger in families of brass instruments and with a greater emphasis on lower instruments for a more homogeneous sound. Any modern conductor looking at the two lists of instruments would know that Sax must win in an outdoor setting. Taking no chances, the manufacturers supporting Carafa kidnapped a number of the players Sax intended to use, including one who was to play the new saxophone. Nevertheless the difference between the two bands was evident, as Berlioz pointed out.

> It was on last Tuesday that this trial took place before a jury composed of members of the Institute, under the Presidency of M. the Général of Rumigny. It was never in doubt for one instant. The military band of Sax, although inferior in number to the bands against which it had to compete, and made incomplete by the defection of some performers, who, for reasons known only to themselves, had feared being compromised by taking his side, showed from the first chords its superiority. The contrast of its sonority, of the fullness, and of the evenness of all its sounds, with the thinness of the intermediate parts of the other bands, was striking from the very first. The superiority of the sax-horns over

the horns (for open-air music), their brilliant agility in the solos and runs, the homogeneity given to the whole by that new instrumental family, the beauty of the low pitches of the tubas, aided by the bass clarinets, compared to the dull and impotent sonority of the bassoons, and to the uncertain and so often out-of-tune pitches of the masses of ophicleides, could not go unrecognized. The numerous audience that curiosity had attracted to the Champ-de-Mars saluted Sax's band several times with its applauding; his regimental fanfare [brass band] was even better received. Therefore, the question seems henceforth settled in his favor, whatever may be the amendments that the Commission perhaps will judge suitable to propose.[40]

40 'Military Band Contest on the Champ-de-Mars,' *Journal des Débats*, April 29, 1845.

The government, after months of delay, finally issued a remarkable document which designated an official instrumentation based on the Sax model together with other recommendations. Berlioz presents these developments in another lengthy newspaper article.

> The Minister of War, by signing the order relative to the reorganization of military bands, has just given an important branch of musical art a progressive movement, whose fortunate consequences people cannot yet fully appreciate. I was forcibly struck, two years ago, during my stay in Berlin, by the magnificence of the instrumental masses, which the Prince of Prussia has at his disposal for the Prussian regiments, and the inferiority of France in this regard seemed to me the more shocking on my return, as the means necessary to remedy it were more evident and easier.
>
> The Prussian military bands are placed under the direction of a man of true talent, at the same time a professor, conductor, composer, and well versed in acquaintances appropriate to instrument makers; this is Mr. Wieprecht. With conscripts more or less well organized for music, he succeeds in making in a short time, if not virtuosos, at least capable instrumentalists, who, reunited into bands, produce magnificent ensembles, harmonious, at the same time both energetic and sweet, and of an irreproachable intonation. The fact is that all the art of the performers, especially for bands of this nature, cannot remedy the defectiveness of the instruments and the system according to which they are grouped. Yet, Mr. Wieprecht, thanks to the special knowledge that he possesses and to the authority with which he is invested, has succeeded not only in prohibiting the use of those frightful, shoddy instruments that the instrumental tinsmiths manufacture by the hundreds, but also in perfecting in a notable fashion some brass instruments, among others, the bombardon, of which he made the five-valved tuba, the true contra-bass of the trumpets and the most precious of the low wind instruments. That is why it happens that his not very advanced students play in tune, while some very able French musicians play somewhat out-

of-tune. One must listen closely to our military musicians to get a good idea of the inconvenience that I am indicating; there is no cacophony comparable to that which results too often from those so-called unisons of ophicleides down low and the clarinets up high, moreover almost completely deprived of the necessary intermediate harmony to unite them properly.

But, if the works of the ingenious manufacturer Adolphe Sax finally brought to light despite the efforts of an interested opposition to keep them in obscurity, the firm will of the Minister to use them, seconded by the cooperation, as active as it is enlightened, of the Générals de Rumigny and de Saint-Yon, has just brought to France an urgent reform, it is true, but which one did not even hope to see enacted so promptly. Still, they have taken great care in implementing this reform; a Commission, composed of all the members of the Institute, has been consulted; still more, a public cooperation has been opened between the best infantry and cavalry regimental bands and the band proposed by Sax. Everyone knows with what applause from the audience Sax emerged from that test, although the musicians responsible for showing off the value of his instruments were as yet very little familiarized with them, and his band had become incomplete because of the defection of some of his musicians at the moment of the experiment. The Minister, by signing the decree that is bringing about this important musical revolution, therefore has on his side, not only connoisseurs, artists of every age and rank, but also the public, whose voice is so rarely counted for anything on such an occasion. Here is the composition of military bands definitively adopted by the Minister of War, following the advice of the majority of the teachers and the music section of the Institute:

Music Personnel of an Infantry Regiment
1 Piccolo in Bb (commonly called in *ut*)
1 Eb Clarinet
14 Bb Clarinets, chromatic (1st and 2nd)
2 curved Bb Clarinets, with brass bells (Sax system)
2 Saxophones
2 three-valved Cornets
2 valved Trumpets (Sax system)
4 three-valved Horns
1 soprano Sax-horn in Eb
2 contralti Sax-horns in Bb
2 tenor Sax-horns in Eb
3 baritone and bass Sax-horns in Bb, with three and four valves
4 contrabass Sax-horns in Eb
1 valved Trombone (Sax system)
2 slide Trombones
2 Ophicleides
5 Percussion Instruments (two pair of cymbals, a bass drum, a pair of timpani, and a snare drum)

50 TOTAL

Music Personnel of a Cavalry Regiment
2 Trumpets (natural trumpets)
4 valved Trumpets
2 Sax-horns in Eb
7 Sax-horns in Bb (1 solo, 3 firsts, 3 seconds)
2 Sax-horns in Ab (to replace the horns)
2 Sax-horns in Eb (to replace the horns)
2 Sax-trombes
2 three-valved Cornets
1 valve Trombone (Sax system)
3 slide Trombones
3 baritone three-valved Sax-horns in Bb
3 bass four-valved Sax-horns in Bb
3 contrabass Sax-horns in Eb

─────

36 TOTAL

The number of instrumentalists for each infantry regiment, including the conductor, will be:
27 musicians
23 students

─────

50 TOTAL

For each cavalry regiment:
22 musicians (called trumpets)
14 students

─────

36 TOTAL

    The student musicians will be chosen freely from among the soldiers and the children of the troop personnel who manifest a particular aptitude for music.

    The replacement of the existing instruments by those indicated above, will take place either as the old ones gradually become unusable, or by means of collections made beforehand, taken from the first portion of the General (regimental) Fund for Maintenance. The annual allocation for the maintenance of the fanfare trumpets in the cavalry regiments is raised from 2,500 fr. to 5,000 fr.: the augmentation of 2,500 fr. will be placed under the aegis of the Fund for Harness and Metal-working. The conductors in the infantry will continue to be chosen from among the students of the Music Gymnase, and must have taken previously a test before a Commission consisting in part of the members of the Music Section of the Institute.

    A sum of 3,000 fr., chargeable to the General Fund for Maintenance of the Corps, proportionally to the allocations accorded for the maintenance of the musicians and fanfare trumpets, will be divided up annually between the composers who have presented musical works judged best by a Commission composed of the Music Section of the Institute.

A metronome will be introduced in each musical group, whether infantry or cavalry.

A fixed-pitch tuning fork in Bb, conforming to the model decreed by the Minister, also will be adopted.

This last article of the new regulation is of the highest importance. Everyone knows about the serious inconvenience which results, on many an occasion, from the variety of tuning forks. One can notice it immediately when the composers of opera use at the same times a band and the theater orchestra. Very rarely are these two instrumental masses perfectly in tune, and in certain cities, even, despite all the precautions and all the efforts of the conductors, a frightful discord results from their combination. The project of giving a prize every year to the composers who have written the best pieces of band music is of a much more difficult realization. As to the choice of the instruments of Sax, we have said quite often what we thought of the inventions and the perfecting of this able manufacturer, so that it would be superfluous to approve of it. Sax is first in his specialty, and Mr. Wieprecht, who recently was with him in Coblentz, after having heard his sax-horns and his new bass clarinet, gave a glowing endorsement of these instruments, whose excellence he, as well as the majority of his Prussian musicians, recognized.

Now there remains to be done the implementation of that decree which goes against so many habits and which conflicts with several industrial interests. Undoubtedly, one can only succeed with the aid of active surveillance confided to a man of the art, independent in his position from any coterie, and who, seeing everything for himself, will know how to act so that the will of the Minister and the desires of the superior officers and the competent men whom he brought together, may have the result that one must expect.

Mr. Kastner, Reporting Secretary of the Commission, seems designated by public opinion as the most appropriate one to fulfill the function, unpaid moreover, of inspecting the bands and of watching over their reorganization. One could not have chosen better. Mr. Kastner knows the problem intimately; he is of an upright and firm character, he is a disinterested party, he loves his art, he will know how to defend it.

It is to be hoped that soon one may do for other branches of music that are languishing under the rust of prejudices and of routine what the Minister of War, guided by his high experience and his profound love of all that concerns the glory of the Army, has just done for regimental music. So many important institutions in the arts of peace should be directed militarily!!![41]

[41] *Journal des Débats*, September 12, 1845.

Things were slow to change, however, and Berlioz complains the following year that even so basic an instrument as the trumpet was not found in sufficient numbers in the French military bands.

Could one believe ... that trumpets have become the rarest of instruments in our military music? There is even a mass of infantry regiments who have none at all. And with what do they pretend to replace them? Not by violins nor guitars, certainly. What instrument possesses a timbre more essentially warlike, brilliant, proud, and of such long carrying power than the trumpet? In Austrian military music, which has excellent sonority and harmony, there are always for the smallest band, without counting the three flugel horns, seven trumpet parts, while those of ours that have kept them, possess two at most, and often only one. The truth to tell, it is an insanity![42]

42 Ibid., July 29, 1846

In 1847 another competition was held and the opportunity presented itself for the new model band to play for the king. Berlioz describes the king's role in helping to move the reorganization along.

In another competition with all the corps of military music in Paris and the suburbs, the band of the 74th Line Infantry, directed by M. Sarus, entirely organized from the beginning according to the system of Sax, has obtained last month three First Gold Medals, consistently beating his adversaries. The band of the 45th Line Infantry, directed by M. Ducler, designated by the Minister of War as the model band, having been called recently to Neuilly to play several pieces during dinner for the King, His Majesty was struck by the superiority of that military band, and above all by the charm of an instrument whose timbre was totally unknown to him: it was the saxophone that had been recently acquired by the regiment. The King wished to hear it again, and had the piece in which this beautiful instrument figured replayed.

Passing through Amiens, on his return from the Castle d'Eu, the King also noticed as well the Band of the 9th Cavalry of Hussards, also organized with Sax's instruments, and had its Director, M. Binon, come in order to express his satisfaction to him. So, everywhere these instruments, so decried by people interested in getting their usage prohibited, are obtaining an evident success ... The cause of Sax's inventions and his perfecting of wind instruments has now been won.[43]

43 Ibid., October 12, 1847.

In a brief review in 1851,[44] Berlioz mentions his friend, Kastner's new *Manuel général de musique militaire*, the most important early study of the history of the wind band, and lists its three sections: a history of earlier military music; a history of the nineteenth-century improvements, and a section of musical examples.

44 *Journal des Débats*, January 17, 1851.

In 1852, Berlioz turns his attention again to the military bands. It is evident he still believed the French bands have not made sufficient progress to be of the level of the German ones.

> Here is the situation of the regimental musicians. Now, whether they work or not, conduct themselves well or badly, whatever may be their merit, the result is the same for them as far as their military position is concerned. It is also the same as to their future.
>
> Whether they are arriving or leaving, recruits or seasoned soldiers, elitist artists or ignorant students, all are equal, and equal, not in splendor, but only in the very pronounced inferiority of their position.
>
> Unfortunate at the beginning, without fortune during their service, they go away still miserable at the end of a career full of fatigues, labors, and at times, of perils: because, after all, the musicians are soldiers, they campaign, and, having nothing to inspire their courage, nonetheless, they still must fear enemy bullets and bombs. We remember the energetic defense of the barrack of Reuilly by the musicians of the 18th Line, and we know that the military musicians were decimated under the walls of Rome.[45]
>
> Such a situation for the present and the future is little conductive, we know, to encourage and to retain artists under the flags. As soldiers, they are acquitting a debt, but, as soon as they can, they leave, and one can only be astonished if they remain. Hence a permanent disorder, continuous and numerous mutations, every-renewed studies, lost expenses of education, and finally the disastrous weakness of the majority of our corps of military music …
>
> What is sure, is that some military music groups, Austrian, Prussian, and Russian, are much superior to ours, but, now, thanks to the ingenious works of Sax, ours can all possess instruments of an incontestable excellence, to which the quality of foreign instruments cannot be compared; that Nature, in reality, hardly gave more to the Russians or the Germans, than to the French, according to the reports of musical faculties, and that today the vices of a deplorable organization alone cause their inferiority in the musical service of our armies.[46]

Now the government began yet another study of military band instrumentation, due no doubt to the continued efforts of the manufacturers who had lost out to Sax in 1845. Berlioz immediately comes to the defense of his friend, Adolphe Sax, who had apparently been accused of ignoring the traditional woodwinds.

---

45 A French colleague at the National Library in Paris told me that some 2,000 French bandsmen died on Napoleon's march to Moscow.

46 Ibid., January 7, 1852.

The question of military music is again the order of the day. This time it is about organization of the National Guard bands. In 1845, M. Sax wrote on that question a *Memoire* in which he examined the value of the instruments then in usage, the position of the music directors, and that of the regimental musicians.

Marshal Soult, at that epoch Minister of War, named a commission charged with the reorganization. Before it, a public competition took place in the Champ-de-Mars between the military bands representing the old system and those of the new. Success was declared from the first for the infantry and cavalry bands as proposed by M. Sax. Today for the National Guard, this subject has arisen again, except that the bands of the infantry and the cavalry are brought together, both organized according to the system presented by M Sax in 1845, almost the only exception being that the infantry band is a little more numerous.

M. Sax complains with reason, it seems to me, about the rumor being accredited among the listeners to this new competition which has just taken place at the Palais-Royal. They accuse him openly of demanding the suppression of woodwinds in the infantry bands, when it was, to the contrary, his two systems that they brought together. M. Sax only proposes today the admission of some new elements introduced by him in the instrumentation, and their addition to flutes, oboes, bassoons, Eb and Bb clarinets of the infantry band. Therefore, he certainly does not dream of suppressing the woodwinds, and I could not quite get him involved in defending himself from such an intention. He only says, 'where would the symphony orchestra be if there were no family of stringed instruments to form the basis of that ensemble?' He now proposes to fill that very function in the infantry band with a complete family of sax-horns, instruments whose sonority is the most powerful. The first requirement for military music is to be bellicose and stirring, yet, in order to avoid monotony, it must offer a great variety of timbres. We possess, in the new system of organization which M. Sax presents, all that is found in the symphony orchestra, minus the stringed instruments and the horns, and plus the Eb clarinets and the two families of saxophones and sax-horns.[47]

47 *Journal des Débats*, February 21, 1852.

...

Since a few days ago there has been talk of a new reorganization of military music. Général Saint-Arnaud is one of that small population of statesmen who are interested in the art of music and truly loves it and is looking to protect it. Therefore, we must have great hopes for his wishes and his special acquaintances on this occasion. One dreams, so they say, of definitely introducing into the military bands the soft instruments of Sax, such as the saxophones (small and large) which are too often confused with the saxhorns and all other families of brass stentors with mouthpieces. We have high hopes that this addition will be adopted and, moreover, maintained if adopted, and that it should be so for all the other projects proposed to the Minister of War for the purpose of improving and making less precarious the position of musicians in the army.[48]

[48] *Journal des Débats*, November 2, 1852.

The following month, Berlioz announced the formation of a new military band based on the instruments of, and organized by, Sax. It was this band which performed at the banquet in honor of Sax, discussed above, under 'Adolphe Sax.'

> Mr. Sax has just been appointed in charge of the organization of the Band of the Guides. The orchestra's instrumentation will be based on a new system which, to me, seems excellent. It will contain in its instrumentation the majority of the older wind instruments and also the new families of sax-horns, saxophones, and the contrabass tuba, of which Mr. Sax is the inventor.
>
> The band, placed under the skilled direction of Mr. Mohr, will function beginning next month. A large number of first-rate theater artists of Paris will be among them and Mr. Arban, the ideal cornetist, has just left London to join them. This will be a caliber of military music the likes of which probably do not exist anywhere in Europe, and to which nothing can be compared, and which is worthy of the high patronage under which it is placed.[49]

[49] Ibid., December 25, 1852.

Finally, in 1854, Berlioz mentions the government's decision, once again, to approve instrumentation models after Sax. This represented the final victory for both Sax and Berlioz.

> The emperor, moreover, has just signed a decree that determines the composition of military bands for each regiment, according to a plan acknowledged by all the masters of the art. This important decision will have as a first result a reasonable and truly good organization of the military bands, then a considerable advantage due to the uniformity of all these musical bands of the army. A composition of well done music for the instrumental resources indicated by the imperial decree thus will be playable by all military bands, without exception, since they will all be organized in the same way, and the composer of this piece will no longer be exposed to the grotesque mutilations that the directors were almost obliged up until now to perform on all scores not written for them, in order to bring them into conformity with the actual forces which they had at hand. Really, from the point of view of art, this is a very handsome, and I hardly hope to see it accomplished without any obstacle, so great still in France is the number of people interested in thwarting, when it comes to music, the power of common sense.[50]

[50] *Journal des Débats*, October 11, 1854.

Bands and the Church

As the result of winning the composition prize, the Prix de Rome, Berlioz was able to spend a number of months in 1831–1832 traveling in Italy and residing in Rome. One of the things which seemed to have surprised him, as a French catholic, was the secular appearance of the celebration of some of the church feast days. Continuing from the older traditions of close relationships between civic and church institutions, the church celebrations also included parades with the inclusion of many civic elements, not the least of which was the town band. There are places in the world where one can still see this tradition today. To Berlioz, reared in the small village traditions of France, these celebrations seemed to appear too secular and too overdone. He was also sensitive to the poor quality of church music he heard in Italy.

His first description of the Corpus Christi celebration he saw in Rome, on 2 June 1831, we read in a letter to his sister.

> In came the monks in all their splendor, and then the small scoundrels from the abbey, grotesquely dressed and making eyes at the ladies who were seated in the galleries, laughing and joking loudly among themselves. Then came a military band, sounding somewhat like the lottery of Paris, or even better yet like the music those tricksters usually have in their company to sell drugs—poor devils of soldiers in white uniforms with blue lining that was so worn out that you could see right through it, wearing their shakos and their arms like a first week draftee. The Swiss, the gold brocaded Cardinals, the flag bearers with holes in their stockings and with bad shoes covered with mud, and the damned little rogues singing an unbearable counterpoint with their off-pitch voices and harmonies, sounding like rusty doors. The pope did not come. So there you have it, in the capital of the Christian world and in the place where we are sent to admire the masterpieces of music that we hear in religious festivals. I miss my beautiful military band of Nice, which at least played music of substance.[51]

[51] Letter to his Sister, Adaele, Rome, June 6, 1831, in *Correspondance*, 230.

By the following Spring, his description of this celebration, now written for the public, had become much more dramatic.

I left Geneva for Rome. Passing back through Florence ... I was listening with the keenest interest to those around me who were talking about the festival of the Fete of Corpus Domini (Corpus Christi), which was to be celebrated soon at Rome. So, I was very anxious to go there, and I undertook the journey to the capital of the pontifical states with several people from Florence who were drawn by the same motive. During the trip, the only subject of conversation was the marvels that were to be offered for our admiration. These gentlemen spread before me a tableau dazzling with tiaras, mitres, chasubles, brilliant crosses, vestments of gold, clouds of incense,—ma la musica?—'Oh, signore, lei sentira un coro immenso.' Then they returned to the clouds of incense, the gilt vestments, the brilliant crosses, the tumult of the bells and cannons ... La musica, I asked again, la musica di questa ceremonia?—'Davero, signore, lei sentira un coro immenso.'—Well so it seems there will be ... an immense chorus, after all. I was already thinking about the musical pomp of some religious ceremonies in Solomon's Temple, my imagination became more and more inflamed, I went so far as to hope for something comparable to the gigantic elegance of ancient Egypt ... Accursed faculty, that makes of our life nothing but a continual mirage! Without it, perhaps I would have been delighted by the piercing and out of tune falsetto of those eighteen castrati that made me listen to a stupid and insipid counterpoint; without it, perhaps I would not have been surprised NOT to find in the procession of the Corpus Domini a swarm of young virgins, in white dress, with pure and fresh voices, with faces imprinted by religious sentiment, breathing towards heaven pious cantiques, the harmonious perfumes of those living roses. Without that fatal imagination, those two groups of duck-like clarinets, roaring trombones, maddened bass drums, clown-like trumpets, perhaps would not have revolted me by the impious and ridiculous cacophony. In this case, it is also true that one would have had to suppress one's sense of hearing. They call that, in Rome, band music. For an old drunken Silenus, mounted on an ass, followed by a group of crude satyrs and impure bacchantes, to be escorted by such a concert ... nothing better; but the Holy Sacrament, the images of the Virgin!!! ... How could the Pope permit it?[52]

52 *Revue européene*, March-May, 1832, 54ff.

53 *Memoirs*, 163.

When Berlioz mentioned this in his *Memoirs*[53] he added the following,

Barbarous! The Pope is a barbarian, like most other sovereigns. The Roman people are barbarians, like all other peoples.

Berlioz has also left a similar, vivid picture of the public celebration of Carnival with a small peasant band participating.

I was as fierce as a chained dog. My companions' attempts to include me in their diversions only made me more irritable. The attraction they found in the 'delights' of the Carnival particularly incensed me. I could not conceive (I still cannot) what pleasure anyone could take in the festivities connected with what are appropriately called, in Rome as in Paris, the fat days, *i giorni grassi*. Bloated days, greasy with mire and sweat and grinning painted faces, gross with brutalities and foul-mouthed abuse, drunken informers, whores, half-wits gaping and guffawing, broken-down horses, the reek of the streets, the boredom and degradation of humanity! In Rome, where they preserved the great traditions of the ancient world, a human victim was sacrificed during the festival. I do not know whether this charming practice, redolent of the poetry of the arena, is still extant. No doubt it is; ideas of such grandeur do not disappear overnight. In those days some poor devil under sentence of death was kept for the purpose and fattened so as to be a worthy offering to the sacred people of Rome; and in due time, when this rabble of fools of every nation (for in justice it must be said, the foreigners are as eager for the sport), when this horde of apes in the likeness of men grew bored with watching the horse racing and pelting each other in the face with plaster pellets, to the accompaniment of shrieks of witty merriment, they went off to see 'the man' die. The worms, they do well to call him that. Generally it is some luckless bandit who, weakened by his wounds, is taken half dead by the valiant soldiers of the Pope, carefully patched up, nursed back to health, and fattened and shriven for shrovetide: and to my mind this wretched prisoner is a thousand times more truly a man than the gloating multitude for whose amusement the church's spiritual and temporal head (*abhorrens a sanguine*) and the representative of God on earth is obliged from time to time to provide the spectacle of a severed head.

It is true that soon afterwards the fastidious crowd repairs to the Piazza Navona to wash itself free of any stains which the blood may have left on its clothes. The square is completely flooded; the vegetable market disappears and is replaced by a stagnant pond, upon whose bosom float not water-lilies but cabbage stalks, lettuce leaves, melon peel, straw and the husks of almonds. On a platform erected towards one side of the enchanted lake a small band of musicians, with a couple of bass drums, tenor drum, side drum, triangle, Turkish crescent and two pairs of cymbals, supported for appearances' sake by a few horns or clarinets, discourse music in a style as pure as the water lapping round the supports of their stage.[54]

54 Ibid., 169.

In a footnote to this passage, written at the time he began his *Memoirs*, Berlioz adds the following reference to another Parisian who was offended by what he saw in Rome.

The Parisians still maintain the standards set by the Romans in 1831. M. Leon Halévy, brother to the well-known composer, has just written a thoroughly sensible and right-minded letter to the *Journal des Débats*, demanding the suppression of the disgusting rites celebrated during the Carnival, when the shrovetide bull is paraded through the streets for three days and finally driven exhausted to the slaughterhouse, where its throat is cut amid scenes of great pomp.

His eloquent protest stirred me to send him the following letter:

'Sir—permit me to congratulate you most warmly on the admirable letter published in the *Journal des Débats* this morning. No, do not believe you have made yourself look foolish. In any case, to be thought foolish by trivial minds is far better than to be thought callous and insensitive by men of feeling for remaining indifferent to the scenes you so justly stigmatize, which turn so-called civilized man into the nastiest of all predatory animals.'

In one of his newspaper articles, Berlioz makes a plea for the Church to improve the quality of the music, at least.

When the ceremonies, so pompous, moreover, of the Catholic cult were delivered from the ridicule which snatches of barbarous music pours over them, but that they fondly believe themselves decorated with, what harm would there be? In the processions of Corpus Christi, for example; instead of the grating falsetto of some hideous castrati, as in Rome, or the savage bawling of five or six cathedral cantors, as here, followed by band music performing popular street ditties, as is done everywhere, if some sacred hymns, written by the greatest masters and sung by an immense chorus young men and women with fresh and pure voices, were accompanied by a hundred harps, the harmonious vibrating of three thousand strings united to the religious melody of the voices, would not that be equal to the pounding of the bass drum beating the time from the duet of THE PURITAINS?

Musical sentiment must be a very rare thing, since the Catholic clergy, so jealous of the splendor of its cult, so prodigal of its treasures when it is a case of attracting to itself the masterpieces of architecture and the arts of sketching, not only does so little for religious music, but would not even wonder that, if the devil in person were to come sing a parody of the Holy Rites, he would not do anything worse than what is heard daily.[55]

55 *Journal des Débats*, July 23, 1836.

Three years later, Berlioz writes of Spontini who, when hearing inferior music in the church, actually made an effort to influence the pope toward reform.

Spontini has just traveled around Italy, which he had not seen again since his youth. Horrified by the state in which he found religious music (people did not want to believe what we wrote on this subject), the famous composer proposed to the Pope a vast plan of reform perfectly conceived and worked over with the heated indignation that such a lowering of the art is well calculated to induce. This project, perfectly welcomed by His Holiness, has already received a beginning of its implementation at Jesi, Spontini's home land, where we see from a mandate from Cardinal Oatini that it is forbidden, under severe retributions, for composers to parody the sacred words in music theater, for organists to play opera overtures during the holy service, and for singers to sing comic songs during the communion. They forgot to forbid also tenors to sing in falsetto ornamented arias written for sopranos; a grotesque monstrosity that I witnessed in Rome in the church of St. Louis of the French. It would not be bad either to request organists to use other registers than the high pitched register for the accompaniment of funeral services.

In Florence I heard a Mass for the Dead played entirely in the piccolo register. One never sees anything of this kind in Germany, nor in France, nor in England, where even amateurs treat sacred music with all respect and dignity.[56]

[56] *Journal des Débats*, May 10, 1839.

There was an old custom, continued in some churches in France well into the nineteenth century, to use the serpent to accompany the singers of chant. It was this practice, for the most part, which kept this instrument alive in France long after it had been retired to the museum in other countries. This was a practice which Berlioz attacked, due, we may guess, to the terrible sound of the instrument.

The truly barbaric tone of [the serpent] would be much better suited for the bloody cult of the Druids than for that of the Catholic church, where it is still in use—as a monstrous symbol for the lack of understanding and the coarseness of taste and feeling which have governed the application of music in our churches since times immemorial. Only one case is to be excepted; masses for the dead, where the serpent serves to double the dreadful choir of the Dies Irae. Here its cold and awful blaring is doubtless appropriate; it even seems to assume a character of mournful poetry when accompanying this text, imbued with all the horrors of death and the revenge of an irate God.[57]

[57] *Treatise*, 348.

Some years later his friend and fellow critic, Joseph d'Ortigue, published a treatise on church music which also attacked this custom, which was still continuing after mid-century. Berlioz, once again, adds his support against the use of the instrument.

> What he censures most is the manner in which plainchant is usually performed; this amounting to its being bellowed, or roared in bull-fashion to an accompaniment of serpent or ophicleide. He is certainly quite right. To hear such successions of hideous notes, with threatening accents, one might imagine themselves transported to a cave of Druids at the moment of their preparing for a human sacrifice. This is frightful, though I must admit that every piece of plain-chant I have heard was so performed, and might fairly be described in this way.[58]

[58] *Journal des Débats*, January 20, 1854.

Bands and Opera

THE FOLLOWING COMMENTARY BY BERLIOZ can only be understood if one remembers that during the nineteenth century the military was at the forefront of society. The military was inseparable from social, church and government events (during the second-half of the century, the American Presidents, from Lincoln on, were the only world leaders who did not wear a military uniform). During these twilight years of the ancient aristocratic world, the battle was the last 'grand adventure,' something which would never again be possible after World War I.

In France, of course, this fascination with all things military began with the dramatic events of the Napoleonic era, and the resultant formation and popularity of civic militia bands. It is no surprise, therefore, that persons in charge of staging opera in Paris, following the interest of the public, began to add to the orchestration of operas the brass and percussion instruments associated with the military. Sometimes full military bands were added as a stage element, even to operas by Mozart. In turn, composers of new operas, including Meyerbeer, Wagner, and Verdi, began to include off-stage military bands in their opera scores.

It was the audacity of adding instruments to the scores of earlier composers which particularly angered Berlioz while a student in Paris.

> It was just as unwise for the performers to change anything in the score, for I knew every note and would have died rather than let the slightest tampering with the great masters pass unchallenged. I had no intention of waiting until I could protest coldly in print at this crime against genius. No, indeed! I denounced the offenders then and there, publicly and in a loud, clear voice; and I can vouch for it that there is no form of criticism so effective. One day—to give an example—*Iphigénie en Tauride* was on. I had noticed at the previous performance that cymbals had been added to the Scythians' first dance in B minor, which Gluck wrote for strings alone, and also that in Orestes' great recitative in the third act the trombones, which are so superbly appropriate to the dramatic situation, had been omitted. I decided that if the same errors were repeated, I should point them out. When the Scythian ballet began I waited for the

cymbals. They came in precisely as they had before. Although seething with rage, I managed to contain myself until the end of the piece: then, in the short pause which ensued, I yelled out, 'There are no cymbals there. Who has dared to correct Gluck?'

There was a buzz of consternation. The public, who are very unclear about such artistic questions and do not care whether the composer's orchestration is altered or not, could not understand what this young lunatic in the pit was getting so angry about. But it was worse in the third act. The trombones in Orestes' monologue were suppressed as I had feared they would be, and the same voice rang through the theater: 'Why aren't the trombones playing? This is intolerable.'

The astonishment of both orchestra and audience was only equaled by the wrath—very natural, I admit—of Valentino, who was conducting that evening. It transpired that the trombones had only been obeying an express order not to play in that particular passage; the orchestral parts complied exactly with the score.

As to the cymbals, which Gluck uses with such felicity in the first of the Scythian choruses, I do not know who had taken upon himself to put them into the dance music as well, thus altering the whole color and disrupting the sinister stillness of that strange ballet. But I do know that at subsequent performances everything was in order. The cymbals were silent, the trombones spoke. I contented myself with growling between my teeth, 'Ah, now that's better.'[59]

59 *Memoirs*, 82ff.

Berlioz objects again, in an article on Gluck, to the casual substitutions of winds, which now he heard in Gluck's *Orfeo*.

At the time when Gluck wrote *Orfeo* at Vienna, an instrument was in use, which is still employed to accompany the chorales at some churches in Germany, and which he calls 'cornetto.' It is made of wood, is pierced with holes, and is played with a mouthpiece of either copper or horn; similar to the mouthpiece of the trumpet.

In the religious funeral ceremony which takes place around the tomb of Eurydice, in the first act of *Orfeo*, Gluck adds the cornetto to the three trombones, in order to accompany the four chorus parts. The cornetto not being known at the Opéra of Paris, was later on suppressed without being replaced by any other instrument; and the sopranos of the chorus, whose part it followed in unison in the Italian score, were thus deprived of instrumental support. In the third verse of the romance of the first act, 'Piango il mio ben cosi,' the composer introduced two English horns; but, as the orchestra at the Opéra did not possess these instruments, they were replaced by two clarinets …

Finally, trombone parts were added, by one of the old leaders of the Opéra orchestra, for certain parts of the infernal scene, where the composer had not supplied them.[60]

60 Berlioz, *Gluck & his Operas*, 5ff.

On the subject of changing the scores of the earlier masters, Berlioz was most incensed and vocal when he heard the addition of the bass drum. It always seemed to him to be the most gross insult, musically, to the composer.

> On my way back through Genoa I went to hear Paer's *Agnese*, which had been a famous opera in the dark ages before the dawn of Rossini.
>
> It left me unmoved and bored; no doubt its beauties were obscured by the performance, which was appalling. I noticed at once that, in accordance with the charming practice of certain persons who, though incapable of writing anything themselves, see it as their mission to rewrite or touch up everything, and who can tell at a glance of their eagle eye what a work lacks, someone had strengthened the score by the addition of a bass drum; with the result that Paer's modest and sensible orchestration, not being designed to stand the shock of such an encounter, disappeared without a trace.[61]

[61] *Memoirs*, 159.

Even where the composer himself scored the bass drum for works to be given in Paris, Berlioz can not fail to make reference to it.

> *William Tell?* ... I think that all the newspapers have gone mad; it is a work which has some beautiful parts, which is not absurdly written, [in places] where there is no *crescendo* and a little less bass drum.[62]

[62] Letter to Humbert Ferrand, August 21, 1829, in *Correspondance*, 134.

Again, in a review of the first performance of Halévy's *La Dame de Pique*, 'In the officers' chorus the voices are just about covered by the noise of the snare drum, the bass drum, and the timpani.'[63]

[63] *Journal des Débats*, January 1, 1851.

After years of objecting to the addition of percussion, in 1853 he published an article which summarized the history of this practice in the Paris Opera.

> Here is how the kingdom of the percussion instruments [in the opera] was established. The readers who are friends of music will excuse me for my long-windedness—at least I hope so. As for the others, I am not worried as I am sure they will not read me.
>
> Unless I am ghastly in error, it was in *Iphigénie en Aulide*, by Gluck, that the bass drum was first heard in the Paris Opéra—but, by itself, without cymbals or other percussion instruments. It was used in the last Greek Chorus to the words, 'Let us leave! Fly to Victory!' It served the purpose of a military parade, beating the strong beats of each measure as it does in vulgar marches ...

Gluck then introduced cymbals (and we know with what admirable effect) in the Seythes Choir of *Iphigénie en Tauride*, and cymbals alone, without the bass drum—which people with a tendency toward routine thought were inseparable. In a ballet of the same opera he uses, with the rarest joy, the triangle—alone. And that was all.

In 1808, Spontini admitted the bass drum and cymbals into the triumphal march and dance of the gladiators in *La Vestale* and later in the march of Telasco in *Fernand Cortez* …

But Rossini came to give *Le Siege de Corinthe* at the Opéra and noticed, not without sorrow, the public's indifference to the execution of these beautiful works—indifference brought on more by the physical reasons of our big theater than for musical reasons … Rossini swore that he would not suffer this indignity: 'I know how to prevent you from sleeping,' said he. And so he put in the bass drum everywhere, and the cymbals and the triangle and the trombones and the ophicleide by handfuls, punching with violent rhythm. He made the orchestra create such lightening sounds and harmonies, and such rumblings of thunder, that the public, rubbing their eyes, took to this new type of vibrant emotion, which was more musical than what they had been hearing up to then.

Encouraged by success, he went even further in this type of abuse by composing *Moïse*, where, in the famous and magnificent finale of the third act, the bass drum, cymbals, and triangle beat, during the *fortes*, each beat of the measure. In doing so, they play *as many notes as the singers*, who try to accommodate as best they can with such an accompaniment. Nevertheless, the orchestra and chorus of this surprising piece are constructed in such a way that the tone of the voices and instruments is so overwhelming that the music floats on the surface of all this din. And further, the music projects waves of sound to all corners of the hall, despite it vast dimension, and grasps the listener and shakes him and makes him vibrate and the greatest effect is produced … But, do the percussion instruments contribute to this sound? Yes, if they are considered as an exciting fury for the other instruments and voices; no, if one only considers the realistic part they take within the musical action, for they smash the orchestra and the voices and substitute a violent sound reaching folly, a sonority of energy, an incomparable beauty.

Be that as it may, starting with the arrival of Rossini at the Opéra the instrumental revolution of the theater orchestras began. Big noises were used in all works, at all times, no matter what style they imposed on their subject. Soon the timpani, bass drum, cymbals, and triangle were not enough and to them were added the side drum, two [valved] cornets coming to the aid of the [natural] trumpets, trombones and the ophicleide. The organ was set up backstage next to the bells and then the military band entered on the scene and finally the big instruments of Sax, which were to the voice of the orchestra what a canon is to a shotgun …

The judicious use of even the most vulgar and offensive of instruments can be done for the sake of art and can truly help increase richness and strength. Nothing should be disdained within the means we have at our disposal today. But the instrumental horrors we have witnessed today will surely become all the more hideous and I feel that I have proven that they have greatly contributed to the birth of excessive singing—and have motivated these too lengthy and, I fear, useless ponderings.

Add these same excesses, as they were in the spirit of imitation, to the Opéra-Comique, with the particular conditions of this [smaller] theater, of its orchestra and singers, and the general tone of its repertoire, and the result is incomparably more revolting.[64]

[64] *Journal des Débats*, February 6, 1853.

In his musical travels Berlioz did not mention this practice as being so common as in Paris—with the exception of London.

I am once again back from London. This time … I heard nothing there by way of music but what was rather painful. At her Majesty's Theater I saw a performance of Mozart's *Figaro* that was trombonized, ophicleided—in a word, copper-bottomed like a ship of the line. That is an English habit. Neither Mozart, nor Rossini, nor Weber, nor Beethoven has managed to escape *re-instrumentation*. Their orchestra is not sufficiently spicy, and it is deemed imperative to remedy the defect. Besides, if the theaters have regular performers on the trombone, ophicleide, bass drum, triangle, cymbals, they are obviously not hired to twiddle their thumbs.[65]

[65] Berlioz, *Evenings with the Orchestra*, 356.

In Paris this perceived freedom to reorchestrate earlier works even extended to Beethoven symphonies. One has to add that this practice spread to other parts of Europe as the century continued; even Mahler, in Vienna, reorchestrated the Ninth Symphony of Beethoven! Berlioz never forgave this practice.

It was recently remarked, at one of the Conservatoire concerts, that, in the duet of Gluck's *Armide*, 'Espirits de haine et de rage,' the voices were frequently overpowered by loud trombone notes, and thus lost much of their effect. These trombone parts, which are very indifferently done, have been added at Paris, I do not know by whom; while at Berlin, this work has suffered to an even greater degree from the same cause. Now, it may be useful to observe in connection with this subject, that, for neither *Armide* nor *Iphigénia in Aulide* has Gluck written a single note for trombones. It is useless to reply that, the reason for his abstaining from the use of this instrument in *Armide* was because there were no trombones at the Opéra at the time; for, in *Alceste* and *Orphée*, both of which were presented before *Armide*, those instruments appear, and, in the first of these, play a highly important part. Moreover, they are also employed in *Iphigénia in Tauride*.

It is strange that a composer, however great he may be, should not be allowed to write for his orchestra as he chooses; and, especially, that he should not be free to abstain from the use of certain instruments whenever he sees fit to do so. It has admittedly happened in several instances, and even to illustrious masters, to correct the instrumentation of their predecessors; to whom they thus made a free gift of their learning and taste. Thus, Mozart added new accompaniments to the oratorios of Handel; but divine justice decreed that, later on, the operas of Mozart himself should be re-instrumented in their turn. This happened in England: where trombones, ophicleides and bass drums were thrust into the scores of *Figaro* and *Don Giovanni*.

Spontini confessed to me one day that he had added, though admittedly with considerable discretion, wind parts to those which were already present in the score of *Iphigénia in Tauride* by Gluck. Two years afterwards, he was complaining bitterly, in my presence, of some excesses of this kind which he had witnessed; and of the abominable crudities added to the scores of dead masters, who were no longer there to defend themselves. Spontini exclaimed, 'It is a shame! it is frightful! And I fear that they will correct me too, after I am dead.'—to which I could only sadly reply, 'Alas! my dear master; have you not, yourself, already corrected Gluck?'

Even the greatest symphonist the world has ever seen has not been allowed to escape from this indescribable kind of outrage; and, independently of the overture to *Fidelio*, which they have 'tromboned' from one end to the other in England (being of opinion forsooth that, in that overture, Beethoven's employment of trombones was too reserved) they have already commenced, in another quarter, to correct the instrumentation of the C MINOR SYMPHONY!

I intend some day, in the form of a special article, to present you with the names of all these ravagers of works of art.[66]

66 Berlioz, *Weber and Wagner*, 1.

Regarding Gluck's *Alceste*, mentioned above, in 1857 Berlioz received a letter calling into question his authority for a comment he had made about the distribution of the trombones.

Now I must tell you that the distribution of the trombones such as you indicated, has never existed in the French edition of *Alceste* ... No, there is no error in the French edition concerning the trombones; the changes introduced in the disposition of their parts have obviously as their purpose the production of this dominant chord, so vehemently characterized by you.[67]

67 Letter from Françoise Delsarte to Berlioz, Paris, April 28, 1857, in *Correspondance*, 2226.

Berlioz immediately responded as follows:

> I would have believed myself quite sure as to the chords Gluck had used to accompany the choirs in the shadows of Alceste. I would have bet a thousand francs against one hundred sous of your's that you were the victim of an error. And I would have won my bet.
>
> I have just come from the Opéra where the autograph manuscript score is kept. [here follows a detailed explanation of how and why a printing error had occurred in the French edition.] … because of this mistake, the cause of the error became impossible to find by anyone who had not seen the score at the Opéra library.[68]

[68] Letter to Françoise Delsarte, Paris, April 30, 1857, in *Correspondance*, 2228.

As one attempt to halt the practice of adding additional instruments to the works of earlier scores, Berlioz tried to remind his readers why these earlier composers were masters and to explain why they made the choices they had. For example, he explains that although Gluck in fact used percussion instruments, it was done so with careful selectivity.

> Gluck has so constantly abstained from employing the low notes of the clarinet, as well as those of both horns and trombones, that he seems not to have known them. A profound study of his instrumentation would lead us too far from our subject. It will be sufficient to say that he was the first in France to employ (only once) the bass drum (without cymbals) in the final chorus of *Iphigénia in Aulide*; the cymbals (without bass drum); and the triangle and tambourine, in the first act of *Iphigénia in Tauride*; instruments which nowadays, are so stupidly employed and so revoltingly abused.[69]

[69] Berlioz, *Gluck & his Operas*, 101.

Berlioz points out the irony that while Mozart and some earlier composers were criticized for making the orchestra too important in their operas, the productions of his own time compounded what had been objected to.

> [Grétry once said of Mozart], *He put the pedestal on the stage and the statue in the orchestra.* But the same criticism had already been addressed to Gluck, and was later applied to Weber, Spontini, and Beethoven. It will never cease to be addressed to any composer who abstains from penning platitudes for the voice; and who gives the orchestra an interesting part, however much learning and discretion he may display.
>
> The people who are so quick to blame the great masters for a pretended predominance of instruments over voices do not greatly esteem this learning or this discretion. Every day for the last ten years we have seen the orchestra turned into a military band, a blacksmith's forge, or a brazier's shop, without this alarming the critics, and ever causing them to pay the slightest attention to these enormities. The critics say nothing if the orchestra is noisy, violent, brutal, insipid, revolting, and

even exterminating the voice and the melody. But it is fine and intelligent if it attracts a certain attention to itself by its vivacity, grace, and eloquence and, if in spite of all this it still plays the part assigned by dramatic and musical exigency, it is blamed. The orchestra is easily pardoned either for saying nothing at all or for uttering nothing but stupidity and coarseness in the event it should speak.[70]

70 Berlioz, *Beethoven by Berlioz*, 52.

Berlioz pointed to Spontini as an example of a contemporary opera composer who used the expanded wind and percussion instruments with intelligence. In a review of Spontini's *Agnes de Hohenstaufen*, he observes,

> Spontini's orchestration, beginnings of which are found in *Milton* and in *Julie*, are his pure invention, preceded by none. His special color is due to the use of wind instruments ... [his] moderate use, but with excessive genius, of the trombones, trumpets, horns and percussion, with the almost absolute exclusion of extreme high pitches from flutes, oboes, and clarinets, give Spontini's works a grandiose make-up, a power, an incomparable energy and often a melancholic poetic nature. Spontini was the first one who, in the triumphal march and the dance aria in *La Vestale* used the bass drum, which today is abused in all the theaters in a most revolting way.[71]

71 *Journal des Débats*, February 12, 1851.

Only in the case of Renaissance and Baroque music does Berlioz seem to modify his stand. He reminds the reader that, in the end, it is the music which matters. If this apparent contradiction were pointed out, he would no doubt say that his point in nineteenth-century opera is that with tremendous addition of instruments one cannot hear the music any longer.

> There is a widespread opinion which attributes the monotony of the works of ancient composers to the slender resources which were at their disposition. It is customary to say, 'The instruments which we employ were not then invented.'
>
> That is an evident mistake. Palestrina wrote only for voices; and the singers of his period were probably fully capable of executing other things besides counterpoint in five or six parts. As to instrumentalists, although, at the time of Lully they were untrained and of incontestable inferiority compared with ours, a modern composer of talent could easily produce excellent effects, even with the moderate executants that Lully had at his command. We must not attribute such great importance to the material means of the art of sounds. A sonata of Beethoven, executed upon a spinet, would nevertheless remain a marvel of inspira-

tion; whilst many other works which I might mention, even if played upon the most magnificent Erard or Broadwood piano, would remain mere nonsense and platitude.[72]

72 *Gluck & his Operas*, 57.

In still another effort to educate his readers, Berlioz gives the perspective of a master orchestrator on the inherent dangers of that art. He begins with the problem of the winds and percussion making true balance with the strings impossible. Regarding the premiere of a comic opera, *l'An Mil*, by Albert Grisar, Berlioz writes,

> As for the choirs, it is impossible for me to discover anything but rhythmic cries and a lack of musical character on the part of the singers, despite the fact that it is obvious that they were doing the best their lungs could do, which makes one believe that they were highly encouraged to do just this. This is too bad, for this no more constitutes energetic singing than those horrible bass drum bangings at the end of each phrase constitute energetic instrumentation. Following this road we will end up in front of the gun, at the broken chair, with hooplas and Musard's orgiastic gallops. But the use of percussion instruments and trombones in a small orchestra, such as in a comic opera where you might have only six or seven first violins and as many seconds, remind one of the grotesque dwarf in *Bal masque de Gustave*, whose head is as big and as high as the rest of his body.
>
> The brass instruments are powerful auxiliary instruments. The bass drum itself, used with reserve and discretion, sometimes produces an excellent effect, if it is used within an instrumental mass, for the mass of great voices makes it seem less out of proportion. The opportunity to use these forces in the context of a small orchestra exists perhaps, but it is rare and I don't think this kind of opportunity has been offered in the opera in question.
>
> But this is not a trait found only in Mr. Grisar—far from it … . The Example, and its homely daughter, Routine, do all the harm. We are afraid to hear the words *weak orchestra* and *dull instrumentation*. When we only need to hear a pin drop, the bulldogs of the orchestra are unchained.[73]

73 *Journal des Débats*, June 28, 1837.

And again, in an article two years later:

> The trumpets, the trombones, the timpani, and the bass drum still dominate in a horrible fashion, and so much so that in the *fortes* one cannot distinguish the sound of the violins. The artists charged with the brass instrumental parts probably belong to the corps of military music, and the habit of playing in the open air makes them blow notes in a way to *brassify* almost always the sound with a crudity destructive to all harmony …

But as soon as you approach the modern operas where the brass dominates, where the bass drum is employed (without any reason, ninety-nine times out of a hundred), where can be counted, besides the wind instruments formerly used, two valved cornets, a third and fourth horn, and an ophicleide, it is necessary to call to your aid an army of stringed instruments, not only to blend and sweeten the crudeness of these rough voices; but also in order that the violin part, which, in the final analysis, is the principal part, may make a way for itself and keep, in the musical hierarchy, the place that the composers of all times have assigned to it.[74]

[74] *Journal des Débats*, August 9, 1839.

In Berlin he appreciated the extra woodwinds he heard in the opera orchestra, for their ability to mitigate somewhat the power of the brass.

The woodwind instruments [in Berlin] are also extremely good, and you see double the number which we have in the Opéra at Paris. That combination is very advantageous; it permits bringing two flutes, two oboes, two clarinets, and two bassoons *ripienni* in the *fortissimo*, and sweetens singularly, then, the harshness of the brass instruments which, otherwise, always dominate too strongly. The horns are of a beautiful intensity, and all with cylindrical valves, to the great regret of Meyerbeer, who has maintained the opinion that I had just a while ago on the subject of this new mechanism.[75]

[75] Ibid., October 8, 1843.

Again, it was the addition of the military band, or its new instruments, as mere stage props, which Berlioz refused to accept as a matter of principle.

What the provincial conductors are always sure of not lacking, for the performance of modern operas, is the ophicleide, the bass drum. There is always, if not in the village itself, at least in the neighborhood, some regiment quartered, whose military band abundantly furnishes the theaters with these gross instruments. In such a place, you will have no oboe, nor clarinets, nor bassoons, but their absence will be compensated for by a gigantic ophicleide, bawling like a five-year-old bull; in such another, there will only be three violins, one bass, no viola, one flute, one horn, and one clarinet, and you will see, in a corner of the orchestra, a bass drum rising triumphantly, large as a twenty-load barrel, escorted by all his family [of] cymbals, triangle, and bells of the Chinese crescent. It is with such means that they want to execute *Robert*. Good heavens! execute certainly is the word; it is certainly as impossible for the work to come out alive from such a test, as it would be for the author to resist an accolade by the guillotine.[76]

[76] 'De l'Instrumentation de Robert-le-Diable,' in *Gazette Musicale de Paris*, July 12, 1835.

On one occasion he ridicules a fellow critic who mistook the saxhorn for a saxophone.

> A Jupiter of the critical press, attacking recently with violence the wonderful instruments of Sax, ranked among the most formidable—those which could easily tear one's ears off—the *saxophone*, a reed instrument with a veiled and delicious tone, which he had confused with the saxhorns which are brass instruments with a mouthpiece.
>
> This illustrious and conscientious hypercritic without doubt studied instrumentation at the Theatre Français.[77]

[77] Berlioz, *Les Grotesques de la musique*, 91.

Let it also be noted that Berlioz also points out those cases where the composer used his instrumental resources with musicianship and skill. One example is found in his review of a performance of Meyerbeer's *l'Etoile du Nord*.

> It is so finely instrumented, there is so much taste, spirit and luxurious reserve in the use of diverse and exceptional resources of which the composer disposes, that it must be for each artist a pleasure to play his part. Never do we find instrumental or rhythmic brutalities anywhere; never these packets of chords which seem thrown in the face of the listener like a shovel full of cement. There is the big orchestra completely full, military band on the stage, small orchestra of fife and drum … and yet for all this there is no noise, but there is music.[78]

[78] *Journal des Débats*, February 21, 1854.

And in a review of one of the first performances of Beethoven's *Fidelio* in Paris:

> Those critics who are so quick to blame the true masters who use a predominance of instruments over the voices have paid no attention to the enormous change during the past ten years when we have seen the orchestra transformed into a military band, a kettle maker's shop into a blacksmith's shop (no criticism intended). If the orchestra is loud, violent, brutal, flat, revolting, exterminating the voices and the melody, the critics say nothing. If the orchestra, on the other hand, is fine, delicate, intelligent, and attracts from time to time attention to itself by its vivacity, its grace, or its eloquence, and remains faithful to the dramatic and musical demands of the opera, it is censured. One easily excuses the orchestra for not saying anything, or, when it does speak, to speak silliness and vulgarities.[79]

[79] *Journal des Débats*, May 19, 1860.

Once when he himself was asked to participate in the employment of a military band in an opera production, he politely refused.

I am very distressed not to be able to do what you ask of me, but everything prevents me … it is contrary to everything I believe to put my hand to such derangements. The March from *Olympie* doesn't need vulgar military brass, it is quite richly enough scored. I pity you with all my heart for having to submit to such demands on the part of your public.[80]

[80] Letter to George Hainl, January 9, 1862, quoted in Humphrey Searle, *Hector Berlioz, A Selection from his Letters* (London: Gollancz, 1966), 174.

With regard to the use of a military band on stage, Berlioz recommends to Paris the stage placement he saw in Berlin, in a production of Meyerbeer's *The Huguenots*.

The military band, instead of being placed, as in Paris, at the back of the stage, from where, separated from the orchestra by the crowd that throngs the stage, it cannot see the movements of the conductor, nor consequently, follow the beat with precision, begins to play in the apron wings on the public's right; then it starts to move and wanders over the stage passing near the ramp and crossing through the chorus groups. In that way, the musicians are located, almost at the end of the piece, very close to the conductor; they rigorously keep the same beat as the lower orchestra, and there is never the least rhythmic imprecision between the two masses.[81]

[81] *Journal des Débats*, October 21, 1843.

On one occasion, Berlioz was criticized for his use of sax-horns in an opera (which he later crossed out in his autograph score). To this criticism, he responded.

In France, as elsewhere, no one disputes my 'mastery of orchestration,' especially since I published a treatise on the subject. I am, however, criticized for an excessive use of Sax's instruments, no doubt on the sound general principle that I have often praised them, even if I do not happen to have employed them anywhere except in one scene of *The Capture of Troy*, an opera of which no one has yet seen a note. I am also criticized for being inordinately noisy and too fond of the bass drum—although I have included it only in a few works, where there is a reason for it, and although I alone among critics have been protesting for twenty years against the abuse of noise, the brainless introduction of bass drum, trombones and the rest into small theaters and small orchestras, operettas and comic patter songs, where even the side drum is now pressed into service.

It was really Rossini, in *The Siege of Corinth*, who first introduced noisy orchestration into France. Yet French critics never mention him in this connection, nor do they blame Auber, Halévy, Adam and a score of others for their odious exaggeration of Rossini's system. Instead they blame me, nay they blame Weber (see his Life in Michaud's *Biographie universelle*)—Weber, who used the bass drum only once in his orchestra, and handled every instrument with incomparable skill and restraint!

As far as it relates to me, I fancy this absurd delusion derives from the festivals in which I have often been seen to direct enormous orchestras. Prince Metternich asked me one day in Vienna whether it was I who 'composed music for five hundred players?' To which I replied: 'Not always, Your Highness. Sometimes I use only four hundred and fifty.'[82]

[82] *Memoirs*, 481.

On another occasion, Berlioz appears surprisingly sensitive on this same issue.

As for the Sax instruments, I don't know who could have given you the idea that I needed any. I have never used them in any of my scores. Only once (a small, high saxhorn) was used in *one piece* of my *Te Deum* and that is all.[83]

[83] Letter to Louis-Joseph Daussoigne-Méhul, Paris, December 13, 1855, in *Correspondance*, 2062.

Among the more 'modern' composers, Berlioz found, in his review of the premiere of Verdi's *Louise Miller*, hope for more intelligence on the part of future opera composers.

The instrumentation seemed to be a bit sober, often elegant, and the bass drum is completely forbidden in it. This deserves recognition: Mr. Verdi needed courage to leave it out! It is a step in the path of reform; let us hope the maestro will walk in this courageous path even more boldly.[84]

[84] *Journal des Débats*, February 6, 1853.

Part 4

On Performance Problems

On Acoustics

All musicians encounter, at one time or another, the mysteries of the acoustics of concert halls. A composer first imagines his music, and then is often surprised in hearing some of its details when rehearsed, is surprised again by the effect of the hall. Berlioz has left one article in which he discusses the two most important halls in Paris where serious music was performed.

> The timpani occupy a quite high rank in the modern instrumental gamut, the great composers have known how to derive the happiest contrasts from them, the most picturesque effects, in the nuances between *piano* and *mezzo-forte*. However, one can only really hear the timpani well and entirely appreciate the importance that they have acquired these last twenty years, in the hall of the Conservatoire. At the Opéra Comique, they only serve to make a dull noise, very disagreeable; the instrument is not bad, the player does not lack ability, but probably the corner of the orchestra where they are placed is damp; this cause suffices to withdraw from the hides all their sonority and to give them the dull timbre, almost ridiculous, that one can note in drums exposed to rain. It is just about the same in the Italian theater. At the Opéra, on the contrary, one hears them quite well in almost all their nuances. An experiment tried during the setting of the SIEGE OF CORINTH, proved, nevertheless, that all places were not equally good for them. The bass drum was just then making its entree into the orchestra, as M. Rossini was making his own on the stage of the Opéra. Before him, on the rare occasions when the bass drum had been employed, it had not dared to sound except from the depths of a hallway; it had not yet acquired its civil rights. But when M. Rossini had accorded them recognition by making it figure in almost all the pieces of his new works, it was certainly necessary to admit the heavy machine, and count it among the musical instruments. Then, to give it elbow room, the timpani good naturedly ceded their spot on the right side of the orchestra to it, and went to be relegated on the left side. From that moment on, there were no more timpani; from afar, or nearby, in the *piano* and *mezzo-forte*, as in the most *violent forte*, it was almost impossible to distinguish them. I do not know the reason for that singular difference, the two sides of the orchestra of the Opéra seeming to be exactly alike; but after some years (because it always requires several years in the lyric theaters for the least musical reform, unless a man with power, because of his name and his genius, comes to effect it by main force), it became necessary to recognize it; if I am not mistaken, it was M. Meyerbeer who demanded for ROBERT the reinstallation of the timpani on the right side. Then I

found again the terrible rolling in the *finale* of LA VESTALE, which had disappeared; I heard that effect that is so dramatic and so original, placed by M. Rossini at the end of the couplets of Mathilde, in WILLIAM TELL, which I had known from having read it [in the score], but which I had never been able to hear very distinctly; then one could note in ROBERT-LE-DIABLE four timpani tuned in G, C, D, and E, executing a menacing fanfare, in somber and heavy pulsations that certainly had not been perceptible on the left side of the orchestra.

At the Conservatoire, the instrumental mass is disposed differently than in the theaters; the percussion instruments, being placed in the depths of the horse shoe and on the last riser of the amphitheater, the timpani thus are found up against the circular decoration that encloses the stage, and consequently, in the center of the amplification. That is why the softest notes travel to the furthermost points in the hall; that is why the perfectly tuned harmony of the two timpani, in fourths, in fifths, in thirds, or in octaves (Beethoven wrote them in octaves in his last two symphonies) there, as is so absolutely necessary, the accuracy of each sound being of easy determination, while it is so little so in the theaters, that often negligent timpanists dispense with changing the pitch, and play boldly in a piece written in F with timpani tuned in E minor, without anyone being aware of it.[1]

1 *Journal des Débats*, July 21, 1835.

In his *Memoirs*, Berlioz makes a brief comparison of the old Berlin Opera House to those in Paris.

The German Opera, which was burnt to the ground only three months ago, was ... well designed from the point of view of musical effect, with fine resonant acoustics. The orchestra pit did not come so far out into the auditorium as in Paris; it extended much farther on either side, and the more vehement instruments—trombones, trumpets, timpani, bass drum—were partly overhung by the first row of boxes, which cut off their extreme reverberations.[2]

2 *Memoirs*, 317.

Another aspect of acoustics which Berlioz contemplated, was the effect which the numbers of performers had on the resultant sound, and its effect on the listener. He mentions this after hearing a festival performance with a very large chorus.

The amazing effect of the unison is due, in my opinion, to two causes: to the enormous number and good quality of the voices in the first instance, and secondly to the disposition of the singers in very high tiers. The reflectors and producers of sound are thus nicely balanced. The air within the church is struck from so many points at once, in surface and in depth, that it vibrates as a whole and its disturbance develops a power and majesty of action on the human nervous system which the most learned efforts of musical art under ordinary conditions have so far not given us any notion of. I may add, as a mere conjecture, that under exceptional circumstances such as these there must occur a good many as yet uncharted phenomena having to do with the mysterious laws of electricity.[3]

3 Berlioz, *Evenings with the Orchestra*, 233.

There was one area of acoustics for which Berlioz had very firm beliefs and this was the aesthetic result when music is played in the open air. First he discusses the detrimental effect on the music and the general impact of space on sound.

There is no music possible out doors, for a thousand and one reasons, the least of which would be that one cannot hear. No, one cannot hear! One can hear neither details nor nuances, not even a single clean, vibrant chord. There, harmony lacks force and power, the melody is without expression, without vital warmth; every poetic idea is inaudible, or becomes a ridiculous non-essential.

Doubtless, people have not forgotten the famous monster concert of the July holidays, where three hundred voices and two hundred fifty wind instruments, backed up to the Tuileries, produced such a miserable result.

The example of military music that resounds with brilliance in the streets proves nothing against what I maintain: far from it, I would cite it, rather, in defense of my opinion. The streets are bordered right and left by houses that serve as amplifiers, one cannot therefore consider what one hears there as open air music. And the proof is that the higher the houses, the greater the echo of the sounds emitted in the street, and if the leading regiment, at the head of which march the musicians, comes along, leaving a street, and entering a plain bare of trees and buildings, the music loses its color instantly, or to put it better, there is no longer any music. Moreover, as popular concerts always take place in the summer, the heat of the atmosphere is still a real obstacle to musical effect. The rarification of the air by the heat deprives it of as much sonority as its condensation by a dry cold gives to it. I have compared the noise of the explosions of firearms on the plain at Rome on one of those burning days of July, and on the plain of Saint-Denis on the ice of the Seine in a quite intense cold; the relationship of the one to the other was about that of ten to one hundred. I frequently have seen guns shot off in Italy where I did not hear them, although the distance that separated me from the hunter was inconsiderable.

Doubtless such observations will seem quite puerile, they can furnish the text for many excellent pleasantries; it is none the less true, however, as it is to quite common causes that one must report the weakening or even the annihilation of musical power on many an occasion.[4]

4 *Journal des Débats*, July 21, 1835.

In another place he concentrates on the dispersion of sound in the open air.

> Reflectors are indispensable. They are found, in various forms, in every enclosed place. The closer they are to the source of sound the greater is their effect. This is why there is no such thing as music in the open air …
>
> An orchestra of a thousand wind instruments and a chorus of two thousand voices, placed in an open plain, would be far less effective than an ordinary orchestra of eighty players and a chorus of a hundred voices arranged in the concert hall of the Conservatoire. The brilliant effect produced by military bands in some streets of big cities confirms this statement, in spite of the seeming contradiction. There the music is by no means in the open air: the walls of high buildings lining the street on both sides, the avenues of trees, the facades of big palaces, near-by monuments—all these serve as reflectors. The sound is thrown back and remains for some time within the circumscribed space before finally escaping through the few gaps in the enclosure. But as soon as the band reaches an open plain without buildings and trees on its march from the large street, the tones diffuse, the orchestra disappears, and there is no more music.[5]

5 *Treatise*, 406.

In another interesting discussion he mentions a very significant question relative to the impact on the sound caused by the spacing of the players and the resultant effect their very clothing has on the formation of the tone. This factor, still rarely discussed today, Berlioz may have first heard of in his classes with Reicha, who, for example, discusses it in the foreword notes to his great *Commemoration Symphony* for three bands.

> I have said it many times, and I repeat it, outdoor music is a chimera: the number and strength of the sound producers will always be insufficient to take the place of reflectors, by means of which sound is concentrated, bends back upon itself, is condensed, and acquires, through its condensation, that vital force which makes of it all its power and all its charm. Five hundred wind instruments in a closed hall would have produced a more completely musical effect than the eighteen hundred musicians of the Hippodrome, casting their harmonies to every breeze.
>
> Still, the considerable space occupied by that army of musicians, the mass of air it put into vibration, the innumerable multitude of unisons not lacking, had, in regard to the ascending force of sound, the result of creating effects of a beauty noted by all people placed in the elevated ranks of the Hippodrome enclosure. They must have been, at certain moments, strongly impressed. Those who occupied, to the contrary, the lower ranks, heard very badly, and the cause is easy to seize upon: the musicians were all placed horizontally in the arena, and in quite close ranks, stifling amongst themselves the sounds, and one knows that there are no mutes comparable to sand, to clothing, and to human bodies.[6]

6 'Military Festival,' in *Journal des Débats*, July 29, 1846.

If, as Berlioz says, one cannot really *hear* the music outdoors, then one cannot fairly judge the value of the music. He was thinking of this when he attended a great celebration on Bonn for the unveiling of the Beethoven monument there.

> One knows the effect that vocal music can produce in the open air, but the wind was blowing in force on the choir and my portion of M. Briedenstein's music was unfairly carried entirely to the spectators at the other end of the square, who also found it, the gluttons, very scanty.
>
> How could composers of these pieces have any illusion for an instant about the reception which awaits them? A score that one does not perform cannot yet pass as admirable …, but the one that is presented to the public in the open air, not necessarily producing any effect, is always reputed mediocre and remains under the charge of that prejudiced accusation until a proper performance, *behind closed doors*, permits the author to destroy it, or the public to justify it.[7]

[7] Ibid., September 3, 1845.

Finally, in one article Berlioz mentions, perhaps inadvertently, the additional effect of stillness of wind and the cool evening temperature on outdoor music. The occasion he describes, in Baden, was one in which perhaps he heard the music more intact, for it clearly carried him away into a mood of poetic contemplation.

> I stayed there with no thoughts, listening to the Hymn of the Austrian Emperor, played at some great distance in the Kiosque of the Conversation [Hall], by a Prussian military band, and which the wind brought me from the depths of the valley. Oh, but that melody of the good Haydn is touching! How one feels a sort of religious affection! It is truly the song of a people who love their king. Notice that I do not say *the good Haydn* with a mocking manner—oh no, God help me! … Of course Haydn was a good man, and not an ordinary man. The proof of this is that he had an insufferable wife and he never beat her, even though, as some say, he let himself be beaten by her.
>
> But, we had to return, night having fallen … I went back via the pine forest full of sounds—and a better sound than most of our concert halls. Quartets could play here … But when one has the inclination to listen to music in the forest, it always follows a lunch of pate and only hears fanfares of French horns, hunting horns, waking only the ideas of dogs, thieves, and wine merchants.[8]

[8] Ibid., September 12, 1861.

On Intonation

Both as a conductor and listener, and as an observer of all technical inventions relative to instrumental music, Berlioz was obviously sensitive to the quality of intonation in the music he heard. One feels some hint of his exasperation on this subject in a humorous review of a new device advertised to end all problems of intonation.

ON THE MEANS DISCOVERED BY M. DELSARTE
FOR TUNING STRINGED INSTRUMENTS
WITHOUT THE AID OF THE EAR

Do you realize this?—all you pianists; guitarists; violinists; violoncellists; contrabassists, harpists; and you, too, conductors!

Without the help of the ear!!!

The discovery is immense; incomparable; and, especially for us poor listeners, who now have sadly to tolerate so many discordant pianos, violins and cellos; discordant harps and orchestras. M. Delsarte's invention places upon you the obligation of not torturing us any more; and of no longer making us perspire with pain, and harbor thoughts of suicide.

Without the help of the ear!!!

By means of this invention, not only does the ear become useless for tuning purposes, and dangerous to consult; but it must absolutely not be consulted. Think of the advantage for those who have not any! Until now, the contrary was the case; and accordingly we pardoned you all the torments you inflicted. But, in future, if your instruments or orchestras are not in tune, you will have no excuse; and we shall give you over to public vengeance.

Without the help of the ear!!!

Help so often useless, deceptive and fatal. The discovery of M. Delsarte only applies to stringed instruments; but that is much, in fact, enormous; for hence it follows that, in orchestras directed and tuned in this way, there will be no more discordance except amongst flutes, oboes, clarinets, bassoons, horns, cornets, trumpets, trombones, the ophicleide, the tuba and the timpani. The triangle might, as an extreme case, be tuned in the new manner; but it is generally recognized that that is not necessary, for, in common with the bells, the discordance between triangle and other instruments *does good*; and they quite like it in all lyric theaters.[9]

9 Berlioz, *Mozart, Weber and Wagner*, 47ff.

Berlioz apparently gave considerably more serious thought to this question, as we can see in a very extended discussion of the history of pitch.

THE PITCH

The Minister of State, uneasy respecting the future, more and more alarming, of musical execution in lyric theaters; astonished at the shortness of duration of the singer's career; and rightly persuaded that the progressive elevation of pitch is a cause of the ruin of the best voices; has just appointed a commission, carefully to examine into this question, ascertain the extent of the evil and discover a remedy for it.

Whilst waiting for this gathering of specialists, consisting of composers, physicians and musical scholars, to resume its labors which have been suspended during the month now expiring, we propose to endeavor to throw some light upon the whole collection of facts; and, without any prejudice to the views which the commission may adopt, to submit to it, beforehand, our observations and our ideas.

HAS THE PITCH REALLY RISEN, AND, IF SO, HOW MUCH DURING THE LAST HUNDRED YEARS?

Yes, unquestionably; the fact of its rise being recognized by all musicians and singers, as well as throughout the entire musical world, the progression followed by the rise seeming to have been approximately the same everywhere. The difference now existing between the orchestras of countries separated by considerable distances, generally consists of nuances not sufficient to prevent the occasional union of these orchestras; and, by means of certain precautions, to form of them one grand instrumental mass, the agreement of which, in respect of pitch, is satisfactory. If there were, as we are very often assured in Paris, a great difference between the pitch of the Opéra, the Opéra Comique, the Theatre-Italian and the military bands, how would it have been possible to form the orchestras of seven to eight hundred musicians which I have often had to conduct in the vast spaces of the Champs Élysées, after the exhibitions of 1844 and 1855, as well as in the church of St. Eustache; considering that the elements of this musical congress necessarily consisted of nearly all the instrumentalists disseminated throughout the numerous musical bodies of Paris.

The festivals of Germany and England, for which the orchestras of several towns are frequently combined, prove that the differences of pitch are, there also, but slightly felt; and that the precaution of *drawing the slide*, in the case of wind instruments which happen to be too sharp, suffices to obviate them.

Yet, however small they may be, these differences exist. The proof of this will shortly be in hand, as the commission has written to all the bandmasters, concert directors and conductors in those towns of Europe and America where musical art is mostly cultivated, to ask them for a sample of the steel instrument which, under various names, they employ, as we do, to give the note A to the orchestra; and in the tuning of organs and pianos. These contemporary intonations, compared with those of 1790, 1806, etc., of which we are in possession, render the difference which exists between our present day pitch and that of the close of the last century both evident and precise. Besides that, the old organs in various churches, on account of the special nature of the functions to which divine service has restricted them, never having been placed in relation with the wind instruments of theaters, have preserved the pitch of the period at which they were constructed; and this pitch is, in general, a tone lower than that which is now in use.

Hence arises the custom of giving these instruments the name of organs in 'Bb'; because their C, being a tone lower than ours, is in unison with our Bb. These organs are at least a century old; and we are therefore bound to conclude from all the facts, which, however different, agree amongst themselves, that, as the pitch has risen a tone in a hundred years, or a semitone in fifty years, if the same ascent continues, it will, in six hundred years, traverse the whole twelve semitones of the scale, and thus necessarily amount, by the year 2458, to the rise of a complete octave.

The absurdity of such a result is sufficient to show the importance of the step taken by the Minister of State; and it is highly regrettable that one or another of his predecessors has not thought of adopting similar measures long ago.

But, until now, music has rarely obtained any enlightened or official protection; notwithstanding that, of all the arts, it is the one which stands most greatly in need of it. At nearly all times, and in nearly all places, its fate has been committed to the hands of agents who had neither the sentiment of its power, grandeur or nobleness, nor the possession of any acquaintance with its nature, or means of action. Always, and everywhere until now, it has been treated like a Bohemian; expected to sing and dance in the public squares, in the company of monkeys and performing dogs, and covered with tinsel to attract attention from the crowd, for the mere purpose of collecting money …

These faults, gross, palpable and evident in themselves, could not fail, when aggravated by the rise in pitch, to produce the sad results which now attract the attention of even the least attentive listeners at our theatrical performances; but the present high intonation has produced a further evil which will now be mentioned.

Horn, trumpet and cornet players can no longer be sure of certain notes which were formerly in general use; the majority not being even able to attack them. Of these, we may cite the high G of the trumpet in D; the E of the trumpet in F; the high G of the horn in G; the high C of this same horn (a note employed by both Handel and Gluck, but which has now become impossible); and the high C of the cornet in A. At every moment, frayed and broken notes, vulgarly called *couacs*, appear to the detriment of an instrumental ensemble, sometimes composed even of the most excellent artists. Thus, we hear it said, 'Trumpet and horn players have no longer any *lip*? Why? Surely, human nature has not changed.'

No; human nature has not changed, but the pitch has; and many modern composers seem to ignore the new conditions.

CAUSES WHICH HAVE LED TO THE RISE IN PITCH

It seems, now, to be an ascertained fact that the evil which we are now all called upon to deplore is one of which the guilt lies with the makers of wind instruments. In order to give more brilliancy to their flutes, oboes, and clarinets, certain manufacturers have clandestinely raised the pitch. The young virtuosi, into whose hands such instruments have first fallen, have been obliged, on entering an orchestra, to *draw the slide*; in order to place themselves in tune with the others. But, as this lengthening of the tube (and especially that of the flute) disturbs its proportions, and consequently diminishes the truth of the intervals, such artists, little by little, abstained from having recourse to it. The whole mass of stringed instrument players naturally followed (possibly even without knowing it) the impulse thus given by these sharp wind instruments … After that, the other musicians, the elders of the orchestra, having charge of bassoon, horn, trumpet, second oboe parts, etc., tired with making useless endeavors to bring themselves up to the prevailing pitch, have quietly gone to the maker to get their tubes slightly shortened; to get them 'cut' and so enable themselves to conform with the new pitch. The latter is thus fully installed, as far as the orchestra is concerned …

SHOULD THE PITCH BE LOWERED?

It is certain, in my opinion, that a lowering of the pitch could only be attended by benefit to the art of music generally, and to that of singing more especially; but it seems to me impracticable to extend such a reform to the whole of France. An abuse which is the result of a long succession of years is not to be destroyed in a few days; and musicians, both singers and others, who might appear to be the most interested in securing a lower pitch, would very likely be the first to oppose it. First, it would collide with their present habits; and God only knows whether there exists in France a force more irresistible than that of habit. But, even supposing that an all-powerful will should intervene to cause the reform to be adopted, its realization would cost enormous sums. Even without counting organs, it would be universally necessary to buy new wind instruments for theaters and military bands, and to absolutely forbid the use of old types. And then, after the reform had been successfully effected, if the rest of the world did not follow our example, France would remain isolated with her low pitch; and excluded from the possibility of musical relations with other nations.

SHOULD WE ONLY FIX THE ACTUAL PITCH?

This is, I believe, the wisest course to take; and the means to effect it are already in our possession. Thanks to an ingenious instrument which the science of acoustics has acquired a few years ago, and which is called the syren, it is now possible to count, with mathematical precision, the number of vibrations given out per second by any sonorous body.

In adopting the A of the Paris Opéra as the typical sound, or sonorous official standard, this A being presumably the result of 898 vibrations per second [A = 449!], all that we should have to do would be to place, in every concert or theater orchestra, an organ pipe giving the exact sound designated. This pipe would alone be referred to for the A, and the present custom entirely discontinued of tuning to the oboe or flute, the former of which can easily cause the pitch to rise by increasing the pressure of his lips upon the reed, and the latter do the same by turning his embouchure a little outwards.

The wind instruments would thus be in perfect tune with the organ pipe. They should also remain, in the interval between the representations or concerts, kept in the same room where the organ pipe is placed; which room should be, like a greenhouse, constantly maintained at the average temperature of the theater when the audience is present. Thanks to this precaution the instruments would not be brought cold into the orchestra, and would not sharpen, in the course of an hour, in consequence of the breath of the executants, or of their being introduced to a warmer atmosphere. It follows that the wind instruments of a theater (of a theater of the government at any rate) should never be taken away under any pretext, but remain in the allotted room as permanently as if they were its fixtures. Should any player remove his instrument—his flute or clarinet—for the purpose of getting it 'cut,' the misdemeanor would be at once discovered; as he would then be out-of-tune with the organ pipe, which, as I have said, should be alone consulted. Finally, the official adoption by the government of the A of 898 vibrations would involve that every manufacturer circulating either wind instruments, organs or pianos pitched differently, would be amenable to certain penalties, precisely in the same way as shopkeepers who sell by false measure or weight.

With such precautions once taken, and the regulations enforcing them well and rigorously maintained, it is quite certain that the pitch would not continue to rise.[10]

10 Ibid., 95ff.

In a newspaper article Berlioz presents much of this discussion, but here he gives a somewhat more extended discussion under the heading, as above, 'Causes which have led to the Rise in Pitch.'

It would seem that the woodwind instrument makers are the ones guilty of what we deplore today. In order to give a bit more sparkle to the flutes, oboes and clarinets, certain instrument makers clandestinely raised the pitch. The young virtuosos into whose hands these instruments fell first had to lengthen the slide in order to be in pitch with the others in the orchestra. But, since elongating the slide disturbs more or less the proportions and alters the pitch (especially for flutes), thereafter these artists little by little abstained from doing this. The mass of string instruments followed in suit, perhaps influenced by these wind instruments, and the violins, violas, and bass tightened their strings, thus adapting a higher pitch. The more senior musicians, responsible for the bassoon, French horn, trumpet, second oboe, etc., tired of not being able to obtain the higher pitch, despite their efforts, finally ended up taking their instruments to have the tube cut in order to achieve the higher pitch.

The same thing occurred, more or less, every twenty years.

Today, organ makers follow the movement and tune their instruments to the higher pitch. We certainly don't know for whom Saint Gregory and Saint Ambrose composed the chants that they bequeathed to the church, but it is obvious that the more the pitch of the churches raised (if the organ sets the pitch for the singers and not vise versa), the more the entire hymn system is altered and the more the economy of the voices is disturbed. The organs should either transpose, if they accompany chant, or be retuned to the old pitch ... Today organs [at the old pitch] are a tone and a half below today's instruments. The orchestral instruments can play perfectly in tune with the organs by playing, for example, in F when the organ plays in Ab.

Unfortunately, some instrument makers took the worst way out. They constructed organs a quarter tone lower than the theater's pitch. I had the cruel opportunity of experiencing the result of this at St. Eustache during a performance of my *Te Deum*. It was impossible, despite the lengthening of all the resounding tubes of the orchestra, to have the entire instrumental mass in tune with an organ that was only finished three years before.[11]

11 *Journal des Débats*, September 29, 1858.

Toward the end of his active career, he seems to have come back to the realization that, in the end, it is the musician, himself, who must play in tune. His patience seems exhausted, in his review of a performance of David's *Perle du Bresil*.

More than once, when I have criticized the orchestra's pitch as compared to certain foreign orchestras, I have been told,

> Sir, our flutes, our clarinets and our trumpets make up the military bands and use, consequently, instruments possessing a pitch a bit higher than our French horns and bassoons; there is no way to tune them.

These reasons are the summit of madness. An orchestra must be in tune. If you have poor instruments, get new ones. An orchestra must be in tune. If the instruments are faulty, get them better ones. An orchestra must be in tune. An orchestra must be in tune. If you want civilized people not to leave your theater, then don't give them a pain in the ear. An orchestra must be in tune. An orchestra must be in tune. An orchestra must be in tune. An orchestra must be in tune.[12]

12 *Journal des Débats*, April 3, 1858.

Part 5

Berlioz's Compositions for Winds

Early Compositions for Flute

Potpourri concertant sur des thèmes italiens

> For flute, horn, 2 violins, viola and bass
> Date of composition: ca. 1818
> Sources: Lost

(Two) *Quintets*

> For flute and strings.
> Date of composition: 1818–1819
> Sources: Lost

Perhaps the earliest reference to music in the life of Hector Berlioz is a letter of his father indicating some instruments had been ordered for the boy.

> Hector asks that you not forget the flageolets that Mr. Eugene ordered in his name.[1]

[1] Letter of Doctor Louis Berlioz to Joseph Faure, April 8, 1816, in *Correspondance*, Nr. 1.

The editors of the *Correspondance Générale* add that a letter dating between January 1816 and March 1817, from Felix Marmion to his brother-in-law, Dr. Berlioz, now in the Reboul Collection, contains the following:

> The flageolets that I am sending Hector are not brilliant, but they are certainly in tune and above all harmonize perfectly. Advise him not to blow too hard, because that makes them go out of tune. I still do not have any music to send him; no one here has any for that instrument.

The town, La Côte-Saint-André, on 20 May 1817, employed a music teacher named Imbert. He was Berlioz's first teacher and also performed in the youthful compositions listed above. The teacher's son was the horn player in the earliest of these works and it is the absence of a horn part from the following two works which suggests that they were written after Imbert's son committed suicide in the summer of 1818.[2] Berlioz recalled these early experiences:

[2] D. Kern Holoman, *The Creative Process in the Autograph Musical Documents of Hector Berlioz, c. 1818–1840* (Ann Arbor: UMI Research Press, 1975), 23.

One day I chanced upon a flageolet at the bottom drawer in which I was rummaging. I immediately wanted to play it and attempted to render the popular air, 'Malbrouck,' but to no purpose.

My father found these squeakings exceedingly disagreeable and begged me to leave him in peace until he had time to instruct me in the fingering of the instrument and the correct execution of the heroic strain I had selected. This he did without much trouble. At the end of two days I was master of 'Malbrouck' and able to regale the whole family with it—an early manifestation of my remarkable feeling for wind instruments which will not, of course, escape the attention of any self-respecting biographer.

The episode of the flageolet gave my father the notion of teaching me how to read music. He initiated me into its basic principles, explaining the meaning and function of musical notation. Not long afterwards he presented me with a flute, together with a copy of Devienne's *Method*, and again took the trouble to show me its mechanism. I worked so hard at it that in seven or eight months I could play pretty well. My father wished to encourage the talent I was showing and persuaded a few well-to-do families in La Côte to join with him and engage a music master from Lyons. The plan succeeded ... His name was Imbert. He gave me lessons twice a day. I ... soon developed into a fearless reader ... and could play Drouet's most intricate concertos on the flute ...

At length, by dint of listening to the quartets of Pleyel, which our local amateurs played on Sundays, and with the aid of a copy of Catel's treatise on harmony which I had managed to procure, I suddenly found that the mysteries of chord formations and progressions had become clear to me. I immediately wrote a kind of medley in six parts on themes from a book of Italian melodies in my possession. The harmony seemed tolerable, and I was emboldened by this first step to undertake the composition of a quintet for flute, two violins, viola and cello, which was performed by three of our amateurs, my teacher and myself.

It was a triumph. Only my father seemed not to share the general enthusiasm. Two months later another quintet followed. My father wanted to hear me try over the flute part before risking a full-scale performance (A characteristic attitude of provincial amateurs, who imagine they can judge a string quartet from the first violin part). I played it to him. At one particular passage he exclaimed, 'Ah, now that is what I call music.'

But this quintet, much more ambitious than its predecessor, was also considerably more difficult. Our amateurs were unable to give an adequate account of it ...

As this happened when I was twelve and a half years old, the biographers who still maintain that at the age of twenty I did not know the rudiments of music are strangely mistaken.

I destroyed the two quintets a few years later, but it is a curious fact that long afterwards in Paris, when I was writing my first orchestral work, the phrase my father approved of in the second of these early efforts came back to me and I adopted it. It is the theme in Ab which the first violins announce soon after the opening of the allegro of the *Francs juges* overture …

Behold me then, past master of those three magnificent instruments, the flageolet, the flute and the guitar. Can anyone fail to recognize in this judicious choice the hand of Nature urging me towards the grandest orchestral effects and the Michalangelesque in music? The flute, the guitar and the flageolet! I have never possessed any other skills as a performer; yet this seems to me already an impressive list. Indeed, I do myself an injustice: I could play the drum.[3]

Indeed, according to local custom Berlioz led school outings with his drum.[4]

At this time Berlioz also made some unsuccessful efforts to interest publishers in these early compositions and, according to Holoman these letters contain the earliest examples of the composer's handwriting.[5]

I would like you to undertake the Edition of a potpourri Concertant, composed of chosen pieces for flute, horn, two violins, viola, and bass.[6]

As the youthful Berlioz continued to become more interested in music, his father, who wanted a career in medicine for his son, tried a kind of bribe to interest his son in reading a medical treatise.

In order, he said, to get me accustomed without delay to the objects I would soon have to have constantly before my eyes, he had laid out in his study a copy of Monro's enormous treatise on osteology, with its life-size illustrations in which the various components of the human frame are meticulously reproduced. 'Here,' he said, 'is a work you will have to study. I cannot suppose you will persist in your hostility to medicine; it is unreasonable and wholly without foundation. If, on the other hand, you promise me to begin really seriously working at your osteology, I will send to Lyons and get you a splendid new flute with all the latest keys.' Such an instrument had long been the object of my dreams. What could I say? The impressive earnestness of the offer, the respect mingled with fear which, for all his kindness, my father inspired in me, and the temptation of the coveted flute, were more than I could resist. I stammered out a faint yes, went back to my room, and threw myself on the bed in utter dejection.[7]

3 *Memoirs*, 39ff.

4 Ibid., 537.

5 D. Kern Holoman, *Berlioz* (Cambridge: Harvard University Press, 1989), 13.

6 Letter to Ignace Playel, April 6, 1819, in *Correspondance*, 4.

7 *Memoirs*, 43.

Berlioz continued his interest in the flute during his study in Paris in 1825–1826 and apparently even had some students of his own there.[8]

8 Ibid., 66.

Messe solennelle: 'Et Iterum Venturus'

For orchestra and chorus
Date of Composition: 1824
Sources: Original Messe destroyed (a revised version of the 'Resurrexit' is extant in Grenoble, Bibliotheque Municipale (Res R 90665)

A discussion of the Messe solennelle is included here because the original version of the *Et iterum venturus* featured six trumpets, four horns, three trombones and two ophicleides.

The premiere of the original version of this music was scheduled for a concert in the St.-Roch church on 28 December 1824, to be conducted by a conductor named, Valentino. A student choir of the church was to sing but also were to copy parts for the performance. Berlioz had printed an invitation reading,[9]

9 Holoman, *Berlioz*, 36.

> You are invited to attend a MESSE EN GRANDE SYMPHONIE composed by M. H. Berlios [sic], student of M. Lesueur ...

Unfortunately, problems with errors in the parts encountered in the rehearsal the day before resulted in the cancellation of the concert.

After recopying the parts himself, Berlioz was finally able to perform the work on 10 July 1825. This performance apparently made a strong impression on some of the listeners. Holoman provides a sample of the reactions:

> Berlioz's teacher, Le Sueur: 'You'll not be a doctor or apothecary, but rather a great composer.'
>
> ...
>
> Mme. Lebrun, a colorful member of the Opéra chorus: 'Damn, my boy: now there's an un-worm-eaten O Salutaris, and I defy those little bastards in the counterpoint classes at the Conservatoire to write a movement so tightly knit, so bloody religious.'
>
> ...
>
> The writer, and establishment figure in Paris, Fétis: 'Everyone came away shrugging his shoulders and saying that what he had heard was not music.'

Berlioz's own reaction is found in a letter written ten days later,

> I believe my Mass produced a hellish effect; especially the strong parts such as the *Kyrie*, the *Crucifixus*, the *Iterum venturus*, the *Domine Salvum*, and the *Sanctus* ... In the *Iterum venturus*, after having announced by means of all the trumpets and trombones in the world the arrival of the Last Judgment, the chorus of humans consumed with horror unfurled; Oh Heavens! I was swimming in that agitated sea, I smelled those waves of sinister vibrations; ... and, after having announced to the wicked, by means of a last broadside from the brass, that the moment of *tears* and of *grinding of teeth* had come, I applied such a heavy gong crash that the whole church shook from it. It is not my fault if the ladies, especially, did not believe that they had come to the end of the world.[10]

10 Letter to Albert Du Boys, July 20, 1825, in *Correspondance*, 48.

A few years later, he added,

> The devout old ladies, the woman who rented the chairs, the holy-water man, the vergers, and all the gapers of the quarter declaring themselves well satisfied, I had the simplicity to regard it a success.[11]

11 Quoted in Holoman, *Berlioz*, 36.

Another performance was given on St. Cecilia's Day, 22 November 1827, in the larger church of St.-Eustache. The brass movement, *Et iterum venturus*, was now altered somewhat to become a description of The Last Judgment, a topic to which Berlioz was drawn again and again. This performance, which Berlioz conducted, caused him such excitement that he had to call for an interval afterwards to sit down and collect his emotions.

> My Mass was performed on St. Cecilia's day, with twice as much success as the first time. The little corrections I made in it have improved it a great deal. The *Et iterum venturus*, especially, which failed the first time, was performed magnificently this time by six trumpets, four horns, three trombones and two ophicleides. The chorus which follows, which I had performed by all the voices in octaves, with a burst of brass in the middle of the phrase, produced a terrific impression on everybody. I kept my composure until then, and it was important not to get agitated, I was conducting; but when I saw this picture of the Last Judgment, this proclamation sung by six basses in unison, this terrible *clangor tubarum*, the cries of fright from the multitude represented by the chorus, everything rendered exactly as I had conceived it, I was seized by a convulsive trembling. I managed to master it until the end of the movement, but

I was then forced to sit down and allow my orchestra to rest for a few minutes: I could no longer stand upright and I was afraid that the baton would slip from my fingers.[12]

12 Letter to Humbert Ferrand, November 29, 1827, in *Correspondance*, 77.

The success of the brass writing remained in his mind, however, as he began thinking about a great Oratorio, in 1831, which again dealt with 'The Judgment Day.' In his description of his plans in a letter to a friend, we see the idea of the four brass bands which would eventually be used in the *Requiem*.

The men, at the height of corruption, always lent themselves to the latest scandal. Some sort of government despotic Anti-Christ … A small number of the righteous, led by their prophet, coming down among this general depravation. The despot tormented them, took away their virgins, insulted their beliefs, made them rip to pieces their holy books in the middle of an orgy. The prophet came to have them confess their sins, announcing the end of the world and the final judgment. The irritated despot threw them into prison and rendering himself again to the ungodly deeds, was surprised in the middle of the party by the terrible trumpets of the resurrection, the dead rising from the grave, lost souls screaming horrors, the world broken apart, the angels thundering in the thick clouds, forming the finale of this musical drama. We must, as you well know, use entirely new musical methods. Besides the two orchestras, there are four groups of brass instruments placed in the four key spots. The combinations would be completely new and a thousand unpracticed new methods would come out sparkling from this harmonic mass.[13]

13 Letter to Humbert Ferrand, Rome, July 3, 1831, in *Correspondance*, 234.

This *Messe solennelle* has long assumed to have been lost, based on the statement in the autobiography of Berlioz that he burned the score. Nonetheless, since I first wrote this book a Belgian school teacher, Frans Moors, has found the score in the organ bench of a church in Antwerp.

Parody on the Symphonie Fantastique

For piccolo and serpent
Date of Composition: 1831
Source: Letter of 12 April 1831

In a description of an organ he had heard in Rome, Berlioz wrote to a friend.

> … having reached the range of the piccolos and played small gay melodies somewhat like the twittering of wrens. You wanted music, well, I send you music. It is nothing like the song of birds even though I am as happy as a lark.[14]

14 Letter to Humbert Ferrand, Florence, April 12, 1831, in *Correspondance*, 216.

Berlioz used the same phrase describing the upper range of the organ in a letter of 6 May 1831, written to a group of his friends.

The music Berlioz promised his friend he included in the letter quoted above, in the form of a parody on his *Symphonie Fantastique*, composed for the highest and lowest sounding wind instruments. The little composition concludes with an 'Amen,' based on a French popular tune, 'I have good tobacco.'

Méditation religieuse

For voice and seven wind instruments
Text by Thomas Moore
Date of Composition: August 1831
Sources: Lost

The original version of this work, for voice and winds, is known only through the composer's mention of it in a letter of 1 January 1832.

Sometime later, Berlioz made a revision of this work for chorus and orchestra and this version survives (Bibliotheque du Conservatoire [in Bibliotheque Nationale, Department de la Musique] MS 1187). Holoman takes the position that, 'there is no certain proof that the lost Version I is the same work as the [second version], only strong circumstantial probability.'[15]

Some background for this work is given in a letter from Berloz to Ferdinand Hiller.

15 D. Kern Holoman, *Catalog of the Works of Hector Berlioz* (Kassel: Barenreiter, 1987), 118.

> You wanted to know what I have been doing since my arrival in Italy. The first overture to King Lear (in Nice) and the second overture of Rob Roy MacGregor (sketched out in Nice, which I had the stupid idea to show to Mendelssohn before it was finished). I finished it and orchestrated it in the Subiaco mountains. Third, *Melologue en six parties*, words and music, composed up and downhill on my way back to Nice, and finalized in Rome. Then, some vocal pieces, detached, with and without accompaniment. The first was a choir of angels for the Christmas festivities; the second was a choir of all voices improvised (as one improvises) in the middle of the fog on my way to Naples, praying for the sun to come back out. Finally, another choir on some words of Moore with accompaniment of seven wind instruments, composed in Rome one day when I was dying of boredom, and entitled, 'Psalm for those who have suffered much and who have a soul sad enough to die.'[16]

16 Letter to Ferdinand Hiller, Rome, January 1, 1832, in *Correspondance*, 216.

Le Dernier Jour du monde

For orchestra, band and chorus (?)
Date of Composition: 1831–1833
Sources: Not completed

In Florence in April 1831, Berlioz drafted a plan for what he called a 'colossal oratorio,' on the subject of the Day of Judgment. The plans he mentions in a letter to Ferrand, his desired librettist, suggest he was perhaps thinking of the kind of combined band and orchestra he would use later for the *Symphonie funèbre*. One also sees here the four independent brass choirs which he would actually realize later in the *Requiem*.

> I had a great project that I wanted to realize with you; it had to do with a colossal oratorio to be performed at a musical celebration in Paris at the Opéra or the Pantheon or in the courtyard of the Louvre. It would be called *Le Dernier Jour du monde*. I wrote the plans for it in Florence, and some of the words three months ago. It would take three or four solo actors, choruses, an orchestra of sixty musicians in front of the theater [in the pit], and another of two or three hundred instruments at the rear of the stage, stacked in amphitheater fashion.
>
> The men, having arrived at the last stage of corruption, indulge in every sin; a sort of Antichrist governs them despotically. A few worthy people, led by a prophet, cut off in the midst of this general depravity. The despot torments them, kidnaps their virgins, insults their beliefs, and has their hold books destroyed during an orgy. The prophet comes to reproach him for his crimes and announces the end of the world and the Last Judgment. The enraged despot has him thrown into prison, and while indulging again in impious sensual pleasure is surprised in the middle of a feast by the terrible trumpets of the Resurrection. The dead leaping from the tomb, the damned crying frightfully, the shattering world, the thunder of heavenly hosts make up the *finale* of this musical drama. As you can see, it is necessary to use entirely new forces. Besides the two orchestras, there are four groups of brass instruments placed in the four main corners of the place of performance. The combination is completely new, and ideas not practical with the ordinary forces will emerge sparkling from this mass of winds.[17]

[17] Letter to Humbert Ferrand, July 3, 1831, quoted in Holoman, *The Creative Process*, 117ff.

The idea floundered in part on his inability to find anyone to undertake the writing of the libretto and it is doubtful that any music, certainly any new music, was actually composed.

Le Retour de l'armée d'Italie

For band (?) and chorus
Date of Composition: 1832–1836
Sources: Sketchbook in La Côte-St.-Andre, Musee Hector Berlioz (Res. 1[I])

In the sketchbook of 1832–1833, Berlioz writes of his initial inspiration,

> The idea for the symphony in two parts came to me in Turin on May 25, 1832, upon seeing the Alps again, my heart full of Napoléonic memories awakened by the countryside I had just traversed.

Berlioz, in a later letter to his father,[18] mentions that the Duc de Montpensier wishes to commission a military symphony with chorus, for three thousand men, on a subject which he had once spoken: *Le Retour de l'armée d'Italie*.

While this composition was apparently never completed, the sketchbook contains sketches and the following outline:

The Return of the Army of Italy: Military symphony in 2 parts
1. Farewell, from the summit of the Alps, to the brave men fallen in the Italian fields.
2. The Victors' triumphal entry into Paris.

Holoman reproduces three of the melodic sketches for this proposed symphony.[19] The third of these is immediately recognizable as a familiar melody from the fourth movement of the *Harold in Italy*.

A final hint regarding this work is found in a review[20] of the *Te Deum* by one of Berlioz's colleagues in the press, Maurice Bourges, who states that this work had its origin in the earlier, 'Retour de la campagne d'Italie,' information which could have only come from Berlioz himself. When Bourges writes of the musical depiction of 'the entrance of General Bonaparte with ... flags waving and drums playing ...,' he was perhaps thinking of the final movement of the *Te Deum*, the *Marche pour la presentation des drapeaux* ('March for the présentation of

18 Letter to his Father, October 10, 1846, in *Correspondance*, 1061.

19 Holoman, *The Creative Process*, 140ff.

20 *Revue et Gazette*, May 6, 1855.

the flags'), which is a virtual march for wind band, with the strings only joining for cadential utterances or for doubling. If any music had been more fully scored for the projected 'Military Symphony in Two Parts,' it might well have been this music.

Chant héroïque

I. Prière de femmes
II. Choeur général

For band and chorus
Date of Composition: 1833
Sources:
  Autograph score: lost
  Manuscript parts: Bibliotheque du Conservatoire, in
    Bibliotheque Nationale, Department de la Musique
    (L.17239, A-J), as follows, with the number of parts given
    in parenthesis:

  Soprano I (39)
  Soprano II (42)
  Soprano III (24)
  Ténor I (27)
  Ténor II (35)
  Basses récitantes I (7)
  Basses récitantes II (8)
  Basses-Tailles (36)
  Piccolo (6)
  Oboe (5)
  Soprano clarinet in F (4)
  Clarinet I (19)
  Clarinet II (15)
  Bassoons (10)
  Horn I, II (6)
  Horn III, IV (6)
  Trumpet I, II (4)
  Trumpet III, IV (3)
  Trombone I (2)
  Trombone II (2)
  Trombone III (3)
  Ophicleide (7)
  Timpani (3)
  Bass drum and tambour (5)
  Cymbals (4)
  Tam-Tam (1)
  Contrabass (12)

A modern edition of this work has been published in 1991 by Bärenreiter in Kassel.

During 1825 Berlioz's friend, Humbert Ferrand, had written the text for a Cantata, called *Scène héroïque grecque*, inspired by the revolution of the Greeks against the Ottoman Empire. This struggle had begun in 1821 and was nearing its climax by the time Berlioz set the work for orchestra and chorus. The work, four movements in this form, was performed once, on 26 May 1828.

In 1833 Berlioz made a new version of the final two movements for chorus and band. An announcement of the forthcoming concert (28 July 1833), in the *L'Europe littéraire* for 24 July 1833, listed an instrumentation similar to that which survives, '100 female and 200 male singers, 12 flutes, 10 oboes, 8 soprano clarinets, 80 clarinets, 18 bassoons, 20 horns, 20 trumpets, 16 trombones, 15 ophicleides, 3 timpani, 6 tambour, 2 cymbal players, tam-tam, and 22 string basses.'

Apparently three rehearsals were held, but a performance in the Tuileries did not occur as the candles ran out and the musicians could not see their music. The first of these rehearsals, in the atelier of the painter Cicéri, is described by Berlioz:

> The first rehearsal of the immense orchestra took place in a closed area, in the painting studio of Cicéri in Menu-Plaisir, and the impression on *high society* was immense, even if half of the singers were non-musicians and could not read music or sing. At one moment, I had to leave because my chest was vibrating too much. When I heard the *William Tell Chorus* (if among us there be any traitors) I almost became ill. In the great outdoors- nothing, no effect at all. The music is simply not intended for the streets in any way, shape or form.[21]

21 Letter to Humbert Ferrand, Paris, August 1, 1833, in *Correspondance*, 341.

In a footnote to this letter, the editors of *Correspondance Générale* add,

> 'The *Révolution Grecque*, transformed into the *Triomphe de Napoléon*, could well be the arrangement for choir and large wind orchestra (with celli) of the *Prière de la Révolution Grecque*, which we have reconstituted from the partial manuscripts recently inventoried in the Library of the Paris Conservatory.'

Le Jeune Pâtre breton

For voice, piano, and horn
Date of composition: 1834
Source: Printed score (Paris: Schlesinger, 1835)

Holoman lists four separate versions of this song.[22] The first, which appeared on a concert in the Salle du Conservatoire on 22 December 1833, was a song for voice and piano, under the title *Le Paysan breton*. The second and fourth versions (1834, 1835) were for voice and orchestra. The version for voice, piano and horn, which was published in 1835, carries a note by the composer indicating that the horn part could be performed, if necessary, by viola or cello.[23]

According to the editors of the *Correspondance Générale*, there may have been yet a fifth version, as they quote from Tiersot (*Le Musicien errant.*, 3) the program of a concert given in Brussels in the Fall of 1842, which included the *Le Jeune pâtre breton*, in a version for singer, orchestra and horn.[24]

22 Holoman, *Catalog.*

23 See *Correspondance*, 365, fn.

24 Ibid., 777, fn. 2.

Fête musicale funèbre

For orchestra (?)
Date of Composition: 1835
Source: Lost

Berlioz spent much of 1835 working on a 'third symphony on a new and vast plan,' as it was described in a letter of 15 April 1835, to his friend Ferrand. The following month he mentions the work again to his father.

> I am going to work a great deal this summer on my new piece that I am pondering on, but it is of such a large dimension that I am right to worry about it being ready for next winter's concerts.[25]

25 Letter to his Father, Paris, May 6, 1835, in *Correspondance*, 435.

It is, however, another letter to Ferrand, in which he gives a proposed title, that attracts our attention.

> I started an immense work entitled, *Fête musical funèbre a la mémoire des hommes illustrés de la France*. I have already written two pieces and there will be seven altogether.[26]

26 Letter to Humbert Ferrand, Montmartre, after August 23, 1835, in *Correspondance*, 440.

The editors of the *Correspondance Générale*, in a footnote, add the following comment:

> Of this work, only the title exists, with its striking similarity with the symphony for military band, *Musique pour célébrer la mémoire des grands hommes qui se sont illustrés au service de la Nation Francaise*, by Anton Reicha (1770–1836), one of Berlioz's teachers. This work, in three movements, foreshadows in some aspects the *Symphonie Funèbre et Triomphale*, but exists only in manuscript and has not been performed. Nothing permits the belief that Berlioz would have known of its existence.

The similarity of the titles is indeed striking, too striking for the present writer to believe that Berlioz had never seen this score. Further, when Berlioz became a student at the Conservatoire in 1826 he was in fact a student of Reicha. There should be no surprise that Berlioz knew this great work of Reicha, as indeed his 1836 eulogy of Reicha, suggests.

There exist more than a hundred printed works of the composition of Reicha, without counting a great number of others, still in manuscript, and among which several are, for art, of the greatest importance.[27]

> 27 'Antoine Reiche,' *Journal des Débats*, July 3, 1836.

This same eulogy reveals that Berlioz remembered very clearly details from his classes with Reicha and speaks of Reicha's interest in innovation and his 'love of abstract combinations and mental games in music.' It seems likely to this writer that the unpublished band symphony, with its extraordinary scheme of short-hand score notation, would be exactly the kind of innovative work Reicha might show his class.

The present writer also disagrees with the editors of the *Correspondance Générale* in their observation that the Reicha symphony 'foreshadows in some aspects' the Berlioz *Symphonie Funèbre et Triomphale*. There are earlier works which have parallels with the Berlioz Symphony, but the Reicha is not one of them. The Reicha is a work which looks backward and is much closer to Haydn and early Beethoven, two composers, by the way, who were personal friends of Reicha.

On the other hand, Holoman believes that one of the movements of the unfinished *Fête musicale funèbre* may have been used later by Berlioz in his symphony.

Berlioz labored diligently at this project through early autumn. As the concert season drew closer, however, it was obvious that the *Fête musicale* could not be finished in time to allow a proper production. Berlioz took one of the two completed movements—the other is almost surely equivalent to the *Marche funèbre* in the *Symphonie funèbre et triomphale*—and refashioned it as the Napoleonic cantata, *Le Cinq Mai*, commemorating the emperor's death on St. Helena in 1821.[28]

> 28 Holoman, *Berlioz*, 168.

Aubade

Version I: for voice and 2 horns
Version II: for voice, 4 horns, 2 cornets
Date of Composition: 1839 (Version I)
Sources:
    Version one is in an autograph album in private hands.
    Version two is an autograph score in La Côte-St.-Andre,
        Musée Hector Berlioz.

This composition is based on a poem by Alfred de Musset (1810–1857) and is dedicated to Alfred de Beauchesne, secretary of the Conservatoire.

Symphonie funèbre et triomphale

For band, with later additions of strings and chorus to the third movement.
Text by Antoni Deschamps (1800–1869).
Dedicated to S. A. R. Monseigneur le Duc d'Orléans
Date of Composition: 1840
Score Sources:
> Original version, Lost (a revealing fragment is given in Hugh Macdonald, ed., *Hector Berlioz New Edition of the Complete Works*, vol. 19, 102, as well as a great deal of additional information.)
> Final version, in partial autograph, in Bibliotheque du Conservatoire, in Bibliotheque Nationale, Department de la Musique (MS. 1164). This score was given by Berlioz to the critic Joseph d'Ortigue (1802–1866); it passed next to Charles Malherbe before arriving at the Bibliotheque du Conservatoire.
> First edition (Paris: Schlesinger, October, 1843)

Parts Source: First edition (Paris: Schlesinger, October, 1843)
Choral Sources:
> Mss vocal score in French and English (by Berlioz) in Bibliotheque du Conservatoire, in Bibliotheque Nationale, Department de la Musique (MS. 17463)
> Mss vocal score in German and Russian in Bibliotheque du Conservatoire, in Bibliotheque Nationale, Department de la Musique (D. 16489)

Modern Edition by David Whitwell, www.whitwellbooks.com

Berlioz composed his great Symphony for band at the request of the Minister of the Interior to be used in a ceremony on 28 July 1840, commemorating the tenth anniversary of the so-called 'July Revolution.' On this occasion the remains of some of the heroes of this revolution would be reburied beneath a new column in the Place de la Bastille. The commission was for music to play during a processional through Paris[29] much

---

[29] Holoman, *Berlioz*, 205 gives the parade route.

like those of the great festivals of the French Revolution, as well as music for the ceremonies at the column. The official commission read,

> 'Sir, I have the honor of informing you that you have been bestowed with the commission of composing a funeral march for the transporting of the remains of the soldiers of July as well as another piece of music that will be played during the time that their coffins are lowered into the tombs.
> You will conduct both pieces yourself.
> Would you be so kind as to come by the Administration of the Fine Arts in order to take care of the formalities as to the expenses.'[30]

30 Letter to Berlioz from the Minister of the Interior, Paris, July 11, 1840, in *Correspondance*, 717.

The editors of the *Correspondance Générale* add, 'The official confirmation came later. Berlioz knew as of the month of April that he would be asked to compose this music.' If this were the case one would suppose that Berlioz had the better part of three months to compose, a minimum amount of time for so large a work even supposing some of the material was taken from earlier, now rejected works.[31] Berlioz's comment to his father that he composed the work in 'forty hours for three or four thousand francs,' may be taken as a son trying to convince a very doubtful father that his career had financial promise after all.

31 Holoman, *Berlioz*, 105, proposes three earlier works may have contributed material.

A rehearsal was held two days before the festival, on 26 July 1840 in the Salle Vivienne before invited friends. A printed program for the rehearsal gives the title *Symphonie Militaire*, as well as the movement titles of the original version: *Marche Funèbre*, *Hymne d'Adieu*, and *Apothéose*.

Berlioz speaks in detail of his work on the composition and its public presentation on 28 July.

> In 1840, as the month of July drew near, the government proposed to celebrate the tenth anniversary of the 1830 Revolution with public ceremonies on an imposing scale. The relics of the glorious victims of the Three Days were to be translated to the monument lately erected to them in the Place de la Bastille. M. de Remusat, who was the Minister of the Interior at the time, happens by a remarkable coincidence to be, like M. de Gasparin, a lover of music. He decided to commission me to write a symphony for the occasion, leaving the choice of the form of the work and the forces entirely to me. In return I would receive ten thousand francs, out of which I was to pay the expenses of copying and performance.

It seemed to me that for such a work the simpler the plan the better, and that only a large body of wind instruments would be suitable for a symphony which was to be heard—for the first time at any rate—in the open air. I wished, to begin with, to recall the conflicts of the famous Three Days amidst the mourning strains of a bleak but awe-inspiring march, to be played during the procession; to follow this with a kind of funeral oration or farewell address to the illustrious dead, while the bodies were lowered into the cenotaph; and to conclude with a hymn of praise at the moment when, the tomb being sealed, all eyes were fixed on the high column on which Liberty with wings outspread seemed soaring towards heaven like the souls of those who had given their lives for her.

I had almost completed the funeral march when a rumor went round that the July ceremonies would not take place. Ah-ah, I thought, this is the Requiem all over again. This is as far as I go: I know these people. And I stopped. A few days later I was strolling through Paris, when the Minister passed me in his carriage and, catching sight of me, beckoned me over. He wanted to know how far I had got with the symphony. I told him bluntly the reason which had led me to stop work on it, adding that I had not forgotten what I suffered over Marshal Damremont's funeral and the Requiem.

'But the rumor which has alarmed you is completely false,' he said. 'Nothing has changed; the inauguration of the Bastille column, the translation of the July dead—everything stands. I'm counting on you. Hurry up and finish the work.'

Although my mistrust had been all too natural, this assurance set my mind at rest and I resumed work at once. The march and the funeral oration were completed and the theme found for the Apothéose; but I was held up for quite a long time over the fanfare which I wanted to bring gradually up from the depths of the orchestra to the high note on which the song of triumph bursts in. I wrote version after version. None of them satisfied me. The effect was either commonplace, or it was insufficiently spacious or too light-hearted, or it lacked sonority, or the transition was badly managed. I imagined a trumpet-call of archangels, simple but sublime, boundless, glittering, an immense radiance swelling and resounding, proclaiming to earth and heaven the opening of the Empyrean gates. In the end I settled, not without anxiety, on the version which is familiar, and the rest was soon done. Later, after I had made the usual corrections and modifications, I added strings and chorus. Though not absolutely necessary, they greatly enhance the effect.

I engaged for the occasion a military band of two hundred. Habeneck would again have liked to conduct, but I prudently reserved that function for myself …

Happily it occurred to me to invite a large audience to the final rehearsal, for it was impossible to get any idea of the work on the day of the performance. Despite the volume of sound produced by a wind band of this size, very little was heard during the procession. The only exception was the music played as we went along the Boulevard Poissonnière, where the big trees—still standing at that date—acted as reflectors. The rest was lost.

In the open spaces of the Place de la Bastille it was worse. Almost nothing could be made out more than ten yards away. To cap it all, the National Guard, growing tired by standing at the slope in the blazing sun to the very end of the ceremony, began to march off to the accompaniment of some fifty side-drums maintaining a relentless barrage throughout the Apothéosis, not a note of which survived. That is how they regard the role of music on public occasions in France: by all means let it figure as an attraction—for the eye.

This I knew. The final rehearsal in the Salle Vivienne was the real performance. It made such an impression that the impresario in charge of the hall engaged me for four evening concerts, at which the new symphony was the main work in the program and a lot of money was taken in.

On the way out of one of these performances, Habeneck, with whom I had had a fresh quarrel (I do not remember why), remarked, 'One must admit the b--- has some damned fine ideas.' A week later he was probably saying the opposite. This time I had no bone to pick with the Minister. M. de Remusat, who behaved like a gentleman; the ten thousand francs were sent forthwith. When I had paid the bill for the band and the copyist, I had two thousand eight hundred francs left. It was not much; but the Minister was pleased and, as each performance made clear, the work appealed to the public more than all its predecessors. People became wildly excited by it. One evening at the Salle Vivienne, after the Apothéose, some young men were moved to pick up their chairs and pound them against the floor, uttering wild yells as they did so. The management promptly gave orders that at subsequent performances patrons would kindly express their enthusiasm in the more customary ways.

Spontini wrote me a long and curious letter on the subject of this symphony when it was performed much later at the Conservatoire, with strings as well as wind but without chorus. I am sorry not to be able to reproduce it here: I foolishly gave it to a collector of autographs. I remember only that it began: 'I write still being under the impression of your vibrant music.'

Despite his friendship for me, this was the only time he praised a composition of mine.[32]

32 *Memoirs*, 253ff.

A more personal description of this experience is found in the letter Berlioz wrote to his father.

Dear Father,

I feel badly that I have not yet announced to you the success that I had. But the service that I did with this musical army was so difficult that I am still getting over it, and yesterday I had trouble writing as my arm and hand were so sore from conducting.

Everything worked wonderfully. The big success took place at the dress rehearsal before the most intelligent audience in Paris. There were not only women who cried. After this ordeal, decisive as the work itself, remained the fact of playing it on stage. Our stage was Paris itself, its docks, its boulevards. And these old crafty military musicians swore that I would never get them to play the funeral march *while marching* and that my 210 musicians would never be able to march together during 20 measures. Experience won out over these routine predictions. I placed the trumpets and drums in front so that they would have freedom of movement, and I myself marched backwards (as I planned when I wrote the piece). The first measures were soli, so they could be heard by the rest of the band. Thus not only the funeral march but the *Apothéose* as well was played six times, while marching, together and with an extraordinary effect. The Minister sent me his division chefs to warmly compliment me, after the second hearing of the triumphal march which impressed all of the people who were around us. Last night, he had Cave send me a letter filled with pompous compliments.

This time I wrote so big that even nearsighted people could read me. Also, extraordinarily, there was no criticism. Even Mainzer, himself, my most intimate enemy of the *National*, let himself compliment my last work in his review.

This in itself does not prove in any way his superiority over my former works.

But it is a sign, a colossal feat and everyone saw it. The artists are all so filled with enthusiasm that it takes me aback. (I tell you this, father, in hope that you will not show this letter to anyone but my sisters.) I received congratulations in prose. So far only three journals speak of my music in detail: The *Galignani's Messenger* (enthusiastic); *Le National* (Mainzer converting himself); and *L'Univers* (enthusiastic). If I can send you these articles, I will be sure to do so.

I will now go to the Ministry, where Mr. de Remusat, so they say, *has a lot of things to tell me*. All of this does not negate the fact that two years ago they asked Rossini to compose the *Requiem* for the Emperor! A *Requiem* of Rossini would be strange indeed! If he does it. In this case, probably, they will ask me to compose some heroic triumphal song for the entrance of the cortege into Paris. Many people would be needed, and a lot of money, and even a lot more time to prepare everything—and strength not to crumble under the emotion of it all. After all, it is for Napoleon. I am really angry that I had to write this triumphal march for our little heroes of July; it was almost done for the big hero.

PS: It seems that they will give me three or four thousand francs for this piece that I wrote in less than forty hours. If that's the case, they should have given me fifty thousand for the *Requiem*. That's how it goes. There is fortune and misfortune for the compositions as well as for the composers.[33]

33 Letter to his Father, Paris, July 30, 1840, in *Correspondance*, 721.

The government representatives were delighted with Berlioz's contribution to the festival. The official letter of thanks came from Edmond Cave in the Office of the Minister of the Interior:

Dear Mr. Berlioz,
Your music is beautiful—very beautiful and it is very successful. All of the connoisseurs have admired your generous and lofty style—it is frank, new and beautiful—therefore it is good. Even those who envy you admit the same.

The Minister was very satisfied. He has asked me to compliment you until he can do so himself. His only regret is that he could not hear the complete work until the end. He has to start the parade that lasted three hours and you know that the military units from the suburbs had quite a long way to travel.

In expressing his regret this morning, the Minister manifested his desire that you be given a prompt opportunity to play these two new pieces. This is also my desire as I myself did not get enough chance to hear your works. But how should we go about this? Do you have any ideas on the subject? Come and tell me what you think?[34]

34 Letter to Berlioz from Edmond Cave, Office of the Minister o the Interior, Paris, July 29, 1840, in *Correspondance*, 720.

The editors of the *Correspondance Générale* add an interesting footnote to the this letter, 'Among those who envied Berlioz was Adolphe Adam, who wrote to Spiker on 23 July 1840, the following:

For the transporting of the remains of the July martyrs, the music will be composed *ad hoc* by Master Berlioz. There will be 200 wind instruments and a cannon as well—it will be beautiful. It is really a shame for us the other French composers to see the government make so many favors on such a detestable man. Le *Journal des Débats* does not even conserve its dignity by opening its pages to Mr. Berlioz, who spreads his hate and poor taste against everything that the public applauds.

But on 12 August, Adam wrote to the same correspondent the following:

I do not like either the man or his manners, but justice forces me to admit that in the second of these works [of the *Symphonie Funèbre et Triomphale*] there is a summing up which has a great impact far superior to any thing that he has written so far. The first piece and the first part of the second are an utter mess, but the last movement is really quite good. It does not have any melodic intervention, but the rhythm is accentuated, the harmony new, and the entrances quite enjoyable. In all, it is great progress, as the phrases are cut completely in four measures and are quite understandable. I would have liked the journals to render justice on this work as I have done and take note of this progress but nothing doing. They continued to persist that this last composition was the same as the others, even though it was greatly superior.[35]

35 Letter published in the *Revue de Paris*, September 2, 1903.

The success of the rehearsal in the Salle Vivienne led the administration of that hall to offer Berlioz four concerts there, the first being 7 August 1840. Berlioz, as usual, played an active role in advertising his own concerts, and, as the following two letters indicate, he began immediately. One will note that he was still using the title, *Military Symphony*.

If, without upsetting the length of your article, could you please print today:

'Mr. Berlioz will give next Thursday in the Vivienne Room a great instrumental concert during which you will hear the *Symphonie militaire* that he has just composed to transport the victims of July.'[36]

……

Madam:

The *Symphonie militaire* that I have just composed for the transfer of the ashes of the victims of the July Revolution is to be played again in a concert I am giving on Thursday next. Yielding to the desire I feel of having you hear this work, I take the liberty of submitting to Your Majesty's gracious notice the program of this musical occasion.[37]

36 Letter to Jules Janin, *Journal des Débats*, Paris, August 2, 1840, in *Correspondance*, 725.

37 Letter to Maria-Amelia, wife to Louis-Philippe, August 4, 1840, in *Correspondance*, 727.

The program for this first of the Salle Vivienne concerts which Berlioz conducted, included:

Overture to Benvenuto Cellini
Harold en Italie, movements I–III
Symphonie fantastique, movements II–IV
Symphonie funèbre, with Dieppo as trombone soloist.

In response to a friendly review of this concert, Berlioz wrote,

> I do not know how to thank you, Sir, for your admirable article in yesterday's *Messager*. I let myself naively go and cried out for joy, not only because you flattered me so, but for a review which (excuse me for admitting it) I found prodigal and profound. At last the first man of letters and a non-musician who seems to understand my music completely.
>
> I do not doubt that my friendship with Brindeau helps and must have added something to your great work. But I find your personal opinion very powerful and encouraging and something that I have not encountered in the past.
>
> Thank you, Sir, and believe me that I am filled with joy and thanks. I would go through many more negative criticisms to end up with such fine praise.
>
> As for your final observation, there is truth. I do not overly salute the audience because I do not want to be accused of taking bows to get extra applause.[38]

A member of the audience who heard this concert wrote Berlioz as follows:

> I must tell you that never before has music made me feel such emotions. It was beautiful, grand and beyond anything I could have imagined. It was beyond what you yourself have done in the past and your past inspirations. Bless you, Berlioz, the people of July could only have had you to so nobly salute them during the hypocrisy of the July 28 parade. You took your work seriously and you accomplished it as a citizen and a poet. Bless you a thousand times! I would like to tell you a little about what I feel now and the admiration and respect that I have for you, but words fail me! My heart is full, too full. I would like to see you and embrace you![39]

On 14 August 1840, Berlioz conducted the second of his four Salle Vivienne concerts, again using his favorite trombonist, Dieppo, in the symphony for band. The program was as follows:

Overture to Benvenuto Cellini
Harold en Italie, movements I–III
Symphonie fantastique, movements II–IV
Fête chez Capulet, Romeo et Juliette
Symphonie funèbre

The following month, one finds a curious letter to his father.

---

38 Letter to Edouard Thierry, Paris, August 11, 1840, in *Correspondance*, 729. The editors add that this article has never been found as the year 1840 of this journal is missing from the Bibliothèque Nationale.

39 Letter to Berlioz from August Luchet, Nogent-sur-Mane, August 12, 1840, in *Correspondance*, 730.

> Upon arriving, I found a letter condemning me to two days of prison for missing the guard of July 30. When I went before the administration that condemned me, I explained that perhaps my performance the day before, conducting 200 musicians during five hours in the heat was worth an exemption for the following day. He cried, 'But you are the Berlioz who did … —but yes, if you please! That stupid sergeant couldn't have known.'
>
> So, I received grace and believe that my prison sentence will be reduced to nothing.[40]

[40] Letter to his Father, Paris, September 22, 1840, in *Correspondance*, 731.

In the Fall, Berlioz managed to obtain permission to use one of the annual benefit concerts offered to the administrative director of the Opéra to organize a 'Festival de M. Berlioz.' The program of the 1 November 1840 concert was held in the Opéra house with Berlioz conducting. Berlioz provides a lengthy and rich account of the difficulties which the young artist encountered in attempting to stage this concert in the Paris Opéra.

> M. Pillet, then director of the Opéra, welcomed the proposal I put to him that I should organize a festival in the theater, and I set to work, without letting any news of the project leak out. The problem lay in my giving Habeneck time to act against it. He was bound to take a jaundiced view of my conducting a great musical enterprise of this kind, the largest yet seen in Paris, in the theater where he was conductor. So I prepared secretly all the music needed for my chosen program and engaged the players without revealing where the concert was being held. When everything was ready and I could safely show my hand, I asked Pillet to inform Habeneck that I was in charge of the proceedings. But he could not bring himself to do it, such was his dread of the formidable old man. The awkward task was left to me. So I wrote to Habeneck and told him what arrangements I had made, with Pillet's approval, and added that as I was in the habit of conducting my own concerts, I hoped he would not take it amiss if I conducted this one as well.
>
> Habeneck received my letter at the Opéra, in the middle of a rehearsal. He read it several times, paced gloomily about the stage for a long time and then, suddenly making up his mind, went down to the manager's office and announced that the whole thing suited him admirably, as he had intended in any case to spend that day in the country. But his annoyance was obvious and it was soon shared by many of his players, all the more vehemently because they knew they would flatter him by showing it. Under the agreement which I had made with Pillet, the whole orchestra was to be at my disposal, together with the players whom I had recruited from outside.

The concert was a benefit for the director of the Opéra; he guaranteed me a mere five hundred francs for my pains and a free hand with all the arrangements. Consequently, Habeneck's players were bound to take part and would not be paid for it. I remembered the gentlemen of the Theatre-Italien and the way they had made a fool of me in very similar circumstances. This time, indeed, I was in an even more delicate position with regard to the players at the Opéra. Every evening I could see private meetings going on in the orchestra during the intervals. The air was electric. Habeneck, with a bodyguard of supporters in angry attendance, was cold and impenetrable. Copies of the *Charivari*, in which I was torn to pieces, were distributed on their music stands. The storm was clearly gathering: a few of Habeneck's henchmen had announced that they would not 'march without their old general'; and now that the full rehearsals were due to begin, I tried to get Pillet to agree that the Opéra orchestra should be paid like the others. When he refused, I said, 'I fully appreciate your reasons. Only, in this way you're endangering the whole performance. I have no choice but to use the five hundred francs which you have set aside for me to pay the players who don't actually refuse to play.'

'What!' he said. 'Get nothing out of it, after all that frightful effort?'

'That is not important. The great thing is that it should go well. My five hundred francs will keep the less mutinous quiet. For the others, I would rather you didn't use your authority to force them to play. We'll leave them to their old general.'

So it was arranged. I had a combined orchestra and chorus of six hundred. The program consisted of the first act of Gluck's *Iphigénie en Tauride*, a scene from Handel's *Athalia*, the Dies Irae and Lacrymosa from my Requiem, the Apothéose from my Funeral and Triumphal Symphony, the adagio, scherzo and finale from *Roméo and Juliet*, and an unaccompanied chorus by Palestrina. Considering how my army of performers was put together, I cannot imagine how I contrived to teach them such a difficult program in so short a time as a week; but I did. I would go straight from the Opéra to the Theatre-Italien (where I had engaged the chorus only), and from the Theatre-Italien to the Opéra-Comique and the Conservatoire, taking a chorus practice in one place, a sectional rehearsal of the orchestra in another; supervising the entire work myself, not leaving anything to anybody else. After that I took the combined instrumental forces, in two halves one after the other, in the foyer of the Opéra: the strings from eight in the morning till midday, the winds from midday till four. I was on my feet, baton in hand, all day. My throat was on fire, my voice had gone, my arm was dropping off. I felt ready to faint with thirst and exhaustion, when a compassionate member of the chorus brought me a large glass of mulled wine; it gave me the strength to carry through this grueling session to the end.

Fresh demands by the Opéra musicians had added to its natural trials. Discovering that I was paying some of the outside players twenty francs, they considered that this gave them the right to come up in the middle, one after the other, and demand to be paid the same amount.

'It's not the money,' they said, 'but you can't have Opéra artists getting less than players from minor theaters.'

'All right,' I said, 'You shall have your twenty francs—I guarantee it; only, for God's sake get on with your job and stop bothering me.'

Next day the final rehearsal took place on the stage of the Opéra, and was satisfactory. Everything went reasonably well except the Queen Mab scherzo, which I had rashly included in the program. The piece is too swift and delicate to be performed by an orchestra of this size, nor should it be. With so short a bar, it is virtually impossible to keep the extremities of such a huge body of players together. Those farthest from the conductor soon get behind because they cannot quite keep up with the very rapid beat. I was in such a state of agitation that it never occurred to me to form a small picked orchestra which, concentrated near me in the middle of the stage, could have carried out my intentions without difficulty. After the most fearful struggles we had to abandon the scherzo, and it was removed from the program. I noticed on this occasion how difficult, indeed impossible, it is to prevent the little cymbals in Bb and F from dragging when the players are a long way from the conductor. I had stupidly left them at the back of the stage, next to the drums, and despite everything I could do they were sometimes as much as a bar behind. Since then, I have been careful to place them right beside me, and the difficulty has vanished.

I had counted on resting the following day, at any rate until the evening; but a friend wrote warning me that Habeneck's partisans were planning to spoil or even to wreck the whole enterprise: the drums were to be slit and the bows of the double basses greased, and in the middle of the concert they would call for the Marseillaise.

This information, the reader will surmise, somewhat disturbed my much-needed rest. Instead of spending the day asleep, I paced feverishly up and down outside the Opéra. As I was prowling about on the boulevard, I had the luck to meet Habeneck in person. I went straight up to him and took his arm.

'I've been warned that your players have some foul play planned for tonight. But I've got my eye on them.'

'Oh, you've nothing to fear,' the old hypocrite answered; 'they won't do anything. I've made them listen to reason.'

'My dear man, it's not I who need reassuring. I'm trying to reassure you. You see, if anything happened it would fall pretty heavily on you. But don't worry: as you say, they won't do anything.'

All the same, when evening came I was not without anxiety. I had stationed my copyist in the orchestra all day, to stand guard over the drums and the double basses. The instruments were untouched. But there was something else that I was afraid of. The four small brass bands in the pieces from the Requiem contain trumpets and cornets in various keys (Bb, F, and Eb). It so happens that the crook of a trumpet in F, for example, differs little from the crook of a trumpet in Bb, and it is easy to confuse them. In the Tuba Mirum some sly dog could slip me a fanfare in F instead of Bb. His excuse would be that he had used the wrong crook. Meanwhile he would have engineered a fearsome cacophony.

Just before the Dies Irae began, I left my stand and went round the orchestra, asking each trumpet and cornet player to let me see his instrument. I inspected them carefully, scrutinizing the inscriptions on the various crooks ... until I reached the band which included the Dauverne brothers (who played in the Opéra orchestra), when the elder made me blush by saying, 'Oh Berlioz, how could you? Surely you don't suspect us? We would never do a thing like that. And we're your friends.' The reproach stung me (though what I had done was only too excusable) and I stopped my investigations.

My worthy trumpeters made no mistakes, everything went well, and the Requiem pieces produced their due effect.

Immediately after this part of the concert there was an intermission. During the ensuing lull the Habeneckists tried to explode their remaining bombshell, the simplest and the least dangerous to themselves. Several voices from the pit shouted, 'The Marseillaise, the Marseillaise!', hoping to excite the audience and upset the carefully planned organization of the evening. A number of spectators, attracted by the idea of hearing the famous hymn declaimed by such a chorus and orchestra, were already joining in the cry, when I came forward to the front of the stage and roared out at the top of my voice, 'We will not play the Marseillaise. That is not what we are here for;' and calm was instantly restored.

It did not last long. A moment later another incident, this time quite unconnected with me, set the house in a greater commotion. Cries of 'Murder! It's monstrous! Arrest him!' were heard coming from the amphitheater, and the whole audience rose in confusion. Madame de Girardin, looking disheveled, was waving her arms about in her box and calling for help. Her husband had just had his face slapped by Bergeron, one of the editors of the *Charivari*, a notorious lampooner of Louis-Philippe, and the man popularly supposed to have fired the pistol shot at the King from the Pont Royal a few years before.

Such a fracas could not but be very damaging to the rest of the concert, which passed without incident but in a general atmosphere of abstractedness.

Be that as it may, I had overcome my difficulties and frustrated the enemy general staff. The receipts came to eight thousand five hundred francs. As the sum which I had surrendered in order to pay the Opéra players was not enough, owing to my having promised them all twenty francs, I was obliged to present the cashier of the theater with three hundred sixty francs. He accepted it, indicating the source in his book with an entry in red ink: *Surplus handed over by M. Berlioz.*

Thus I succeeded, alone and unaided, in organizing the largest concert that had yet been seen in Paris, despite Habeneck and his men, and by giving up the modest amount allocated to me. The takings were eight thousand five hundred francs, while my part in the proceedings cost me three hundred and sixty francs.

That is the way to get rich! I have often employed this method during my career.[41]

41 *Memoirs*, 258ff.

It would seem that the efforts of his enemies extended even farther than Berlioz indicates above. Apparently a review of this concert was written and given to a critic, who must have published it even though he did not actually attend the concert. While the reader might believe such practice is not possible, in fact it continues today. This writer has also had a European concert with a published review, very favorable, thank Heaven, by a critic who did not attend. In the present case, Berlioz tried to embarrass the critic by writing the paper to supply corrections of such a nature to make it clear to all that the critic could not have attended the concert.

> Sir, in the review of the *Revue des Deux Mondes* of the festival that I gave at the Opéra, there were several factual errors which I would like to bring to your attention for correction.
>
> The author of this review would make me guilty of the crime of *lèse-majesté* regarding the music of Gluck and Palestrina. 'Poor Gluck, he says, would not have imagined that the sound of his trombones, which evoke just feelings of hatred and rage, would someday be replaced by Mr. Berlioz with some poor ophicleides. And Palestrina, the peaceful maestro we tore away from the Sistine Chapel, for whom a few soprani would suffice for his contrapuntal melodies, [would never have imagined] that his suave and religious inspiration would be crushed under the pomp of instruments.'
>
> Well now! The music from *Iphigénie* was played absolutely as the composer wrote it; no poetic license was taken. As for Palestrina, this madrigal, *Alla riva del Tebro*, is a trite secular work which was never performed in the Sistine Chapel. It takes an active imagination for the critic to hear the singers crushed by instruments, since we performed it WITHOUT ACCOMPANIMENT.
>
> These are the errors which damage me in my role of interpreter of the masters I admire so much.[42]

42 Letter to Franois Buloz, Director, *La Revue des Deux Mondes*, Paris, November, 1840, in *Correspondance*, 737.

In any case, the concert was a success for Berlioz and his accounts of this concert to his sisters speak of the great enthusiasm which the last movement of the *Symphonie funèbre* so often produced.

> I continued with the *Lacrymosa*, the *Fête chez Capulet*, and the *Symphonie militaire* in its entirety which were all received with enthusiasm rarely seen in the Opéra—especially of a public who paid more than usual. The 'Apothéose' was interrupted five times by applause. At the return of the triumphal theme, all of the audience was on its feet moving about, screaming—it was superb. I am exhausted, but less than the day before yesterday.[43]
>
> …
>
> The princes stayed until the final note of the Apothéose, which the audience listened to standing up, as if it were a national anthem.[44]

43 Letter to his Sister, Adele, Paris, November 2, 1840, in *Correspondance*, 734.

44 Letter to his Sister, Nanci, Paris [in prison for missing a Guard appearance], November 13, 1840, in *Correspondance*, 736.

On 1 February 1842, Berlioz conducted the third of his Salle Vivienne concerts. Once again the *Symphonie funèbre* was performed, but now for the first time with strings added. The program for this concert was,

Berlioz, *Reverie et Caprice*, for violin, in its premiere performance
Weber, *Invitation to the Dance*
Beethoven, *Triple Concerto*
Symphonie funèbre

Berlioz wrote his sister of this concert,

> You know that I gave a great concert last Tuesday. You will all never be here, neither father, nor uncle, nor sisters, nor brothers-in-law, when these great things happen; you witness them in writing! You cannot be among the shouts, the cries, the entire feeling that excited the *Apothéose* of my *Symphonie Militaire* that I have just rescored for two orchestras. The moment the second orchestra played part of the audience stood up in a great agitation and the two hundred musicians could no longer be heard, such was the force of the unsuppressed shouts. People tell me how strange crowds can be at such times. If my father had been there, with all the rest of the family around, with active thoughts attached to the work and the three days that we killed ourselves so bravely in the streets of Paris, he would have no doubt felt a great feeling that he had not yet experienced. The room was splendid with standing room only. Despite the expense of a double orchestra and the new copy, I still made money.[45]

45 Letter to his Sister, Naci, Paris, February 5, 1842, in *Correspondance*, 765.

On 15 February 1842, Berlioz conducted the fourth of his concerts in the Salle Vivienne in the following program:

Harold in Italie, movement II
Symphonie Fantastique
Grand Symphonie Funèbre et Triomphale
Rêverie et Caprice
Heller, *A Grande Caprice* for piano

He had evidently invited Victor Hugo to attend, but received the following apology:

> You know, my dear great poet, that God disposes. Feel sorry for me. Your admirers at the Place Royale are going to spend the night at the bedside of a sick child, instead of going to applaud you along with all of Paris who admire you. I send two of your fans in our place.[46]

46 Letter to Berlioz from Victor Hugo, Paris, February 15, 1842, in *Correspondance*, 766.

During the months that followed it is evident that Berlioz conceived the idea of adding a chorus to the final movement of the *Symphonie funèbre*. He also seems to have been under the impression that the symphony would soon be published, although we know this did not happen until the following year. In preparation for publication, Berlioz had obtained permission from the Duke of Orléans to accept the dedication, only to lose any potential political value to the dedication by the duke's almost immediate accidental death. Berlioz speaks of these things in letters to his family.

> Speaking of the Duke of Orléans, I have just dedicated to him my Grand Symphonie Funèbre et Triomphale that is being published at this moment.
> Speaking of this symphony, let me tell you that I have reread, corrected and strengthened the choir, along with the two orchestras, and we will present this new version this month (around the 15th) at the Opéra, a little bit before the festival of July ...[47]
> ......
> I will soon publish in succession all of my symphonies; one always does so in the end. The first to appear will be the last one I wrote—it is the Grande Symphonie Funèbre, composed for the transport of the victims of July and which the poor Duke of Orléans had just accepted the dedication when, alas, he passed away so cruelly. I cannot tell you how sad this awful event has made me. I seem to be surrounded by funerals and catastrophes.[48]

47 Letter to his Sister, Nanci, Paris, July 5, 1842, in *Correspondance*, 771.

48 Letter to his Brother-in-law, March Suat, Paris, August 10, 1842, in *Correspondance*, 772.

The widow of the Duke eventually sent Berlioz a gift for his thoughtfulness in offering to dedicate the symphony to her late husband. Perhaps to impress a family member, Berlioz describes the gift as follows:

> The Duchess of Orléans has just sent a rather expensive bronze. It is a gift for the symphony that I had dedicated to the Duke of Orléans.[49]

Actually the widow 'sent Berlioz a paltry bronze trinket in gratitude for what turned out to be a posthumous honor.'[50]

The reader will also notice in the first two letters above that Berlioz had changed the title of the symphony from 'Military Symphony' to the one we know today. Another letter at about the same time, to the President of the Jury of the Academy of Fine Arts, contains a list of his compositions, where we find,

> Symphonie Funèbre et Triomphale pour un orchestre d'Harmonie, un second orchestre d'instruments a cordes et un Choeur.

The first performance of the symphony with the new choral part (but here without strings) occurred on 26 September 1842, in Brussels, in the Concert Hall of the Royal Brussels Military Band. On this occasion Berlioz conducted the following program:

> Portions of *Romeo et Juliette*
> *Le Jeune Pâtre breton*
> *Harold en Italie*, movement II
> *Symphonie funèbre*, with a local trombone soloist named Schmidt
> A wind orchestra work composed by Snel
> An *Elegie and a Fantaisie on Othello* by Ernst

There are three extant letters by Berlioz to his host, Joseph-François Snel, conductor of the orchestra and wind orchestra of the Société de la Grande-Harmonie in Brussels, regarding this concert. These interesting letters reveal Berlioz's careful interest in all the details of his concerts.

> After your answer I will send you, via the stage coach, the choral music for my symphony ... and the tambour parts of the *symphonie*, which is rather difficult and should be studied ahead of time, as well as the trombone solo. You did not tell me if we will have a symphony orchestra. It

---

[49] Letter to his Sister, Nanci Pal, Paris, July 12, 1843, in *Correspondance*, 843.

[50] According to Holoman, *Berlioz*, 285.

would be important to have [at least] 18 to 20 violins, six viola, six celli, and eight bass ... the symphony would lose a lot of its value if these strings instruments were missing.

You also did not tell me how many Bb clarinets you have, but the day I had the pleasure of seeing you, you told me that you had more than 20, so I am reassured on this point. Your letter tells me about three small clarinets in Eb and then two clarinets in Eb—that is where the error lies, I think. Will I need to transpose the third flute parts for your Db flutes? Please choose your best tenor trombonist for the *Orasion funèbre* solo. I will send you the music so he can study ahead of time. With it you will find the music for the valve horn, alto valve trombone, and the bass clarinet (meant to replace the tenor trombone part if you cannot find a talented enough player). I will not be able to send at the same time the score for the Apothéose, with the choir's music, as the printer still has it in order to finish his work. But, as soon as I have a copy, I will send it to you.

The words for the final chorus are just what you need for your Belgian Revolution, sister to our own. It would be a good idea to have something printed in any newspaper announcing at least that I will be performing on the 27th a concert in which will be played [1] *Grande Symphonie Funèbre et Triomphale composee pour la Translation des restes des victimes de Juillet et l'inauguration de la colonne de la Bastille* ... It seems to me that this program is very respectable and will be much appreciated by the audience.

Now, let me know the exact number of members of the Society who will expect to enter free of charge to the concert and those who are entitled to tickets at 2 francs. You understand that I cannot make this trip and bring two singers, who I am paying rather well, if the probable intake of money will be reduced to a point (as I hear here) due to free tickets to the Society. You will have to clarify this subject for me. You have put your heart and soul in this affair and I do not hesitate mentioning this potential problem. My fear is founded also a bit due to the fact that we are going to have to use some of the intake of the general seats to pay for the double orchestra, if we are to also have the string instruments and the choir. You told me, if I am not mistaken, that there will be four hundred free seats and as many seats at 2 francs, and that the hall could only hold three thousand people. If this is so, then we should set the ticket price at 5 francs and if we get sixteen to seventeen hundred people that would be OK. Let me know in your next letter what your feelings are on this matter, after which I will answer your letter so we can officially announce this concert.[51]

......

You are a wonderful man! Thanks for all of your excellence. There has been neglect in the stage coach which delivered to you my package. Therefore, I am bringing the entire package with me for reasons more than the fact that this damned score will only be printed tomorrow.

I will bring some extra music for the chorus as well ...

51 Letter to Joseph-François Snel, Paris, August 28, 1842, in *Correspondance,* 772 bis.

I will leave on the 20th at 10:00 AM by stage coach and will arrive in Brussels, so they tell me, the next day at noon …

I will write the King [Leopold I, of Belgium] and I will see all of my colleagues, the journalists of Brussels that had the goodwill to announce me. As for the copy of my *symphonie* that you requested, I hope that you believe that my intentions have always been and always are to offer it to the Grande Harmonie, even if we have to delay the publication a bit …

P.S. You have not forgotten the number of music stands that are necessary for a double orchestra. You must place the string instruments in the center. I am enchanted that the trombone solo is in able hands. These arrangements are very disagreeable to me. And the tambours, will they play? You know we need 8 tambours and three pair of cymbals, one *pavillon chinois*, and a gong; plus a bass drum and a pair of timpani sticks with sponge-heads.

I have just seen Meyerbeer and he has not decided if he can come yet. Give my best to A. Sax. I have included in my *Treatise on Instrumentation* a long note on his new instruments.[52]

......

As soon as my *Treatise on Instrumentation* comes out, you will receive a copy. Previously I will send you … the Symphonie funèbre which perhaps you can have performed out-of-doors.[53]

52 Letter to Joseph-François Snel, Paris, September 16, 1842, in *Correspondance*, 776.

53 Letter to Joseph-François Snel, Paris, October 12, 1842, in *Correspondance*, 780.

After this brief taste of foreign adulation, Berlioz began to intensify his plans for a much more extended tour. At the same time he began working towards the idea of a 'farewell concert' for himself at the Opéra.

I am in the midst of putting together my *Symphonie funèbre* at the Opéra before leaving. I probably cannot have this piece played at Frankfurt, but I would like very much to have it played at Mainz by the fine wind orchestra there that I have heard so much about. Do you know the name of the director of this orchestra and could you tell me what I must do to be able to play there?

Sorry for all these questions. A thousand sincere thanks.[54]

54 Letter to Ferdinand Hiller, Paris, October 29, 1842, in *Correspondance*, 785.

In a no longer extant letter, one can see Berlioz answering what must have been one of many obstacles placed in his path by Habeneck. Regarding details concerning the preparation of the final rehearsal of the *Symphonie funèbre*, Berlioz thinks the rehearsals for Wagner's *Flying Dutchman* would, on the contrary not interfere with his project, but rather would help as he would have the subsequent players for the symphony.[55]

55 Letter to François Habeneck, Paris, October 23, 1842 [summarized but not quoted] in *Correspondance*, 783.

Nevertheless this 'farewell concert' in the Opéra occurred on 7 November 1842, in the form of a performance of the *Symphonie funèbre* pressed between performances of the second act of *Gustave III* of Auber and *Giselle* by Adam. It was this performance in which the Symphony was heard for the first time with band, strings and chorus all together, with Berlioz conducting both the choir and band on stage with the strings conducted by Habeneck from the pit.

According to the *Revue et Gazette musicale*[56] the choir was not large enough, but the success of the *Apothéose* was great. Berlioz, obviously delighted, continued his plans for the extended tour.

[56] November 13, 1842.

> I have been very busy putting together my Symphonie funèbre at the Opéra. It was played the other day in a flamboyant way and the success was splendissimo. Tell that to our excellent friend Zani [a critic]. Well before the end of the Apothéose, you could hear neither the orchestra nor the chorus as the audience was so loud and agitated. I got two curtain calls—all in all it was a great success and its importance was great in view of the fact that the audiences are rather lukewarm and preoccupied about an opera which was chosen over another one. You see the difference in the hall. We can no longer perform this symphony in your hall. We need a completely different orchestra … If the concert is still on for December 10, write me … when everything is in order and we will make the program. Our friend should mention in the Belgian newspapers the effect my symphony has just had at the Opéra.[57]
>
> ……
>
> I have just made a musical voyage to Belgium and Frankfurt. And I am ready to go back. But this time, it will be for a longer time, as I must do a big tour there and include Vienna and Berlin. They are organizing two concerts in Frankfurt for Christmas. I will give a third one in Belgium on my way through. And to say goodbye to Paris, last week I organized my Grande Symphonie funèbre at the Opéra—the one played during the July festivities with the addition of a chorus. The performance was wonderful and the success was overwhelming. I had two curtain calls and was forced to go to the front of the stage after the Apothéose as the applause interrupted the performance long before its finale. Even the loges, which are never generous in applause at the Opéra, were moved to a standing ovation.[58]
>
> ……
>
> The Prince of Hohenzollern-Hechingen wrote me yesterday to ask me to have some of my works played for him at a private concert. I will go there tomorrow, and then I will come back here as I am waiting for an answer from Berman of Munich [Clarinetist in the court there and friend of Weber]. If his answer is not satisfactory, then I believe, following your advice, that I will go directly to Breslau. If you write me to tell me that everything is ready and sure, and that I can count on at least 1,000 francs for the first concert, then I wouldn't hesitate. You suggest that I should go first where I have friends like you to prepare

[57] Letter to Joseph-François Snel, Paris, November 12, 1842, in *Correspondance*, 787.

[58] Letter to his Sister, Adele Suat, Paris, November 24, 1842, in *Correspondance*, 789.

the path and take care of my interests, before presenting myself in a city like Vienna where I know no one and where the expenditures will be great. So, as soon as you arrive in Breslau, would you be good enough to see if they can assure two concerts in which we would perform my three symphonies, *La Fantastique*, *Harold*, and the *Symphonie funèbre* (with two orchestras). The wind band will cost a lot, perhaps, as we need 80 instrumentalists, or at least 70 …

When you have time, could you go to the theater and ask Guhr to please give you a package of music, which you can then ship to me here right away at my address (Hotel du Roi de Würtemberg). The package should contain: [1] [string parts] to my *Symphonie Fantastique* and *Harold* …, [2] the score and printed parts of the *Symphonie funèbre* that I have left for him during my first trip.[59]

59 Letter to Ferdinand Friedland, Stuttgart, December 30, 1842, in *Correspondance*, 794.

The only concerts on this tour on which Berlioz conducted his *Symphonie funèbre* were in Dresden. Following is a letter in which he discusses these plans and in particular the number of additional winds needed for the band symphony.

Thank you very much for your rapid answer. I will leave tomorrow for Leipzig, where Mendelssohn waits for me, and will try to come see you on Monday or Tuesday to settle the final details of my first concert in Dresden.

The concert I have here was brilliant and very successful. The population of Weimar welcomed my music, and myself, with rare goodness. I will be happy if my compositions please the tastes of the gentlemen of Dresden.

If possible, at the first concert I want them to hear my big *Symphonie Funèbre et Triomphale* for two orchestras and chorus. Would the superintendent agree to the extra cost of a second orchestra made up of wind instruments? We would need about 60 wind instruments, plus those already in the theater's orchestra. They should be placed on the stage with six tambour and the chorus. All the strings, which make up the second orchestra, will stay in the pit in their regular place …

P.S. If Baron Luttichau absolutely does not want to cover the expense of a second orchestra, then we shall have to make up a different program and that would really be a shame.[60]

60 Letter to Karol Lipinski, Weimar, January 27, 1843, in *Correspondance*, 807.

The first of the Dresden concerts occurred on 10 February 1843 in the Dresden Royal Theater, with Berlioz conducting the following program:

King Lear
Symphonie fantastique
Requiem (two movements)

Symphonie funèbre et triomphale, second and third movements, with Reis-
   siger conducting the strings in the pit
Cavatina from *Benvenuto Cellini*
Absence, song with piano by Berlioz

A second concert occurred on 17 February 1843, also in the Dresden Royal Theater with Berlioz conducting. The program was,

Overture to *Benvenuto Cellini*
Requiem (two movements)
Berlioz, *Rêverie et Caprice* for violin
Le Cinq Mai (in German)
Harold in Italy
Excerpts from *Roméo et Juliette*
La Belle Voyageuse
Absence, with piano
Symphonie funèbre et triomphale (third movement only)

For these concerts the choral part of the *Apothéose* was sung in German.

> I did not have a translation of the chorus part in the symphony, but the stage manager, Winkler, a man of wit and intelligence, very obligingly extemporized, as it were, the German verses that we needed, and rehearsals for the finale could begin … The Funeral Symphony produced the same effect as in Paris.[61]

61 *Memoirs*, 310ff.

A letter written after these concerts reveals an exhausted composer–conductor.

> I was sick and am still incredibly tired from the rehearsals in Dresden and Leipzig. Can you believe that in Dresden I had to do 8 rehearsals, each 3 1/2 hours long, in 12 days, as well as two concerts. And I had to go once from Leipzig to Dresden and return again on the same day, that means [240 kilometers] by rail, as well as preparing my two concerts and come back to attend one given by Mendelssohn here. Mendelssohn was charming, excellent, attentive and in a word a good friend. We have exchanged our conductor's batons in a sign of friendship. He is a great master and I say this despite the fact that he has had only a word of compliment *for my Romances*, with not a word for my *symphonies*, nor *overtures*, or my *Requiem* …
>
> You can tell Dieppo that I have not yet found his match and that the trombones which have tried to play the Oraison gave me a pain in the chest, not to mention the ears.[62]

62 Letter to Joseph d'Ortigue, Leipzig, February 28, 1843, in *Correspondance*, 816.

An extant letter to Berlioz from Meyerbeer indicates that Berlioz had planned to perform the *Symphonie funèbre* in Berlin, but this performance of the symphony did not materialize.

> Dear Maestro,
> I will start looking for the 9 timpanists, but I am afraid that I will not find them. All of the rest will be easy to complete due to our excellent military music. You know that, for the *Symphonie funèbre*, the Prince of Prussia, Supreme Chief of the Military, has given us the use of all of the Berlin and Potsdam military bands, but not the Royal Chapel, giving us a total of 400 musicians.
> You can therefore give a second concert in Hamburg, for we have more work during the holidays and are, consequently, a little late ... The day after tomorrow the rehearsals for the *Huguenots*, which will be given on the 28th and the 29th, will begin ... The rehearsals of your chorus and the orchestra can not, therefore, begin before the 30th. But, in the meantime, you can send the parts of the *Symphonie funèbre*, for the military bands will not be rehearsing during the theater rehearsals. Beginning April 1 ... we can put some body and soul into the rehearsals of your concerts.[63]

63   Letter from Giacomo Meyerbeer to Berlioz, Berlin, March, 1843, quoted in *Correspondance*, 823.

Returning to Paris, Berlioz, inspired by his success abroad, continued to explore future possible performances of the *Symphonie funèbre*.

> For a long time, I have had the desire to have some of my works heard in Italy, but I did not dare to attempt this experience which has the possibility of producing good results ... It would be best to have at least two big festival concerts, at La Scala, during the most appropriate season, with four or five hundred musicians. I plan to perform my *Grande Symphonie funèbre et Triomphale*, for two orchestras and chorus and my symphony for 3 choirs from *Roméo et Juliette* ...
> This is an opportunity that could be a great success, if we take the necessary precautions, especially for the first evening—not to offer the public of Milan music too far from what they are used to hearing, but rather choose those which are sure bets. I think that the vocal and instrumental resources are not what will be lacking, thanks to the Conservatory and the military bands, which we will add to the resources of the theater.[64]

64   Letter to Giovanni Ricordi, Paris, June 15, 1843, in *Correspondance*, 842.

At this time Berlioz also began correspondence with the famous pianist Sigismund Thalberg, who had offered to write a Fantasie for piano on themes of the *Symphonie funèbre*, a project which he eventually realized.

> I have arrived in Berlin and hurry to send you the score of my Symphony and ask that you write, as soon as possible, the work [Grand Caprice pour le piano sur la marche de l'Apothéose, published in 1845] as you promised. This symphony which has not yet been published [made public] was printed 6 months ago by Schlesinger, whom I have asked to release it for sale upon my return. I thought he would give up the printing blocks to Richaut, but this has not been the case, and all of your works and mine will be published by him. He is ready, so he says, to give me the same terms as Richaut.[65]
>
> ......
>
> If in the midst of your honeymoon you have a moment to give me, please write me a note and tell me if you have received the music from my symphony and when you will be able to send me the piece you so kindly promised to write.
>
> All has come to a standstill because of the absence of your manuscript and this delay greatly distresses me. Although you are married, be a good boy and rid me of my problem as soon as possible.[66]
>
> ......
>
> I thank you forty thousand times; no one can be more gracious than you. Your arrangement is superb and you know this as well as I. What you refer to as my inspirations will win even more praise due to the new form you have given them.[67]

A letter from the Paris publisher, Schlesinger, confirms his offer to buy both the piano work and the symphony.

> It has been agreed between us that when Thalberg composes a fantasie on the themes of the *Symphonie funèbre*, that I will buy the entire property of this work for the sum of 1,000 francs.[68]

During 1843 Berlioz gave one more performance of the *Symphonie funèbre* in Paris, in what would turn out to be his final concert in the Hall of the Conservatoire. It was this concert in which Spontini heard the symphony, resulting in the comment quoted above from Berlioz's *Memoirs*. This letter which Berlioz remarks he gave to a collector is now preserved in Paris, Bibliotheque du Conservatoire in Bibliotheque Nationale, Department de la Musique (Hugh Macdonald, ed., *Hector Berlioz New Edition of the Complete Works*, vol. 19, ix).

In an extant letter, Berlioz asks a fellow critic to help advertise the concert.

65 Letter to Sigismund Thalberg, Paris, June 4, 1843, in *Correspondance*, 837.

66 Letter to Thalberg, Paris, August 1, 1843, in *Correspondance*, 844.

67 Letter to Thalberg, undated, in *Correspondance*, 941.

68 Letter from Maurice Schlesinger to Berlioz, Paris, October 10, 1843, in *Correspondance*, 854.

Please see if you can, in your next article, introduce a few words to announce my concert on the 19th at the Conservatory. Duprez will do a piece that I wrote in Germany and Duprez, Massol and Madame Gras will sing a trio. Then there will be a cavatina for Madame Gras, a violin solo for Alard, the overture of *King Lear*, the Scherzo of Queen Mab, the *Harold* symphony, and the finale for two orchestras of the *grande Symphonie funèbre et triomphale* for the Duke of Orléans (the Apothéose). Mix all this with my return from Germany and the long time that has past between my last concert in Paris.[69]

69 Letter to Hippolyte Lucas, critic for the journal, Le Siècle, Paris, November, 1843, in *Correspondance*, 844.

The program for this concert was,

Le Roi Lear
Rêverie et Caprice
Trio and *Cavatine* from *Benvenuto Cellini*
Harold en Italie
Excerpts from *Roméo et Juliette*
Absence
Symphonie funèbre, second and third movement, with Dieppo as trombone soloist

During 1844 Berlioz conducted the *Symphonie funèbre* on two concerts. The first was given on 6 April 1844, in the Opéra-Comique. Berlioz conducted the following program:

Concert spirituel, for Palm Sunday
Le Roi Lear
Cavatine from *Benvenuto Cellini*
Le Cinq Mai
Le Carnaval romain
Sanctus from the *Requiem*
Symphonie funèbre, third movement
Works by Le Sueur, Meyerbeer, and Sivori
An Aria from Meyerbeer's *Robert le Diable*, arranged for and played on five brass instruments of Sax by the famous Distin brothers.

For this concert we have an extant press release written by Berlioz and sent to the newspaper, *Le Menestrel*.

The concert announced for next Saturday at the Opéra-Comique promises to be brilliant. We will have the presence of the principal artists of this theater, Mr. Camille Sivori, who has come specially from Brussels, Mr. Alard, Mr. Alexis Dupont, and most likely also Mr. Liszt who will be arriving soon. The principal compositions on the program are the overtures to *King Lear* and *Roman Carnival* by Berlioz, a piano solo, a

Concerto for violin by Beethoven, another Concerto by Sivori, a *Motet* by Lesueur, the Sanctus from Berlioz's *Requiem*, a Duet from *Armide* by Gluck and the finale (the Apothéose) from the *grande Symphonie funèbre* by Berlioz. A total of 180 performers will be conducted by Mr. Berlioz.[70]

[70] Letter to Jacques-Leopold Heugel, Paris, March, 1844, in *Correspondance*, 892.

The second of these 1844 concerts was a 'monster concert,' on 1 August involving approximately one thousand musicians, sponsored by a Festival of Industry organized by the government. Berlioz, who shared the conducting with a conductor named Tilmant, gives the program in his account in his *Memoirs*. For the performance of the *Apothéose*, Berlioz had a handbill printed with the text, perhaps for the audience to sing along.

> I engaged for my concert virtually every orchestral player and chorister of any ability in Paris and succeeded in mustering a body of a thousand and twenty-two performers …
>
> In selecting my program I duly confined myself to music which was broad in style or which the performers knew already. The program was as follows:
>
> Overture to *La Vestale* (Spontini)
> Prayer from *La muettte* (Auber)
> Scherzo and finale from Symphony in C minor (Beethoven)
> Prayer from *Moses* (Rossini)
> Hymn to the French Nation, which I had composed for the occasion
> Overture to *Freischütz* (Weber)
> Hymn to Bacchus from *Antigone* (Mendelssohn)
> March to the Scaffold from my Fantastic Symphony
> Song of the Manufacturers, also written expressly for the festival,
>   with text by Adolphe Dumas and music by Meraux
> A chorus from *Charles VI* (Halévy)
> Chorus of the Blessing of the Daggers from *The Hugue-
>   nots* (Meyerbeer)
> Garden of Delights scene from *Armide* (Gluck)
> Apothéose from my Funeral and Triumphal Symphony
>
> We planned to hold the general rehearsal in the great central area of the exhibition building, known as the Hall of Machinery, which I had chosen for the concert. Yet on the eve of this crucial trial, while the carpenters were constructing the platform, the hall had still to be vacated. A large number of heavy iron machines lay encamped on the space intended for the audience. No arrangements had been made to have these monsters removed.
>
> I will not attempt to describe what I felt …

> Of the remaining pieces the most successful were the Funeral Oration and Apothéose from my Funeral and Triumphal Symphony (with the trombone solo impressively played by Dieppo) and the scene from *Armide* …
>
> In short my Musical Exhibition was brought off not only without mishap but with brilliant success and the hearty approbation of the immense audience attending it. On the way out I had the unspeakable satisfaction of seeing the proceeds being busily counted at a huge table by the poor-house tax collectors. The sum came to thirty-two thousand francs, of which the tax-collectors took an eighth—four thousand francs. The proceeds of the concert of dance music, which my partner Strauss conducted two days later, and which was not a success, were meager in the extreme; the deficit had to be made up from the profit on the big concert. In the final reckoning I had a grand net profit of eight hundred francs and a receipt for four thousand francs signed personally by the chief tax collector, to show for all the difficulties endured, the risks run, and the endeavors accomplished.
>
> Oh, the delights of living in a free country, where artists are serfs, humbly paying their heartfelt tribute to its liberal and equitable laws![71]

71 *Memoirs*, 358ff.

Although this 'monster concert' would eventually include only the final movement of the *Symphonie funèbre*, a letter to the trombonist, Dieppo, whom Berlioz often complimented on his performance of the second movement, suggests that at some point at least the second movement was also scheduled. Dieppo had apparently requested the solo part in advance and Berlioz writes,

> Here is the trombone solo part that you always play so admirably … [Berlioz regrets that he can only pay Dieppo 50 francs] This time, it is not the government which pays, and you know I am not quite so rich as Rothschild.[72]

72 Letter to Antoine Guillaume Dieppo, Paris, June 25, 1844, in *Correspondance*, 911.

During the summer of 1845, Berlioz made a tour within France, giving concerts in Marseille and Lyon. The Marseille concerts, with Berlioz conducting, were on 19 and 25 June 1845. The concert included,

> *Le Cinq Mai*
> *Hymne a la France*
> *Symphonie funèbre*, movement III

The next pair of concerts, in Lyon, were perhaps more important to Berlioz because Lyon was the second largest city in Paris, and because it was near his home. In fact his sisters attended the first of these concerts.

An extant letter, which again demonstrates the careful interest Berlioz had in all the details of arranging this concert, is valuable for its list of the additional winds necessary, beyond those in the orchestra, to perform the *Symphonie funèbre*. In other words, one can see here some idea of the size of the forces deemed necessary by the composer, on at least this occasion.

> I would like to give a concert in Lyons only if we can do something important. We would have to raise the ticket prices and send posters to neighboring towns, such as Chalon, Macon, Vienne, Bourgoin, Nantua, Belley, etc., and place them on the steamboats on the Rhone and the Saone in order to take in nine or ten thousand francs. If this is just dreaming, then let's forget the whole thing. It is not worth stirring up the entire musical world of Lyons to end up with only average results. Besides, I am so weary of rehearsals, this drill-instructor life at Marseilles has so exhausted me that I really would need to make a great effort to start up again.
>
> For the program I should like to present I will need:
> 34 violins at least
> 10 violas
> 11 celli
> 9 string bass
> 2 flutes
> 2 oboes, one of whom plays English horn
> 4 bassoons
> 4 horns
> 2 natural trumpets
> 2 cornets
> 3 trombones
> 1 ophicleide in C
> 2 timpanists
> 1 cymbal player
> 1 bass drum player
> 1 triangle
> 1 tambourine
>
> Plus, for a composition for two orchestras:
> 4 first clarinets in Bb
> 4 second clarinets in Bb
> 1 Eb clarinet
> 1 Eb flute

1 Db piccolo
2 horns
2 trumpets
2 ophicleides, one in C, one in Bb
3 trombones
2 oboes
4 percussionists (musicians)

And lastly, a chorus of 80 men and 20 women …

For each performer of the large orchestra there should be one section rehearsal and two full rehearsals. For the members of the military band, one would be enough, two at the most …

I am ready to accept the arrangement of sharing the receipts after deducting five hundred francs for the expenses, but in that case these expenses must include not only the cost of lighting and service in the theater, the fees of the orchestra and chorus, but also the cost of raising a four level platform, and also the cost of the posters (two-sided ones) which must be issued four different times and printed at the rate of 60 at least per issue; plus 50 more to be sent around as I have indicated above.

Also please find out if the poor will agree to collect only a tenth [refers to an entertainment tax], as they did at Marseilles and as they invariably do at my concerts in Paris …

P.S. The expenses of the additional wind orchestra will be split between the theater administration and myself; we must try to recruit volunteer singers and string players.[73]

73 Letter to Georg Hainl, July 2, 1845, in *Correspondance*, 972.

Georg Hainl (1807–1873) was the conductor of the orchestra at the Grand Theater of Lyons and organized these concerts for Berlioz, who conducted. The program, for the 20 and 24 July 1845 concerts in Lyon was,

Le Carnaval romain
Symphonie fantastique, movements II–IV
Hymne à la France
L'invitation à la valse
Harold en Italie, movement II
Symphonie funèbre, movement III
Works by Gluck and Weber

Later during this year, Berlioz gave three concerts in Vienna in the Theater an der Wien. Only the first of these concerts, on 16 November 1845, included the *Symphonie funèbre*. The program Berlioz conducted on this occasion was,

Le Carnaval romain
Chant sacré
Cavatine from *Benvenuto Cellini*

Harold en Italie
Le Cinq Mai
Symphonie funèbre, movement III

In the Spring of 1846, Berlioz was commissioned to compose a cantata to celebrate the opening of a new railroad line from Lille to Brussels. This concert, on 14 June 1846, which was outdoors, included a performance of the *Apothéose* of the symphony for band with the extra wind players being members of military bands in Douai and Valenciennes. The organizers of this concert, in which Berlioz conducted the only known performance of the 'railroad cantata,' *Chant des chemins de fer*, had made arrangements for cannons to be fired at the end of the *Apothéose*. This great finale, as Berlioz describes, failed to occur.

> Upon my arrival in Lille, Mr. Dubois immediately put me in touch with the singers whose audition was necessary for the performance of my cantata and with the military bands coming from Valenciennes, from Douai, and from some other neighboring cities. These instrumental groups would form an orchestra of about 150 musicians to play my Apothéose in the public promenade that evening before the princes and the civil and military authorities who were brought together for the festivities. The cantata was soon learned by the choir, made up of young people and children from all walks of life who had been instructed at an institution in Lille known as the Singing Academy … As these young singers had voices far superior than our best singers in Paris, and had been trained under the supervision of Mr. Ferdinand Lavainne, who is known as an eminent composer, and Mr. Leplus, the talented conductor of the Artillery Band of Lille, they mastered in no time the difficulties of singing.
>
> The rehearsal of the Apothéose by the combined military bands [however] gave us much difficulty. The rehearsal had begun before my arrival and, due to a big error in the tempo by the director in charge of this rehearsal, the movement produced only a spinning dizziness. Mr. Dubois, my guide among the embarrassment of the agitations of the festival, who bravely assumed complete responsibility for the musical part, seemed rather agitated and worried when I spoke to him about our military and this great devil of a composition. I did not know that he had been at the first rehearsal, nor that the first rehearsal had produced such a monstrous result. It was only after hearing the chaos again that he admitted his fears. Be that as it may, his fears quickly disappeared and, after the third rehearsal, all went well. If I remember correctly, all three music corps belonged to the city of Lille, those of the national guard and the fire brigade and the artillery did not want to, or couldn't, take part in this festival. They told me why, but I don't remember the reason.

It was really too bad, because these bands are excellent and, most likely, few other military bands in France can be compared to them. I came to appreciate their individual merits as each of them honored me by coming and playing below my window on the day before the concert. It was, on their behalf, a cruel but honest attempt to please me.

They gave me an excellent, small orchestra (the one belonging to the Theater, I believe) to accompany the cantata. One rehearsal was enough. Everything was ready when Mr. Dubois presented to me the Artillery Captain of the National Guard.

'Sir,' the officer said to me, 'I have come to discuss with you the subject of the *pieces* that will be played.'

'Ah, there is a dramatic performance! But, I know nothing of it. It is none of my business.'

'Excuse me, sir, will you perform the pieces with the cannons.'

'Oh my God! What am I supposed to do with those?'

'You are supposed to use them,' said Mr. Dubois with wild effect, 'in your Apothéose,' said Mr. Dubois, 'they are *on the program*. Furthermore there is nothing more to discuss about them—they are on the program and the audience is waiting to hear them and we cannot disappoint them.'

'Now my colleague-enemies of Paris, the good police of the critical press, will say that I am putting artillery in my orchestra! Will they have fun on my behalf! Good God, what luck for me. Nothing will be more enjoyable for me than to give them the opportunity to say, speaking of me, that something stupid was shot from a cannon. OK, go ahead with the cannons! But first, how is your orchestra[74] composed?'

'Our orchestra?'

'Yes, your artillery. What pieces do you have and how many do you have?'

'We have ten pieces of twelve.'

'Well ... that is not much. Couldn't you give me pieces of twenty-four?'

'My God, we only have six twenty-four cannons.'

'So, allow me the use of these six 'chorists,' and then we shall put all of these 'voices' at the edge of the great ditch which is next to the promenade, as close to the military band as possible. The Captain should watch me carefully. I will have a fireworks technician at my side. When the princes arrive, a rocket will be shot off and we will then fire ten cannons successively. When we begin the Apothéose you will have time to reload. Toward the end of this composition another rocket will be shot off, whereupon you count to four and then on 'five' you will have your chorists of twelve and your six first subjects of twenty-four hit a chord in such a way as to coincide exactly with my last instrumental chord. Do you understand?'

'Perfectly, sir, that will happen, you can count on it.'

I heard the Captain say to Mr. Dubois, 'That is magnificent! Only musicians can come up with ideas like that.'

---

74 In his *Les Grotesques de la musique*, Berlioz changed this to a 'Chorus' of cannons.

When the night came the military band was well-rehearsed and my fireworks technician was in place. The Duke of Nemours and the Duke of Montpensier, surrounded by the Major of the area, the mayors and prefects, all the stars of the military, administrators, civilians, lawyers, etc., were on the terrace prepared to receive the orchestra 'full blast.' I said to the fireworks technician, 'Be ready,' whereupon the Artillery Captain comes quickly up the stairs to our platform and says in a trembling voice, 'For the grace of God, Mr. Berlioz, don't give the signal; our men forgot their fuses for the cannons and we have to run get them from the arsenal. Five minutes, please!'

Ignorant as I am (whatever anyone else may say) about the style, or at least the mechanism of these voices, I am surprised that you cannot light these miserable pieces of twenty-four and twelve with a cigar, or a tinder, and that these fuses are as indispensable to the cannons as a mouthpiece is to the trombone. Yet, I allow them five minutes. Even seven. After seven minutes another messenger, climbing the same stairway that the Captain had just descended, said that the princes were waiting and that it was time to begin.

'Go!,' I said to the fireworks technician. 'Too bad if we don't have what we need to light these chorists.'

The rocket was launched with an ardent force that made us think it was destined for the moon. A big silence [as the first cannons did not sound]. Apparently the fuses did not come back from the arsenal.

I began conducting and our military band made miracles. The piece was played majestically and without the least musical flaw. As it was of great dimension, I thought to myself while conducting, 'We lost nothing for having waited—these cannoneers will have had the time to get their fuses by the time we get to the final chord—we will have a noise loud enough to knock down all of the neighboring crossfire.' At the measure indicated in the coda, I made another sign to the fireworks technician to send up another rocket and then, just four seconds after its ascension … My God!

I don't want to seem braver than I am, but my heart beat so hard against my chest as we approached this solemn moment. You may laugh if you want, but I almost fell face forward—the trees trembled, the waters of the canal rippled, in the gentle breeze of the night. A profound silence set in after the last measure of the symphony—a majestic silence, grandiose, immense, which ended only by the great applause of the multitude, obviously satisfied by the performance. And the audience left ignorant of the importance of the lighting fuses, without any regret for the joy they might have missed and that had not expected, forgetting the promises of the program and persuaded that the two flying rockets that had whistled their way through the sky and given off their sparks, were merely my rather pleasant invention for the eye.[75]

75 *Revue et Gazette musicale*, November 19, 1848, reused in his *Les Grotesques de la musique*.

In his later publication of this story, Berlioz added a reference to a review in another journal.

Le Charivari, abundant in its positive reaction, published a series of astonishing articles of the grandest style. 'What would he have done if the fuses …!' It is fatal! I won that night a new promotion, an immortal name, I received a baptism of fire[works]. New and astonishing proof that while you often see guns which are not loaded go off, then you can also see loaded cannons that do not go off.[76]

76 *Les Grotesques de la musique*, 305.

In a letter to his sister after this concert, Berlioz speaks of the invariable success of the *Apothéose* and well as the fate of the 'railroad cantata.'

I have just come from a run, which will help me keep my legs in shape. First, I was an inhabitant of Lille where I was most busy, and certainly the most serenaded for I had to suffer four serenades by three instrumental and one vocal group. The inhabitants of the large square on which I was lodged must have found my company a bit annoying.

All in all, the *Apothéose* was a success and the 250 military bandsmen stubbornly did their part. The Cantata was sung with much verve and with such fresh voices that we could not find their like in Paris if we tried.

While I was talking with the Ducs of Nemours and of Monpensier, who had asked me to come to their side, my hat was stolen, and then my music—the Cantata, then the score and then the choral and instrumental parts. So there goes a great work lost and for which I cannot summon the courage to begin again.[77]

77 Letter to his Sister, Nanci, Paris, June 29, 1846, in *Correspondance*, 1045.

In July 1846, the Association of Artists–Musicians in Paris organized a 'monster' concert in the open-air Hippodrome. In an article to help advertise the concert, Berlioz gives the readers a lengthy preview.

A very interesting solemn occasion is being prepared through the auspices of the Committee of the Musicians Association. I want to speak of the military festival announced for the 24th of this month in the Hippodrome de l'Etoie. An army of seventeen hundred musicians will perform, under the direction of M. Tilmant, some pieces drawn from the works of the principal modern masters, and of Handel and Gluck … These pieces, arranged carefully for military band by MM. Klosé, Fessy, Mohr, and Brepsant, have been rehearsed with the greatest attention by the musicians of the diverse infantry and cavalry regiments quartered in Paris, Versailles, and Saint-Germain, supported by all those of the National Guard and the best students of the Gymnase Musical. Already the experiments made with groups of five hundred and six hundred men, in the Popincourt and Poissonière barracks, as well as at the Military School, have given the most beautiful results. One cannot have any idea of the majesty of these masses of wind instruments especially in the larger works, and everything leads one to hope that the effect will be even more grandiose still, and more beautiful, and the ensemble itself (so difficult to obtain in such a case) more precise, when, at the end of the rehearsals, all the forces are united. This gigantic concert, the biggest of this kind that they ever have given, will take place at noon, in the middle of the Hippodrome. The receipts are destined for the relief fund of the Association of Artist-musicians. They very probably will make 30,000 francs; and the gathering of the performers being free, thanks to the backing lent to the Association by M. le duc de Montpensier and by the Minister of War, the expenses should only amount to a modest sum, without the unfair tax always levied on musicians' work under the name of *droit des indigenes* (indigents' tax). The proprietors of the Hippodrome, moreover, generously have offered their arena to our concertizers without charge. The best places to see and hear well apparently are those to be reserved, in a small number, on the top of the Arc de Triomphe.[78]

78 *Journal des Débats*, July 18, 1846.

This concert, which was given on 24 July 1846, included a performance of the *Apothéose* by no fewer than 1,800 wind players. After the concert, Berlioz published the following review:

There is something quite beautiful in these immense reunions that gives one an idea of festivals of Antiquity. Not only the power of music breaks forth there with incomparable pomp when nothing opposes its manifestation, but also the impressions of the audience become much more sensitized and increase by being sympathetically propagated …

Paris possesses incalculable musical resources whose power still is not entirely known, their action having been heretofore more or less paralyzed. With the least encouragement, an enlightened protection, a little liberty and justice, and our musicians would make miracles. Last Friday's attempt, that the kindness of M. the Duke of Montpensier allowed them to furnish, is proof. At first, everyone began by saying: 1,800 musicians will not be able to perform anything with *ensemble*, they will not be in tune, they will only produce a monstrous cacophony. Experience has completely belied these irritating pre-visions. The ensemble was almost always satisfying, the intonation only rarely left anything to be desired, and the performance, such as we heard it, must seem all the more surprising, since among those regimental musicians, there had not perhaps been even one who ever in his life had taken part in a great ensemble of this nature. The first piece (a *paso doble* by Brepsant) was expressed with a truly miraculous precision; and for those of us who occupied the center of the orchestra seats, the solo of the second *reprise*, played by 150 trombones in unison, gave the impression of being a war song of the Titans marching to scale Olympus; it was sublime. This piece, moreover, is very well composed. I should say the same of that of M. Mohr, which had a great effect. As for the marches of

Fernand Cortez, arranged with talent for the military band by M. Klosé, no one doubts their success; Spontini is the father of the music of war, and Cortez, if such accents had been available to call his soldiers to the conquest of Mexico, would not have needed to burn his vessels. Moses' prayer, ingeniously arranged by M. Fessy, impressed the audience, but much less, however, than it did two years ago, at the Industry festival, with your masses of harps and voices; this work needs to be sung. The choir of Judas Maccabeas, to the contrary, lost nothing of a rare religious splendor; people believed that they were hearing a vast cathedral resound with the victory chant of ten thousand voices. I can but thank the musicians and their leader, M. Tilmant, for their beautiful execution of my *Apothéose* [from his band symphony]. The two waltzes and the hunting tune did not seem properly placed in such a program. There is really something shocking to see such a gigantic band used in the performance of works in a style, at the least, very familiar. The overture of *Fra Diavolo*, very difficult because of the details that it contains, went along with as much ensemble as if there were only forty musicians, and gave everybody extreme pleasure; the trumpet solo, especially, was noted …

 People generally criticized, in the placement of the band in the Hippodrome, especially the diffusion of the high-pitched instruments. The piccolos and Eb clarinets (moreover too few) found themselves separated from one another by an interval of twenty or thirty paces. Was it possible to obtain togetherness for the runs and the melodic ornaments confided to the most piercing instruments of the band being so dispersed? I do not believe so. The Committee had determined to adopt such an order, fearing that the presence of the conductors, who almost all play Eb clarinet was indispensable at the head of their groups in order to maintain discipline. And in so doing, I think that they were oddly mistaken; these fine soldiers are of incomparable submissiveness, patience, and attentiveness, and in regards to this, I certainly would have preferred to conduct ten thousand military musicians than one hundred Parisian theater artists. In any case, one could have easily have made up for the absence of the conductors by using officers of an equal grade, or even superior, to theirs: for one either plays music, or one does not! … The setting was, besides, very beautiful and admirably arranged, those uniforms of diverse colors and forms, grouped in even blocks, those flags, those twinkling helmets, that ant-hill of brass instruments reflecting the sun's rays, and around them that immense group of people that decorated the tiers and a part of the arena of the Hippodrome … It was a festival worthy of Paris in many respects; it bodes well for others which may be worthy of France, if they permit the artists to offer them to her. The conductors of the diverse infantry and cavalry rivaled one another in zeal and patience in the preparatory rehearsals which preceded that great instrumental Congress …

 We believe we should make known the names of the regiments and legions whose musicians figured actively at the Hippodrome last Friday. They are:

LINE TROOPS	CONDUCTORS
1st	Viala
9th	Schillé
11th	Ennés-Berr
14th	Maréchal
16th	Garrouste
23rd	Verzinger
24th	Berr
25th	Sweingruber
26th	Luce
35th	Renault
37th	Guerra
45th	Declerk
46th	Dallée
48th	Henricet
52nd	Goecke
72nd	Blanckman
73rd	Regheer
74th	Sarrus
CAVALRY	
3rd Dragoons	Gentil
4th Dragoons	Maroel
7th Dragoons	Nachbaur
4th Lancers	Péclier
5th Artillery	Landfersicht
8th Hussards	Usse
NATIONAL GUARD	
1st Legion	Louis
2nd Legion	Barizel
3rd Legion	Melfred
4th Legion	Landelle
5th Legion	Fessy
6th Legion	Moúcrux
7th Legion	Lamour
8th Legion	Claveau
9th Legion	Bauller
10th Legion	Klosé
11th Legion	Dossion
12th Legion	Tolbecque
2nd Banlieue	Dorus
3rd Banlieue	Dumouchel

The principal students of the Military [Music] School, conducted by M. Rakoski.[79]

Berlioz mentions this concert, and his review, in a letter of the same date.

[79] 'Military Festival,' in *Journal des Débats*, July 29, 1846.

I have just given this morning an account in the *Débats* of the great military band concert in the Hippodrome, so I won't mention it in this letter. This was the only musical event going on at the moment. The Opéra is more and more atrocious.[80]

80 Letter to Josef Fischoff, Paris, July 29, 1846, in *Correspondance*, 1050.

Spontini also read Berlioz's review of this great concert and wrote the latter in what must be taken as an humorous attempt to write in the extravagant style of Berlioz.

> The so-designated [by Berlioz in his account above] father of the music of war, setting aside this pompous new baptism and all the flattery with which you were pleased to cover him, would excuse you, dear Berlioz, if you had known all the hundreds of military compositions, heroic, triumphal, and national pieces, which during the past years have fallen daily on the Prussian, Russian, Polish, Saxon, and other German armies. Yes, this improvised father has a great hear and has been applauded energetically and written up in the *Débats* for the gigantic and important military band festival. It was performed in a poor arena, an unfortunate race track [the Hippodrome], but this was a true work of art, so perfect in its performance, its definition, and in its theoretical reason in the practice of military music. The instruments in their nature and specially and in their distribution and placement made such a great and varied effect. And the whole performance was directed with such logic, such truth, such knowledge, philosophy and spirit—the experience of national goodness and justice, rendering the audience all the colors—pink, white, black—following the men and their souls, it was impossible for your readers not to have been strongly touched with emotion and admiration, penetrated with wonder in front of such an historic setting, so real, so vigorous, so breathtaking in our art and of our artists, who are so often reduced to a powerless, discouraged and impotent state before the corrupt, meaningless, sordid ignorant state of art today. They must have cherished this rich experience … [and have been] swept away by this fresh experience.[81]

81 Letter from Gaspare Spontini to Berlioz, Passy, July 30, 1846, in *Correspondance*, 1051.

In the Spring of 1847, Berlioz gave a series of concerts in Russia. The first two of these concerts, on 15 and 25 March 1847, included the *Apothéose* of the *Symphonie funèbre*, with Berlioz conducting. The program, in Dvoriansky Hall, St. Petersburg, was,

Le Carnaval romain
La Damnation de Faust, Parts I and II
Roméo et Juliette, movements IV, V
Symphonie funèbre, movement III

Berlioz recalled one of his concerns for the performance of the *Apothéose* in the first concert.

> I had a large and well-rehearsed orchestra and chorus, and a military band to boot, chosen by General Lvov from among the musicians of the Imperial Guard ... The program, consisting of the *Roman Carnival* overture, the first two acts of *Faust*, Queen Mab, and the Apothéose from my Funeral and Triumphal Symphony, was in fact very well performed ...
>
> I had been getting a little anxious about my military bandsmen. They were to play in the final piece, the Apothéose; but there was no sign of them. I was afraid they might enter the orchestra in the middle of a movement and in doing so make a noise which would spoil the effect. I had reckoned without military discipline. On turning round after the scherzo—I beheld my sixty men drawn up in position, each man at his post, instruments at the ready. They had come in and taken their places without anyone noticing it. *Bravissimo!*[82]

82 *Memoirs*, 422ff.

Writing to his father about this concert, Berlioz, notes,

> I had an excellent orchestra, composed of German artists, who played my compositions with a faithfulness and extraordinary verve. They put at my disposal the singers of the theater chorus as well as those of the imperial chapel, in addition to those of other regiments of the Guard who marched [ie., performed] perfectly. The effect that was produced by my last work was magnificent.[83]

83 Letter to his Father, St. Petersbourg, March 1847, in *Correspondance*, 1100.

An additional concert on 27 March, in St. Petersburg, was a benefit concert for invalids. Berlioz conducted a program which included *Apothéose* of the *Symphonie funèbre*.

Early in 1848 Berlioz traveled to London for a series of concerts. Berlioz had been promised a suitable fee by the organizer and conductor, Jullien, who just before the concerts went bankrupt leaving Berlioz without his fee.

The first concert, on 7 February 1848, in the Drury Lane Theater, London, consisted of Berlioz conducting the following program:

Le Carnaval romain
Le Jeune Pâtre breton
Harold en Italie
La Damnation de Faust, Parts I and II
Cavatine from *Benvenuto Cellini*
Offertoire from *Requiem*

Symphonie funèbre, movements II, III, with trombone soloist, Konig

On 18 February 1848, Charles Godfrey conducted the *Symphonie funèbre* at Buckingham Palace. We know this from a reference in one of Berlioz's letters.

> The *Symphonie funèbre* is being played next Thursday at Prince Albert's residence. The director of the Prince's military music told me yesterday; everyone is enchanted *except our own composers*.[84]

84 Letter to Auguste Morel, London, February 12, 1848, in *Correspondance*, 1173.

In a letter to the same correspondent the following month, Berlioz mentions arranging the *Apothéose*.

> At this moment, I am arranging the *Apothéose* in Eb for voice, chorus and piano.[85]

85 Letter to Auguste Morel, London, March 6, 1848, in *Correspondance*, 1184. If Berlioz was serious about this he must have added a great deal of additional text.

During the Summer, 1848, a letter of Berlioz to Pierre Duc, architect of the column which figured in the commission of the *Symphonie funèbre*, and friend of Berlioz from his days at the Villa Medici in Rome, announces the publication of the *Apothéose*.

> Our piece, the *Apothéose*, has been published at last. It was thought necessary to tamper with the sub-title. I had written, 'Composed for the inauguration of the Bastille Column.' This made it clear why the column came into it at all and why the dedication was appropriate. But since the last Chartists' agitation the London bourgeois has a deep fear of anything remotely or nearly related to revolutions, and as a result, my publisher refused to consider any mention on the title page either of your monument or of those to whom it was erected …
>
> I shake your hands in hopes that … hmmm … I don't remember in hopes of what I was going to say. Oh yes, to never again allow the Duke to sing the *Apothéose*.[86]

86 Letter to Louis-Joseph Duc, May 26, 1848, in *Correspondance*, 1200. 'Duke' in the letter is a play on words standing for the recipients name.

During the Spring of 1849 Berlioz heard a mass civic chorus sing their own arrangement of the *Apothéose*.

> The next day another musical group performed with the same joy the overture of the *Carnival of Rome* and a few days before that about 800 members of the Orphéon sang a hymn that they had arranged on the theme of the Apothéose. Now that Berlioz no longer gives [his own] concerts, they play his music all over. Enough of walking toward the mountain, the mountain goes to Mohammed.[87]

87 Letter to Jules Janin, Paris, April 21, 1849, in *Correspondance*, 1256.

During the season of 1850–1851 Berlioz received a request from Lyon for loan of the parts for the *Symphonie funèbre*, a request which he could not, at least at first, honor.

> … the *Symphonie funèbre* I would send you with great pleasure if our philharmonic group were not in need of this piece one day or another.[88]

88 Letter to George Hainl, Paris, December 14, 1850, in *Correspondance*, 1366.

This concert nevertheless went forward and the following month Berlioz sends an interesting letter with advice on the instrumental forces needed to perform the *Symphonie funèbre*. Berlioz, who would never again conduct the entire symphony, now makes the recommendation that only the final movement be performed.

> In order to perform the *finale of my Symphonie funèbre et triomphale* in the Grand Theater in Lyon you will need the following parts:
>
> 7   1st Violin
> 7   2nd Violin
> 6   Viola
> 12 Celli and string bass together
> 2   Flute (*flutes tierces*)
> 2   Piccolo in Db
> 2   Oboe
> 6   1st Clarinet in Bb
> 6   2nd Clarinet in Bb
> 2   Horn I
> 2   Horn II
> 2   Horn III
> 2   Horn IV (if you have four separate parts)
> 2   Trumpet I
> 2   Trumpet II
> 2   Cornet
> 2   Trombone I
> 2   Trombone II
> 2   Trombone III
> 3   Bassoons
> 2   Ophicleides in C
> 2   Ophicleides in Bb
> 2   Timpani
> 3   Tambour I
> 3   Tambour II
> 1   Cymbals
> 1   Bass drum
>
> for a total of approximately 164 performers. In addition, you will need for the chorus:

> 46 Soprano I, II
> 40 Tenor I, II
> 40 Bass I, II
> for a total of 126 singers.
>
> I hasten to ask that George Hainl not to perform the *marche funèbre* nor the *l'oraison funèbre*, but to begin at the *Apothéose* and also remove only the G major chord that is found at the beginning of this piece, which also happens to be the last chord of the preceding piece.
> *Pass this letter on to him.*
> If he does not rehearse the 1st and 2nd tambours separately, they will not play a note of their parts. They must be placed fairly near the conductor and a long way from the bass drum and cymbals. The chorus part is very difficult.[89]

89 Letter to Adolphe Catelin, Paris, January 10, 1851, in *Correspondance*, 1373.

In a review of *Le Muletier de Toledo*, an opera by Adam, Berlioz mentions the *Symphonie funèbre*, in connection with the subject of text-painting.

> A very kind music critic wrote that he heard, in a passage making reference to the death of a mule, a very ingenious orchestral imitation of the last sigh of this poor animal. The poor composer surely thought no more of a poor mule than of a horse of the Apocalypse when writing for the orchestra …
> On another occasion, fourteen years ago, the present musician (Berlioz) wrote a funeral march for the remains of the 1830 Revolution and used in the military orchestra certain drum effects on the weak beats of the measure. One critic found there the perfect imitations of the welcome gun shots heard in the streets of Paris during the famous 'Three Days.' Well, what do you know! The effects of the drums were actually solely to accentuate the energy through a rhythmic form.[90]

90 *Journal des Débats*, January 9, 1855.

Napoléon III had organized, in November 1855, a great industrial exhibition during which Berlioz conducted another concert with a great number of players. On the concert of 15 November 1855, for the awards ceremony, Berlioz conducted the following program, in the Palais de l'Industrie, Paris, with five assistant conductors!

L'Imperiale (premiere)
Symphonie funèbre, movement III
Mozart, *Ave verum corpus*

In a letter written just two hours before this performance, Berlioz writes to the famous lady friend of Liszt,

> Everything is ready—my heart is beating so hard it takes my breath away.[91]

Two days later, Berlioz describes yet another enthusiastic reception of the final movement of the band symphony.

> On the day of the official ceremony the orchestra caused a scandal. After my Apothéose piece, in spite of protocol, my boys sent up a barrage of hurrahs and applause and threw their hats into the air as if they had been at a rehearsal.[92]

Berlioz conducted again the following day, 16 November 1855, in the following program.

L'Imperiale
Symphonie funèbre, mvt. III
Te Deum, mvts I, II, VI, VII
Works by Handel, Mozart, Gluck, Beethoven, Weber, Rossini, and Meyerbeer

On 24 November 1855, Berlioz conducted again in the Palais de l'Industrie, repeating the program of 16 November, and this occasion marked the final time he would ever conduct his *Symphonie funèbre*.

After this series of concerts Berlioz left for another brief concert tour in Germany. Upon his return to Paris, he found himself called before a judge to explain why four players who participated in the big Palais de l'Industrie concerts had not been paid.

> Due to an error made by Sax in recopying the list of military musicians for our concerts for the Exposition, four of these gentlemen were not paid. I was this morning brought before a judge (you can imagine my surprise) and now these men have given me the key to this affair. I think that it is not possible to make Sax responsible for this accident. On my side, I was not aware at all of this error when I had the signature lists submitted. Despite all of the impatience that such a tardy request may cause you, I am obliged to ask you to be so kind as to pay these four artists.[93]

---

[91] Letter to Princess Carolyne Sayn-Wittgenstein, Paris, November 15, 1855, in *Correspondance*, 2045.

[92] Letter to Franz Liszt, November 17, quoted in Humphrrey Searle, *Hector Berlioz, A Selection from his Letters* (London: Golancz, 1966), 143.

[93] Letter to Ernest Beer, Paris, April 15, 1856, in *Correspondance*, 2118.

Chasse a la grosse bete

For: oboe and 'fagot de sapin'
Date of Composition: 1842–1848
Source: Sketchbook, La Côte-St.-Andre, Musee Hector Berlioz

This ten-bar sketch is found in a sketchbook kept by Berlioz on his concert tours. Among other sketches found in this book is the theme from the last movement of the *Symphonie funèbre*.

Chant sacré

For valved piccolo trumpet in Eb, valved piccolo bugle in Eb, large valved bugle in Bb, soprano clarinet, bass clarinet, and saxophone (and orchestra?)
Date of this version: 1844
Sources: Lost

In 1829 Berlioz became interested in the works of the Irish writer Thomas Moore and had Thomas Gounet translate material for nine songs. The sixth of these, the *Chant sacré* was performed at the *Athénée musical*, a series of concerts intended to introduce young conductors, in a new version for solo singer, chorus, and piano on 18 February 1830. Berlioz writes his father of this concert,

> I shall tell you, my dear papa, that I received last evening quite a handsome success. They performed two of my works, one with full choir and one for voice accompanied by piano, at the Musical Athénium before a very numerous public. I had the pleasure of seeing everyone who had listened with a good bit of indifference to the preceding pieces welcome mine with a doubling of attention, a long *shhh* asked for silence in all parts of the hall and my name pronounced on all sides, indicating that they were expecting something from me ... Although the two pieces, *La Reverie* and *Le Chant sacré*, are of the calm and melancholic type, consequently not the type to move the masses, nevertheless they were greeted with several salvos of applause ... The newspapers spoke so much of the originality of my music, that presently it is an agreed upon thing that should I write only six notes, they would still see in them some originality. So, for the *Chant sacré*, which, if it has some merit, has rather that of expression and grandeur than any other, they found that it did not resemble anything known before, that it was entirely new, etc. Nothing is less true, but one must let the good public talk![94]

A letter of this period indicates the work also found favor with some of his friends:

> You are in agreement with Onslow ... he prefers the following four: first, the *Chanson à boire*, the *Elegie*, the *Rêverie*, and the *Chant sacré*.[95]

94 Letter to his Father, February 19, 1830, in *Correspondance*, 155.

95 Letter to Humbert Ferrand, May 13, 1830, in *Correspondance*, 162.

A new version, now for chorus and orchestra was apparently performed in December 1843, in Marseilles. It was this version which Berlioz rescored for six solo winds for a concert in the Salle Herz on 3 February 1844—a concert which also included the premiere of the *Roman Carnival Overture*! Holoman assumes the six winds replaced the voices with the orchestral accompaniment of the 1843 version being retained.[96] However, in the review quoted below the critic speaks of Berlioz 'reducing' the work in order to make an instrumental sextet (*réduisant pour en faire un sextour instrumental*), so it is possible that the work was heard without orchestra at all.

The purpose of this performance was to allow his friend Sax to present some of his new instruments to the public. Sax himself was one of the woodwind performers, together with Duprez and Lepers (or Leperd?), joined by trumpeters Arban, Dauverné, and Dufresne. I believe this was the very first time the saxophone had been heard in a public concert. The following review appeared a few days after the concert.

> L'Hymne, transcribed for the six wind instruments of M. Adolphe Sax, originally did not have the aim that M. Berlioz assigned to it in this concert. Composed with text, this hymn was sung in Marseille with great success. By reducing it in order to make of it an instrumental sextet, the composer wished simply to offer to M. Adolphe Sax the opportunity to produce in public some inventions or improvements, whose merit almost all the composers and distinguished critics of the epoch have appreciated. Here is the impression experienced generally by the audience. The valved piccolo trumpet in Eb, the valved piccolo bugle in Eb also, the large valved bugle in Bb, the soprano clarinet, the bass clarinet, and the saxophone, seemed of a beautiful timbre and of a sonority as full as it was satisfying. If the practitioners alone have the right to hold forth on the difficulties of the mechanism, of which they are the natural judges, every well-trained ear, somewhat attuned, is also competent to appreciate the quality of the sound of an instrument. Public opinion ratified by its applause the endeavors of M. Adolphe Sax, while still recognizing that, despite their incontestable talent, the players had not had the time to familiarize themselves enough with these new instruments; but this is only secondary. Other tests, more specialized and prepared with more time will finally carry the day in all minds free from partiality.[97]

96 Holoman, *The Creative Process*, 46.

97 'Concert de M. H. Berlioz,' *Revue et Gazette Musicale*, February 11, 1844.

Regarding the musical source of this work, Cairns, the editor of the Berlioz *Memoirs*, notes that this music had been earlier used as an *Andante* in the Cantata which Berlioz had composed for the Prix di Rome in 1828.[98] Berlioz remembered this portion of the Cantata as being one of its merits.

> … and without doubt if there was anything good in my score, it was that andante.[99]

Cairns adds that the Cantata also provided some music used later in the *Symphonie fantastique*.[100]

98 *Memoirs*, 116.

99 Ibid.

100 *Memoirs*, 585.

Part 6

On Composition

On Composition

IN HIS WRITING, Berlioz almost never discusses, in a serious way, his actual process of composition. Sometimes one finds details hidden in other stories, as for example a border incident in Italy.

> 'Now, sir, I know perfectly well that's not the way people compose, without a piano, simply wandering about the beach with a sketch-book and a pencil. Tell me where you wish to go and your passport will be made out. You can't stay in Nice any longer.'
> 'Very well, I'll return to Rome, and by your leave continue to compose without a piano.'[1]

1 *Memoirs*, 158.

He is somewhat more forthcoming about the subjective, or experiential goals of his art.

> The predominant features of my music are passionate expression, inward intensity, rhythmic impetus, and a quality of unexpectedness. When I say passionate expression, I mean an expression bent on reproducing the inner meaning of its subject, even when that subject is the opposite of passion, and gentle, tender feelings are being expressed, or a profound calm.[2]

2 Ibid., 478.

He tells us his technique is also subjectively inspired, rather than being driven by academic formulae.

> At first a succession of consonant chords, with a few suspensions here and there, was considered 'music.' When later Monteverde dared to introduce the dominant seventh chord without preparation, he was violently blamed and abused for this innovation. In spite of all this, the chord was soon generally accepted; and so-called learned composers eventually came to look down with contempt upon any harmonic sequence which was simple, clear and natural. They admitted only compositions which, from beginning to end, abounded in the harshest dissonances (minor and major seconds, sevenths, ninths, etc.). That these chords were used without reason or method did not matter; it almost seemed as if there were only one intention: to make this music as unpleasant as possible to the ear. These musicians took a fancy to dissonant chords, as certain animals prefer salt, prickly plants or thorny shrubs. What originally was mere reaction had grown into exaggeration.

Melody did not exist in these supposedly beautiful musical combinations. Yet, when it gradually started appearing here and there, people decried the decline and ruin of art and of its sacred rules; they believed that everything was lost. But in the course of time melody gained its place, and the usual exaggerations did not fail to appear. Soon there were fanatics of melody who abhorred any piece of music in more than three voice-parts. Some even demanded that the melody should be accompanied only by a bass. Apparently they wanted to give the hearer the pleasure of guessing the missing inner voices. Others went still further and rejected any kind of accompaniment; to them, harmony was a barbarous invention.

Then came *modulation's* turn. At the time when modulation was limited to nearly-related keys, the first who ventured into more distant keys were censured. One might have expected this. Whatever the effect of these new modulations, the masters rejected them vigorously. The innovator pleaded vainly: 'Listen to it attentively; convince yourselves how smoothly it is introduced, how well prepared, how skillfully linked with the preceding and the following passages, and how wonderful it sounds!' 'That does not matter,' was the answer; 'this modulation is prohibited and that's why it cannot be used.' However, modulations into distant keys soon appeared in important works, producing effects as felicitous as they were unexpected. Almost immediately a new kind of pedantry arose; there were people who considered any modulation to the dominant a weakness; even in the simplest rondo they sauntered gaily from C major to F# major.

By and by, time restored a reasonable balance. People learned to distinguish use from misuse, reactionary vanity from stupidity and obstinacy. Concerning harmony, melody and modulation, there is now general agreement to approve whatever produces a good effect, and to reject what has a poor effect. Even the authority of a hundred old men (be they as old as a hundred and twenty years) will not persuade us that what is ugly, is beautiful; and what is beautiful, ugly.[3]

3 *Treatise*, 1.

Berlioz also clearly spells out that his aim is art, not popularity.

All that remains to compensate artists who compose their works with so much labor, and without thinking of their commercial value, is the inner satisfaction afforded by their conscience and the profound joy which they experience in measuring the amount of their progress on the road to the beautiful. One such artist advances hundreds of kilometers; and falls at the very moment when he thinks he has obtained the prize. Another one advances still more; but without arriving, for the ideal is never attained. Another may advance less; but they all progress, however, and all prefer their progress, whatever it may be, with all its blazing sun and with all its thirst and fatigue to the fresh open shelter and invigorating drinks poured out by popularity for those aspirants who are unmindful of the inaccessible goal, and who turn their backs upon it.[4]

4 Berlioz, *Mozart, Weber and Wagner*, 135.

Berlioz had to suffer, as composers sometimes do, hearing their music and most intimate emotions laid bare to the technical and human inadequacies of the performer. He gives a dramatic account of the public performance of his Prix de Rome winning Cantata, conducted by Grasset, a former conductor of the Italian Theater.

> Ten million curses on all musicians who do not count their rests! In my score the horn was supposed to give the cue to the timpani, the timpani to the cymbals, the cymbals to the bass drum; the first stroke of the bass drum was the signal for the final explosion. But the accursed horn-player failed to play his note. Without it, the timpanist was afraid to come in. In consequence, cymbals and bass drum also kept silent. Absolutely nothing happened. The violins and cellos went on with their futile tremolo; otherwise, not so much as a pop. The fire went out without a crackle; the much-heralded holocaust had turned into a damp squid—*ridiculus mus*. Only a composer who has himself been through such an experience can conceive the fury that possessed me. I could hardly breathe. A cry of horror burst from me. I hurled my score into the middle of the orchestra and sent the two nearest desks flying. Mme Malibran started back as if a mine had exploded at her feet. The whole place was in an uproar—the orchestra in confusion, the academicians scandalized, the audience mystified, the composer's friends in high indignation. Another musical catastrophe had overtaken me, the cruelest I had yet experienced. Would that it had been the last![5]

5 *Memoirs*, 138.

The personal account of this incident, which he sent his father, contains even more pain.

> Would you believe that ill fortune acted to destroy the grand effect of my conflagration? The end, the crumbling of the palace, the bouquet of my fireworks, an immense, new thing which is mine alone, as I discovered it, failed. The instruments that were to produce this effect count rests before, and start up then like thunder; well, no they did not start! … an inconceivable distraction, a panic terror! … And I, who was in the orchestra, who signaled them to commence, they believed that I was mistaken, they did not start, then the measure passes and there is no longer time. Oh! there is not anything like it; in a fury like unto death, I could not contain myself, I threw my score across the orchestra, upsetting the stand that was next to me, I would have exterminated everything if I could have.[6]

6 Letter to his Father, October 31, 1830, in *Correspondance*, 188.

Such incidents no doubt caused Berlioz to sometimes reflect on the fate of the composer in general. In one newspaper article he gives the reader a virtual catalog of the horrors that can befall the serious composer.

> Recently, people have been discussing a project of a wandering orchestra, that was heard about at different points on the Boulevards on the same evening. It is quite difficult to conceive how the aim of such speculation could be accomplished. An immense wagon certainly can, it is true, transport the orchestra; but as one cannot equally transport a concert hall, it follows that it will be necessarily be open air music, a banal music that any passerby can listen to gratis. What benefit do those who undertake this hope to reap? Will they, like clowns, go extend their hats to 'the honorable society' grouped around the musicians? ... They are really capable of it. The director would appear on the nomadic stand, and, addressing the strollers: 'A moment of your time, gentlemen, one moment! We are going to let you hear with a big orchestra the famous Overture of THE ENCHANTED FLUTE by the divine Mozart, with the perfections of modern instrumentation. I am not afraid to say, the quality of the instrumentation that we are going to offer you is incontestably superior to all the others in the capital; since in the other Parisian orchestras, they persist to this day in following sterilely the composer's instruction. We, to the contrary, gentlemen, persuaded that art cannot remain stationary; convinced that the divine Mozart himself, if he were to return to the world, would hasten to approve the fortunate boldness which makes us add new riches to his magic inspirations, we have, imitating the Italians, introduced into his orchestra the instruments favored by the Modern School, which did not exist at the time of Mozart; two instruments, gentlemen, with the most powerful effect; two instruments of simple and easy use, like everything that is great and beautiful; two instruments that have carried farther the sound of success of the new composers than could the hundred voices of Renown; in sum, gentlemen, we have added to the brilliant accompaniments of THE MAGIC FLUTE, cymbals and the bass drum. As for these instruments themselves, they are made by the premier instrument manufacturers. The cymbals were addressed to us from Peking by the famous Plank-Tsin, the special cymbal player of the Chamber of His Majesty, the Emperor of China, the fifteen-foot circumference bass drum was created in the shops of Bellange, under the eyes of the first artists of the capital. That says it all. This is the way it will be, gentlemen, with every work of any merit whose instrumentation lacks this nerve that is the life of music. We will render it completely worthy of you' (To the musicians): 'Let's go, gentlemen, lots of energy!' And the crowd applauds the harangue, and the boobies come running, as if it were a question of a premiere production of the Opéra-Comique. And at the last blow on the bass drum, the director descends, and addressing the dazzled audience: 'Something for the divine Mozart, gentlemen, if you please!'

All said and done, one must confess that it would be a bias, very completely and frankly. When art thus has become a merchandise at a cheap price; when, instead of bringing to her feet a cultivated public, sensitive and intelligent, music, like a prostitute, sets out in pursuit of the indolent of every kind that hang about on the streets and crossroads of the capital, and do not blush to importune them with ignoble irritations, she certainly may also become a beggar. Nothing more natural. But facts of this sort are well calculated to cast discouragement into the souls of artists. It is the last degree of degradation that it would be possible to inflict on the object of their adoration ...

Everything necessarily is reduced in an orchestra out of doors to a rhythmic noise, above which floats here and there some remnants of leaping melodies that the piercing timbre of the flageolet or the piccolo causes to he heard, despite the strokes of the bass drumstick, and the bawling of the bull-ophicleide. That cannot be tolerated except for galops and contredances. The public that goes, from lack of anything else to do, to hear this quasi-music, asks for nothing more, and even prefers dance tunes to everything else. What good is it then, to expend oneself in pure futility to scratching out great instrumental compositions, [when they are heard] even to the point of rendering them unrecognizable to the composer himself? For what poorly understood vanity, profiting from the legal privilege that authorizes the first comer to have performed, wherever and however he may wish, *every published work*, to go take by the throat unfortunate composers, who were hardly dreaming of it, solder an iron collar around their necks, and in a grotesque position, place them in the pillory of the public wayside, while the assembled spectators ask, in return for their money, only for the capering of the monkey and the niceties of the trained dog? ... Composers really are to be pitied. If they are young and inexperienced, every musical institution closes its doors to them and scornfully refuses to play their attempts; if they succeed by the sweat of their brow to be played, they have no way to prevent their works from being ruined by orchestras incapable of giving even the shadow of their thinking. And they are always sighing for the moment when their works will be published ... To correct this imprudent ambition of theirs, a single word will suffice: Beethoven, last year, was hissed at Bordeaux. It is true that on *the shores of the Garonne*, when they go to a spectacle, *they laugh, kid around, and they reason, and they have a good time for a moment*, a performance, even though perfect, could not make, then, the HEROIC SYMPHONY seem very *amusing* to the Gascons. In any case, in the interest of art and in respect for our European glories, one should make all these unworthy profanations impossible. If a sign painter, aided by some stone cutters, decided to open a museum, in which, soliciting some pennies, he would show the public ignoble copies of the TRANSFIGURATION, and of MOSES, saying: This is Raphael, this is Michelangelo ... Well, if that were to happen ... Why ... They would let him do it! Oh! well, I do not doubt it; I do not know, actually, what blind confidence my optimism was about to drag me into saying. All right, I, myself, shout at you with all the strength of my lungs that it would be infamous! And that this is what happens every day to music. They told us recently of the deed of that French officer who, attending a melodrama in London in which Napoleon was represented on the knees of Lord Wellington, rushed upon the stage to cut down the unfortunate actor charged with the role of the Emperor. In the arts, there are also men who wear the double crown of genius and misfortune, Beethoven and Weber, for example. These are our Emperors, and, for the rest of us musicians, we do not like, either, seeing them travestied, nor mutilated, nor dragged about on scaffolding like clowns.[7]

7 *Journal des Débats*, July 21, 1835.

And, of course, Berlioz suffered from the surest truth of all, that you are never a prophet in your own home town.

One must have a tricolor flag over his eyes not to be able to see that music in France is dead and that it is the last of the arts our rulers are going to take any notice of. They tell me I'm remaining aloof from my country. I don't remain aloof from it: I flee from it as one flees from a barbaric shore when one is looking for civilization … For a long time now I have stifled my love of France and uprooted from my heart the foolish habit of centering all my thoughts on her. During the past seven years I have lived entirely on what my works and concerts have earned me in foreign countries. Without Germany, Bohemia, Hungary, and especially Russia I would have starved in France over and over again …

I have tried enough, suffered enough, waited enough. I shall not fulfill it there. In France I have experienced nothing but frustration in greater or lesser degree. I have found only stupid opposition, because the national mentality is stupid where serious matters of art and literature are concerned. I have an invincible and ever growing contempt for those 'French ideas' which are quite unknown to other nations. Under the previous government I found nothing but scorn and indifference: I now find preoccupation with other, weightier questions added to scorn and indifference.[8]

8 Letter to Louis-Joseph Duc, May 26, 1848, in *Correspondance*, 1200.

There are also great rewards for the composer, to state the other side of the case. In Germany the rewards sometimes came in the form of a special fanfare, which for Berlioz, with his aversion to fanfares in general, must have been a mixed blessing indeed. Three examples will suffice.

One Sunday in the public gardens I was acclaimed by the crowd, and the band played fanfares when they saw me. In short, the whole town is gripped by a tremendous revival of interest in my music.[9]

9 Letter to his Sister, Adele, Hanover, November 17, 1853, quoted in Searle, *Hector Berlioz, A Selection from his Letters*, 123.

…

The day following the first concert, the military bands of Dresden came to wake me with a morning concert, which led to drinking, as you can well imagine, many glasses of punch. All of these people are in a state of splendor and enthusiasm, which they couldn't express in any other way than handshakes, and it embarrassed me since I couldn't speak a word of German.[10]

10 Letter to Auguste Morel, Dresden, February 18, 1843, in *Correspondance*, 815.

…

Hardly had the last chord sounded when an appalling hubbub engulfed the hall. The entire audience were shouting, in the stalls, in the boxes, everywhere, and trombones, horns and trumpets blaring out fanfares in a selection of keys, energetically accompanied by the clatter of bows on the wood of the stringed instruments and the din of percussion.

The German language has a word to designate this peculiar way of applauding, *Tusch*. My first reaction was one of anger and abhorrence: they were spoiling the musical experience I had just been enjoying. For a moment I almost hated the players for choosing such a deafening method of showing me their appreciation. But it was impossible not to feel deeply touched by their tributes when the Kapellmeister, Georg Muller, advancing upon me laden with flowers, addressed me, in French:

'Permit me to offer you these wreaths in the name of the whole ducal establishment, and allow me to lay them on your scores.'

At these words the audience shouted louder than ever, the orchestra resumed its fanfares, and the baton dropped from my hand: I no longer knew what was happening.[11]

11 *Memoirs*, 313.

In a letter to Adolphe Sax of 1853, Berlioz counted a concert in this same city as one of his greatest moments of appreciation as a composer.

I got everything—receipts, dinner for 100 guests, the baton offered by the orchestra, popular ovation in the garden, an institution founded in my name and a marvelous performance. I must admit that I have never had such success anywhere else.[12]

12 Letter to Adolphe Sax, Brunswick, October 26, 1853, in *Correspondance*, 1638.

On Orchestration

BERLIOZ, DUE TO HIS ARTICLES and later treatise on instrumentation, not to mention the art he demonstrates in his own music, was widely recognized for his skill in orchestration during his life time. In his *Treatise*, he speaks of the important dimensions of this facet of composition for orchestra.

> Considered in its poetical aspect, this art can be taught as little as the art of inventing beautiful melodies, beautiful chord successions, and powerful rhythmical forms. One can only learn what is suitable for the various instruments, what is practicable or not, what is easy or difficult, what is weak or sonorous. It can also be indicated that one instrument is more appropriate than another for creating certain effects or expressing certain feelings. But as for their blending in groups, in small orchestras or large masses; as for uniting and combining them so that the tone of some instruments is modified by that of others, producing an ensemble tone unobtainable by one instrument or by a group of similar instruments; all this can be demonstrated only by studying the achievements realized in the works of the masters and by analyzing their methods.[13]

13 *Treatise*, 2.

Today, of course, we identify the generation of Berlioz as the point where composers really begin to think of instrumentation as a vital part of the compositional process. Berlioz, with his genius in this regard, could see around him many examples of errors in, and even ignorance of, this new art.

> This branch of the composer's art has made great strides in the last few years and its achievements have attracted the attention of critics and public. It has also served with certain composers as a means of faking inspiration and concealing poverty of invention beneath a show of energy. Even with undeniably serious and gifted composers it has become a pretext for wanton outrages against good sense and moderation, so you can imagine what excesses their example has led to in the hands of imitators. These very excesses are a measure of the practice, or malpractice, of orchestration, which is for the most part mere whistling in the dark with blind routine to guide it, when it is not sheer accident. For it does not follow that, because the modern composer habitually employs a far larger number of instruments than his predecessors, he is any more knowledgeable about their character, their capacity and mechanism, and the various affinities and relationships that exist between them. Far from it: there are eminent composers so fundamentally igno-

rant of the science that they could not even tell you the range of some of the instruments. I know from my own experience of one to whom the compass of the flute was an undisclosed mystery. Of brass instruments and the trombone in particular, they have only the most shadowy notion; you can see this from the way most modern scores, just as in the old days, cling to the middle register of these instruments and avoid taking them high or low, simply because composers, not knowing their exact compass, are afraid of overstepping it; as they have no inkling of what can be done with the notes at either end of the scale, they leave them strictly alone. Orchestration today is like a foreign language which has become fashionable. Many affect to speak it without having learnt to do so; consequently they speak it without understanding it properly and with a liberal admixture of barbarisms.[14]

14   *Memoirs*, 405ff.

There are two reviews published by Berlioz which contain much information regarding his views on orchestration. The first is a review of the earliest important book written on this subject, Georges Kastner's *Course of Instrumentation, Considered vis-a-vis the Poetic and Philosophic Relationships of the Art*.

M. [Georges] Kastner, whose compositions would merit being better known in Paris, was already placed among the able and conscientious theoreticians by the *Traité général d'Instrumentation*; a very different work from that which we will deal with here, and which is merely an indispensable introduction to it. In the *Traité général*, in fact, the author only has attempted to make well known the range and the properties of each instrument; and if the Conservatoire rushed to adopt it for the teaching in its composition classes, it is with just that much more pertinence and reason as not only the students, but also many justly famous masters, needed to dip into it for the concepts that they lacked.

I could not believe, if experience had not furnished me with incontrovertible proof, the singular ideas that several great composers entertained on the subject, hardly ten years ago. One of them that I know quite well, doubtless was ignorant about the range of the flute; I already had observed many times that his wind instrumental phrases were truncated in the upper register when their ascending direction in the part assigned to the flutes should have required them to exceed natural high G. Having asked him the reason for it, he responded that he stopped on high G because the instrument could not go any higher. I took the liberty of contradicting him and affirming that flutes climbed, not only to A, but to Bb with difficulty, to B natural, and that today they even write, in certain cases, high C. He did not want to believe me, and it would evidently have filled him with chagrin [for me] to deliver him from an error in which he had been living for such a long time ...

Hummel, in his magnificent Septet, gave the horn the low E natural. This factitious note among all factitious notes, which very few hornists can succeed in making heard even with long notes, descending chromatically from G in slow movement, is almost impossible, and in any case, dull, false, and ridiculous in the descending arpeggio C, G, E, C, written by Hummel. Most composers would suppose that such a knowledgeable artist would be free from such errors (probably due to distraction), so his example has misled several young ones.

I must, relative to the horn and the trombone, reproach M. Kastner for not having given in his general treatise details about their true range. Thus, he says nothing concerning three low tones of the horn, Ab, F sharp, and F natural, which sound out very well, prepared by a G, and from which Weber and Beethoven obtained such beautiful effects. Also, he omitted, in the range of the tenor trombone, the low notes called the pedal tones, Bb, A, Ab, and G, on descending the staff (key of F). They appear in some method books for that instrument, and before using them, I often have had the occasion to appreciate their beauty when attending the lessons that the able Swedish virtuoso M. Dieppo gives with so much intelligence to his Conservatoire students. Of course, these pedal tones cannot be written like the other notes; and it is necessary to lead down to them in a very slow movement, the Bb by a leap of a fifth or an octave, from the F or from the Bb above, the three other notes by connecting degrees; taking care, progressively, as you descend, to provide the performer with an opportunity to breathe; because in this case, in order to make the instrument vibrate well, it is necessary to have a quite considerable volume of air. Moreover, one must avoid giving to the trombone high notes in the passages preceding the one in which the pedal tones are to be employed. Without this precaution, the lips would be badly prepared for the embouchure habits which the emission of sound in the lower registers requires. Also, I shall prevail upon M. Kastner, for the next edition of his general treatise, to cut back, in the range of the two-valved cornet, the low B, which our best artists carefully avoid and declare should not be counted among the actual notes of this instrument.

After having made these observations, which prove at least to M. Kastner that we have read and carefully studied his work, we can only repeat, citing M. Meyerbeer and the music section of the Institute: 'This treatise will be of an immense usefulness to young composers who consult it. By putting under their eyes all the resources of the modern orchestras, they will learn without difficulty that which, ordinarily, is only acquired after long experience, preceded by many aborted attempts.' We have seen recently how *young* composers could still find colleagues among those of a more advanced age.

Let us go now to the new *Course of Instrumentation*, in which the author teaches the art of making an appropriate application under the triple relationship of harmony, character, and expression. This work is divided into three big categories. The *first* contains the accompaniment and use of instruments in the orchestra. The *second* includes a certain number of analyses of some remarkable fragments from the best masters in the different genres. The author succeeded perfectly with this method, and it was the best, to tell the truth, to explain well to the students how the famous composers distributed orchestral parts, why, in such and such a case, they chose such and such an instrument, or such and such a combination; why they acted in a contrary fashion in such another, and how these diverse procedures are always, with them, in direct relation to the character of the harmony and melodic expression.

Finally, the *third* part gives some useful information on the military band.

One finds, besides, in the first chapter, an historical glance over instrumentation since its origin up to our days, and it is not of a mediocre interest for the musician to follow the course of that art which was so simple in the first ages of civilization, so weirdly allied in Antiquity to religious ceremonies and to oratory art, and finally so complicated and so powerful with modern Europeans.

For a century now, some new instruments have been invented, others have been developed, and performers have acquired a degree of ability that our forefathers certainly did not suspect. However, completely taking into account these unquestionable advantages, one must state that before obtaining them, the art ought to have been able, nevertheless, to make more rapid progress, and that these recent improvements are almost equaled by the excesses and the inexpressible disorder that they brought in their train. Still, of all the arts, that of instrumentation is the freest, by its very nature: based on experience and guided by it, it ought to have been able to march with a more agile and surer step. But routine was attached to it, and for a long time it paralyzed its movements, seconded as that was, by the naive ignorance of some, by the preoccupation of others, and by the calculated reserve of some savant egotists. When a teacher says to his student: 'One must not use that instrumental arrangement.—Why?—Because that is never done.'—that teacher is a fool. One cannot forbid the use of a means, without demonstrating that the means is vice-ridden or less good than another, and yet, this is what we see done every day. So, in the usage of certain wind instruments, the first thing that is taught is always to arrange them in the following way: the flutes on top, the oboes below them, then the clarinets and bassoons. Doubtless this arrangement is logical, since it is, by reason of the facility with which each of these instruments extends from the high to the low; but why say to a student ... 'It must always proceed thus,' when experience can at each instant prove you wrong? What is wrong with making, for example, the oboe sing in the high register, while the flutes have the harmony below? Does this reversal of the established order produce a bad effect? Not at all, to the contrary; the low tones that our artists today project from the flutes have a special character which blends very well with certain other sounds of the oboes, and whose application can be in this case extremely successful. Therefore, could one destroy the instrumental hierarchy to the point of making the cellos sing in the upper register and the clarinets perform the low notes in the chalumeau register? An intelligent artist, after a moment's reflection, will respond in the affirmative; others will say that it is the proposition of a madman, that you might as well walk on your hands, place the branches of the tree in the ground and the roots in the air, etc., etc. Weber, with the delicious and poetic Andante of his *Overture to Oberon*, took it upon himself to cause to be appreciated the strange charm of that association of timbres, and did not take into account, fortunately, either usage or preconceptions.

This does not mean, as they will not fail to give out, that I propose the senseless overthrow of the entire instrumental ladder, and that I seek the new, or rather the bizarre, by putting the lambs with the wolves; far from it, I am only thinking that it is necessary for instrumentation, as for harmony, as for melody, as for rhythm, not to adopt anything without a profound examination, not to do anything without a reason, but also, not to reject anything without a motive, and to recognize no authority save that of experience, and *well-done* experience. This opinion, which guided M. Kastner in his work, appears to have been that of many great composers; and if, with some it has not been, for instrumentation, more productive of results, it is rather to the preoccupation they were in with another branch of musical art to which one must, in part, attribute it.

Gluck found by instinct some prodigious orchestral effects; and, absorbed by the search for dramatic expression, he did not notice that, in the accompaniment of the recitatives, his stringed instruments hummed in a tiresome fashion, and that it would have been of much more benefit for himself than for any other to change that bad system that he had established. He gave to the clarinets, in the mid-range, accents of irresistible tenderness, and never, without one's knowing why, did he take advantage, in the numerous infernal scenes that he had to deal with, of the sounds of the lower octave, of the chalumeau, which could have appeared there to such advantage. On the other hand, he used with a rare good fortune the two characteristics of the flute, witness the dance tune in B minor of the Champs-Elysées of *Orphée*, everything written *in the mid-range and the high register* of the instrument, and the religious march of *Alceste*, where the two flutes play in unison *in the low range*. With the exception of the famous call of Caron in the same opera, he gave to the horns only a quite obscure role; like his predecessors and his contemporaries, he limited himself to giving them open tones. He obtained from the trumpets, to the contrary, some effects not dreamed of before him, and which one has almost never made use of since then; effects certainly not startling nor warlike, but sweet and calm, as the holding on the dominant in the Andante of the introduction of *Iphigénie en Tauride*.

As to the trombones, who better than Gluck knew how to make them speak? Whether he demanded from them a pompous harmony, or whether he joined them in a terrible unison, or he made them dully menacing, or moaning with the specters of Tartarus, each of their notes, as he said himself, *drew blood*. More often than any other, he rendered pathetic or touching the plaintive sounds of the oboes and bassoons. He knew nothing about the timpani. No one in that epoch suspected the importance that they would acquire later in the hands of the chiefs of the German school. For him, as for the Italians of his time and ours, the timpani served merely to produce a greater or lesser sound. It was reserved to Beethoven, Weber, and Meyerbeer, to make of them musical instruments. The composers then suspected so little that the sounds of the timpani could be properly appreciated, that the majority of the Italian masters did not bother to annotate whether they were to be tuned in fourths or in fifths, limiting themselves to designation of the tonic and the dominant, and not imagining that it could enter into the thought of anyone to tune them otherwise. Today they are used in pairs and in groups of three or four, and even in greater number: they are tuned in fourths, fifths, major and minor thirds, sixths, sevenths, and in octaves (in the key of F). Beethoven, in two of his symphonies, produced charming contrasts by means of this last tuning of two timpani. Gluck never used the bass drum; only one time the cymbals and the triangle appeared in his orchestra, and everyone knows with what success: People will not forget the chorus and the ballet of *Les Scythes* ...

Mozart, soon after him, came along to perfect each of the branches of instrumentation, which he applied to the accompaniment of song with that admirable sagacity and that exquisite taste which formed the principal traits of his genius. If Gluck made of certain instruments inspired voices; Mozart, without raising any of them so strongly above the others, spread civilization in the orchestra. The inhabitants of his harmonious city did not count many men of genius, but they all had, in general, a more cultivated mind; richness and the purity of language are, with them, the inheritance of the greatest number.

Beethoven went farther than Mozart on the same route.

The fiery orchestra, contrasting, dreaming, tender, passionate, of Weber, is only an extension of Gluck's.

The orchestra of Meyerbeer has a little of those of Beethoven and of Weber, combined and blended with a superior intelligence, but with some concessions, however, to contemporary habits which neither Beethoven nor Weber ever wanted to recognize. His 'Resurrection of the Nuns' in *Robert*, and all the fourth act of *Les Hugenots*, are incomparable masterpieces of instrumentation. This leads us naturally to argue with M. Kastner about the complete precision of one of his definitions. *Instrumentation*, says he, *is the art of appropriately applying the different kinds of instruments to a given melody*. No doubt, but it is still another thing: it is the art of coloration through the use of harmony and rhythm; even more, it is the art of creating emotion by the choice of timbres, independently from any effect from melody, rhythm, or harmony. So I would include vocal music as instrumentation; because certain very striking effects of melody are only due to timbre, or depend solely on the choice of the voice register.

Some examples will make me better understood: in his *Robert-le-Diable*, at the moment when Robert approaches to pluck off a grave the enchanted branch, an orchestral chorus sounds only the Ab of the mid-range. In this instance, there is no melody, since the Ab is alone, nor harmony, nor rhythm, for the same reason; and yet there is a musical effect, there is emotion produced by a tone; and nothing of all that would exist if, among the innumerable varieties of timbre which the orchestra possesses, the composer had not chosen precisely that of the stopped note of a horn which comes out as raucous and painful as the rattle in the throat of a dying man …

To sum up, that art [instrumentation] should be, therefore that of causing emotion, whether by combination of diverse timbres of instruments and of voices applied to enhance, to color melody, harmony and rhythm; whether by impressions *sui generis*, or produced without the assistance of the three other great musical powers. But we do not need to say that this art is as little learned as that of discovering beautiful melodies, beautiful successions of chords, and original and powerful rhythmic forms. One can only draw attention to the general results often obtained in certain circumstances given, but which strength or weakness of the genius of the composer must, however, still modify for better or worse in a thousand ways.[15]

15 'Course of Instrumentation, Considered vis-à-vis the Poetic and Philosophic Relationships of the Art, by Georges Kastner,' in *Journal des Débats*, October 2, 1839.

In a letter to his uncle, Berlioz provides a personal note on Kastner.

Finally, we needed to leave, but we stopped off two days in Strasbourg at Mr. Kastner's, who had invited us to come and visit his rich and beautiful property. Mr. Kastner is a wise musician and theorist. He married Mr. Boursault's daughter and consequently possesses an immense fortune. His wife is one of the most distinguished people in France, in her spirit, her rare education and above all in her modest reserve with which she hides many qualities—great musician among others—she knows almost all of my music by heart.[16]

16 Letter to his Uncle, Felix Marmion, Paris, September 5, 1858, in *Correspondance*, 2308.

The second important review on the subject of orchestration is a study of the choice of instruments to reflect the drama in Meyerbeer's *Robert the Devil*.

We are going to examine several of the most striking passages. First, the entire introduction is an artistic masterpiece of managing effects. The grandiose and terrible theme, which appears in the fifth measure, is proposed by the three trombones, in unison *without ophicleide*; that instrument joins them only on the third entrance of the theme. Then the bassoons, underneath a tremolo in the second violins and violas. Then the contrabasses seize it with the bow, and when, underneath a pattern of imitation in the flutes, oboes, and clarinets, the entire orchestra, little by little, becomes more excited in its full mass, the bass drum and cymbals strike their first blow on the re-entrance of the theme *tutti* in the main key. This unexpected effect is gigantic, and nothing, to my mind, could replace this terrible striking by two instruments whose usage generally is so insanely unregulated.

In the first act, I shall point out the orchestration, so full of agitation and horror in the third couplet of the ballade, 'Jadis regnait en Normandie …'; that of the fresh romanza of Alice 'Va! va!', where the violoncellos, the horns, and the timpani play such an important role; that of the entrance of Bertram during the conference between Alice and Robert, where two horns in E and a bassoon, reproduce in three parts in minor the theme of the ballad, …; that of Bertram's 'aside' in C sharp minor, 'Fortune ou non propice, …' where the muted sounds of the horns and the low B of the ophicleide are used to such happy effect.

The second act is less rich in this respect, and the reason for it is in the situations, which do not motivate such slashing effects. However, in the magnificent duet, 'Mon coeur s'elance et palpite,' one notes a very expressive chromatic dialogue between the flute and the soprano; the danced Chorus, 'Accourez au devant d'elle,' seems to me to be deliciously orchestrated, everything there is fresh and engaging; I am not speaking of the melody, which is ravishing, or of the rhythm of a piquant novelty, but only of the instrumental coloration; the solo triangle works wonders through those violoncello and clarinet arpeggios in the chalumeau register. Yet I reproach the composer of having introduced there towards the end the trombones and the ophicleide, whose presence is not motivated by any dramatic intent, and whose crude and violent timbre, forte, can only attenuate the color of such a gracefully gay piece. Of course, I know that *everyone* does that in dance tunes, just to produce a little more noise, but I also know that there is nothing more revolting that to see Ariel's dance, or that of Mlle Taglioni, accompanied by an instrumentation worthy of Caliban; I also know that it is through the absurd use of violent means in every little bit of song or dance, that we have arrived at this frightful orchestral anarchy whose results we see each day in the organization of the public and in the expressive power of new compositions; and as M. Meyerbeer is not *everybody*, I think I must indicate what seems to me a fault in his magnificent work.

Farther on, to the contrary, one must admire the success that the composer was able to derive from the unison of the contrabasses, pizzicato, with the three timpani; it is at the moment when the Prince of Granada crosses the stage; the trumpet fanfare, which soon will burst forth to announce the opening of the tourney, therefore first appears veiled; and the muffled strokes of the string basses and of the timpani, used melodically, produce an impression of terror that the situation renders profoundly dramatic. Instead of this simple pizzicato, if they had taken it upon themselves to perform *col arco* the bass part and to substitute for the timpani some wind instrument, horn or bassoon or trombone, that striking effect would have disappeared completely; and there are some people who still deny that instrumentation is an art!

We shall note the disposition of the horns in the infernal waltz of the third act. In this piece the F sharp is often present, sounded at the octave by the three trombones, the ophicleide, two horns in E, a horn in B and a horn in G. In order to obtain the F sharp from a horn in G, it is absolutely necessary to give it a 'stopped' B natural, as everyone knows. These pitches attacked with strength have a singular savage character; such is the reason that determined the composer to put in use a fourth horn in G, instead of a second horn in B, which would only have had to sound an open tone in order to produce the F sharp, or of a third horn in E, sounding D, an open tone which also gives the F sharp. Another instrument is employed with a rare discernment in this piece: the cymbals. They strike alone, against ordinary usage. These high-pitched vibrations, though mordant and incisive, are perfectly in their place; add to them a bass drum, and that would be commonplace, a platitude, an absurdity …

The ritournelle of the entrance of Alice, which follows the infernal scene, produces an impression of calm and delicious freshness. It is ever the instrumentation to which this contrast is due. Instead of the cohorts, barking, moaning, scraping metallic instruments of all kinds, horns, valved trumpets, cymbals, triangle, tam-tam, trombones, reinforced by all the violence that the *tremoli* of stringed instruments offer, one hears here pure and virginal voices; the orchestra is composed of merely a sextet of the sweetest instruments: two flutes, two oboes, and two clarinets. Farther along, in Alice's duet with Bertram, on the words, 'Nothing! Nothing!' the flute has a descending chromatic run, six notes long, which translates in an astonishing manner the trembling, the hesitation of the voice of a terrorized girl.

But it is in the piece entitled, *Resurrection des Nonnes* [Resurrection of the Nuns], that one must give the award for instrumentation. This scene, the most striking of the drama, could not have been treated more musically nor in a newer or more poetic manner. There is no longer the immobility of death, without, however, there already being the movement of life. Everything is as frozen, dusty, and heavy as the marble tombs that slowly open. The violins, violas, flutes, oboes and clarinets are hushed. The horns, the valved trumpets, trombones, ophicleide, timpani and tam-tam, alone moan several syncopated chords *pianissimo*, preceded on the down beat by two pizzicato plucks by the violoncelli and contrabasses. Then, after each of its horrible strophes, two bassoons alone come in clucking a more animated rhythm which nearly prefigures the movement of the dances over to which the nuns, half-resuscitated, soon will deliver themselves; but it is so pale, so sullen, so dazed, the hand of death weighs still so heavily on these miserable creatures, that one believes he hears the dull sound, the cracking of the joints of the galvanized cadavers, and sees the hideous movements which are developing there. Horrible! Horrible! Frightfully grotesque! These few pages are in my opinion the most prodigious inspiration of modern dramatic music. So then, keep in the rhythm, the nuances and the harmony, do not change a single note, but put some woodwinds, or violins in the place of brass instruments, or play the score on the piano, and presto, that sublime inspiration is nullified, not even a trace of it remains. The bassoon duo especially cannot be translated; nothing can give an idea of it except … two bassoons!

I shall not end yet without stressing the fortunate daring that conferred to the valved trumpet the melody, so nobly beautiful, of the famous trio of the last act. As to the details of this rich instrumentation, it would be necessary to write a book to make them all known and as appreciated as they deserve.[17]

As a conductor, on the other hand, Berlioz knew that not every orchestra was able to provide the instrumentation of his scores. In these cases he proved to have a more practical side and he was willing to offer alternative choices, as in the case of this letter to Liszt.

> I fear that Weimar will be missing a few wind instruments. You will therefore have to arrange a few sparse passages. I have often used four bassoons—when they form a solo chord, replace the first and the second by two clarinets if they don't have anything else more important to play at the same time.
>
> I have also put a bass clarinet in the *Septet* and in the overture. If we can only have one, it is better to have his part given to an ordinary clarinet.
>
> Do you have two harps? Two valve cornets? The latter can be replaced by ventil-trumpets in A and Bb. As for the three timpani, we will eliminate one and the second player will be easy to find in order to perform the rolls simultaneously with two instruments.[18]

But there was one instrumental substitution which caused Berlioz general agitation. The generation of Berlioz was also the one in which the modern piano became so widely popular as an amateur instrument. A manifestation of this popularity was the thousands of arrangements for the instrument of orchestral music. For Berlioz, the piano, because it makes everything sound the same, was an unacceptable substitute.

> There is a wonderfully touching solo for the oboe. Play it on the piano, and in place of the poignant, plaintive effect Gluck intended, you hear so many disconnected notes like the separate strokes of a bell … The piano, in short, by destroying all sense of instrumentation, places every composer on the same level. The master of the orchestra is shrunk to the size of the fumbling incompetent who lacks the first idea of that branch of his art. The fumbler can write trombones for clarinets and ophicleides for bassoons, he can make the most colossal blunders and not even know the compass of the various instruments, and the expert can produce a splendid orchestral work, without its being possible from

17 'De l'Instrumentation de Robert-le-Diable,' in *Gazette Musicale de Paris*, July 12, 1835.

18 Letter to Franz Liszt, Paris, August 29, 1851, in *Correspondance*, 1430.

such a rendering to tell the difference. The piano, for the orchestral composer, is a guillotine which chops off the aristocrat's head, and from which only the poor have nothing to fear.[19]

19 *Memoirs*, 112.

Berlioz on other Composers

IT IS ALWAYS INTERESTING TO READ the impressions of one master of composition for another. Often one finds a curious lack of appreciation, due to the lack of historical hindsight. Berlioz's writing, on the other hand, seem very perceptive in this regard and we present here a sampling.

Beethoven

Berlioz's understanding of the importance of Beethoven was considerably ahead of his Parisian contemporaries, as can be seen throughout his writings. His admiration can be seen in the following discussion of an aria from *Fidelio*.

> The allegro theme of this admirable aria is introduced by three horns and solo bassoon, confining themselves to sounding five notes: F, E, G, B, E, occupying five bars of incredible originality. You might give these five notes to any musician who does not know them, and I wager in a hundred combinations there will be not one to equal the proud and impetuous phrase Beethoven draws from them, as the rhythm used is entirely unforeseen. This allegro strikes many as having one great fault: it does not have any little phrase they can remember easily. These amateurs, insensible to the many and striking beauties of this aria, just look out for their four-bar phrases like children looking for a prize in a Christmas cake.[20]

20 Berlioz, *Beethoven by Berlioz*, 55.

There were some things in Beethoven's music which Berlioz did not understand. One of these he mentions in a discussion of one of the overtures (*Leonore Overture*, op. 72b, no. 3) to this same opera.

> Beethoven wrote four overtures to his only opera. Having completed the first he began again, no one knowing exactly why, retaining the original arrangement and all the subjects, but joining them by different modulations, rescoring them, and adding a crescendo as well as a flute solo. In my opinion the solo is not up to the great style of the rest of the work.[21]

21 Ibid., 50.

The curious, and famous, 'early' horn entrance in the first movement of Beethoven's third symphony was confusing to musicians and critics for many years. Many thought it was simply a mistake to be corrected. Berlioz seems inclined in that direction, only to be held back by the simple fact that it was written as it is by the master.

> Our ears are inclined to protest this terrible anomaly, a vigorous tutti interrupts the horn and, concluding *piano* on the tonic chord, allows the celli to return to state the entire theme in its natural harmony. Considering these things from even the most elevated and detached view; it is difficult to find serious justification for this musical caprice.
>
> Without doubt the master must have so intended it, as it is related that during the first rehearsal of this symphony, his friend Ries stopped the orchestra by crying out, 'Very fast, as fast as possible, the horn made a mistake.'
>
> His only reward for his indiscreet zeal was a sharp slap from the hand of the master.
>
> No other such eccentricity is found in the rest of the score.[22]

22 Ibid., 18.

On the other hand, another passage which was criticized by some, the imitation of birds and various peasant idioms in the sixth symphony, were taken by Berlioz as being charming and appropriate.

> Some berate Beethoven for having tried to reproduce the songs of three birds at the end of the Adagio. In my opinion the absurdity or otherwise of such attempts is decided by their success or their failure. I may tell the adverse critics in this instance that their stricture appears justifiable as far as the nightingale is concerned, as this bird's song is scarcely better imitated here than in the famous flute solo of M. Lebrun; for the simple reason the nightingale only emits sounds inappreciable and variable, so these cannot be rendered with instruments having fixed tones playing in a certain key.
>
> It seems to me this does not apply to either the cuckoo or the quail; their respective cries are two notes in one instance, and one in the other—notes true and determined, and therefore admitting to exact and complete imitation ...
>
> But let us continue. The poet now leads us into the midst of a 'Jolly Gathering of Countryfolk.' They laugh and dance in moderation at first, while from the oboe comes a gay refrain accompanied by a bassoon seeming able to intone only two notes. Beethoven probably intended this to represent some good old German peasant mounted on a bar-

rel and armed with a dilapidated instrument from which he succeeds in drawing the two principal notes of the key of F—its tonic and its dominant.

Each time the oboe gives out its musette-like melody, appearing as simple and gay as a young girl dressed in her Sunday clothes, the old bassoon brings out his two notes. Should the melodic phrase modulate in the least, the bassoon is silent, quietly counting his rests until the return of the principal key allows him to come in again with the imperturbable F, C, F. This effect, so excellently grotesque, seems to almost completely escape the attention of the public.[23]

23 Ibid., 32.

Reicha

Berlioz was a student of Reicha in Paris, as he mentions in his *Memoirs*.

> Cherubini, whose orderly mind showed itself in everything he did, knew that I had not been through the regular Conservatoire mill to get into Lesueur's composition class and had me enrolled in Reicha's class in counterpoint and fugue, which came before composition in the hierarchy of courses.[24]

24 *Memoirs*, 67.

Sometimes one will find in some author's writing on Berlioz the implication that Berlioz did not gain much from this study. However, a eulogy Berlioz wrote on the occasion of his teacher's death reveals a sincere appreciation for the man and his contributions as a teacher.

> The death of Reicha ... could hardly be foreseen. Although he had already arrived at his sixty-sixth year, he had conserved a robust health, a juvenile vigor that an existence consecrated to tranquil works could not alter, totally exempt of the ambition and cares that even the most just brings in his wake. Of a naturally cold temperament, and given to observation rather than to action, Reicha quickly had recognized that the difficulties, chagrins, disappointments of all kinds that the composer must necessarily encounter at each step, above all in France, before arriving at the exhibition of his works, were too great in number for the perseverance with which he felt himself gifted. Making his choice philosophically, he determined, therefore, early on, to profit by the occasion when it was presented, but not to waste his time nor his labor to cause it to happen, and above all never to be painfully attached to its pursuit. He wrote tranquilly what he pleased, accumulated work on top of work, masses, oratorios, quartets, quintets, piano fugues, symphonies,

operas, treatises; causing some to be heard when his resources permitted; trusting to his star for the fate of the rest, and always tranquil in his pace, deaf to the voice of criticism, very little sensitive to praise ...

He attached great value to his knowledge of mathematics. 'It is to this study,' he said to us one day during one of his lessons, 'that I owe having been able to succeed in making myself completely the master of my ideas; it tamed and cooled my imagination that earlier dragged me about madly, and by subjecting it to reason and to reflection, it doubled its strengths.' I do not know if this idea of Reicha is as correct as he believed and if his imagination gained much by this study of the exact sciences; perhaps the love of abstract combinations and mental games in music, the real charm that he found in solving certain thorny propositions which only served to make him deviate from his straight road by making him lose sight of the result for which he was continually reaching; to the contrary, did they damage a good deal the success of his work, and did they make them lose something in melodic or harmonic expression, in purely musical effect, what they gained (if to be sure, it was gaining) in arduous combinations, in conquered difficulties, in curious works made rather for the eye than for the ear? However that may be, his first attempts that he had performed at Bonn received the most encouraging reception. Dating from that moment he abandoned himself more specially to the study of composition, with his colleague and childhood friend Beethoven. Still, the intimacy does not seem to have lasted long between the two great musicians, and probably the complete divergence of their ideas on certain important points of the art's poetics, must have been the cause. What makes me think so is that I often have heard Reicha express himself quite coldly regarding Beethoven's works, and to speak with a badly disguised irony about the enthusiasm which these created ...

The desire to perfect his art and to profit by the counsel of J. Haydn caused Reicha to make the resolution of spending some years in Vienna near that great artist. Upon his arrival in Austria, towards the end of 1802, Reicha received, from Prince Louis-Ferdinand of Prussia, an amateur as zealous as he was distinguished, the same who perished some years later in the Battle of Jena, a flattering letter in which the Prince made the most brilliant offers to Reicha to entice him to come stay with him, and to teach him counterpoint. But Reicha preferred to sacrifice all these advantages to the one more precious to him, the society of Haydn ...

From 1809 he accepted a professorial chair, and, in the doubly difficult art of teaching music, which is, at one and the same time, both an art and a science, he proved to be so superior that to fill his shoes seems to us today, if not impossible, at least terribly difficult. The most famous among his disciples, the one whose name, by its very celebrity, came the least naturally under my pen when I was speaking of students, is our great instrumental composer, an author besides of two dramatic compositions, where beauties of the first order shine forth, M. Georges Onslow. It is to be noted that, despite the apparent severity of Reicha's precepts, none of the living professors has been more prompt than he to recognize an innovation, even if contrary to all admitted rules, if a happy effect resulted from it, and he saw there the germ of progress. In considering how tight the diapers still are in which they would like, in the schools, to keep musical art, one must confess that this merit reveals, in one so gifted, a great honesty of talent and a reasoning ability of the highest order.[25]

25 *Journal des Débats*, July 3, 1836.

Rossini

Berlioz was a keen and interested observer of opera in Paris and wrote of the composers and their latest works, as the reader can find in many places in this book.

Rossini was a composer Berlioz held in considerable contempt for his apparent eagerness to write whatever would please the public and for the lack of variety in his music, however good much of it is. The depth of Berlioz's feeling are evident in the following,

> Rossini's melodic cynicism, his contempt for dramatic expression and good sense, his endless repetition of a single form of cadence, his eternal puerile crescendo and brutal bass drum, exasperated me to such a point that I was blind to the brilliant qualities of his genius, even in his masterpiece, the *Barber*, exquisitely scored though it is. More than once I debated with myself the possibility of mining the Theatre-Italian and blowing it up one evening, along with all its congregation of Rossinians. Whenever I met one of the hated tribe of *dilettanti* I would glare at him with the eye of a Shylock and growl, 'Dog! Would that I might impale thee on a red-hot stake.'[26]

26 *Memoirs*, 77.

Bellini

Berlioz also wrote a brief notice on the death of another famous opera composer, Bellini.

> Bellini, perishing at twenty-eight, in the middle of his career, adulated, caressed by all of dilettante Europe, hardly distracted from time to time by well-meaning admonitions that the critic's hand wrote on sand, and that the wind of success erased the next day, must necessarily have caused grief the more penetrating because his type of talent had made him a star, and because his death was more unexpected.[27]

27 *Journal des Débats*, July 3, 1836.

Berlioz makes the interesting, and accurate, observation that once a composer's fame has been sealed by death, even his minor works are brought out for reverence—even if it is at the expense of the composer.

> The concert of the Gymnase, which I attended last Monday, began with the Overture to Bellini's THE PIRATE. It is a quite weak and quite poor composition that they should not have chosen and placed in evidence, as they are wont to do these days to honor the memory of the young maestro. If the sentiment that presides over these homages given to the great artists after their death had some reality, and weren't basically for show, they probably would abstain from revealing them on their weak side. But hardly had Boieldieu, Herold, or Bellini breathed their last breath, when their names were in all mouths, one must exploit this circumstance. They only excelled, it is true, in dramatic music, their instrumental compositions are extremely weak, but singing is forbidden in the majority of the concerts, and, to be able to place on an advertisement a name recently consecrated by death, they do not hesitate to pull from oblivion some miserable overtures that the composer repented many times of having published, and which only were staged thanks to the profound indifference into which the public has fallen in regard to them.[28]

28 *Le Rénovateur*, October 12, 1835, 171.

Spontini

Spontini was both a friend and a composer for whom Berlioz had considerable respect. In one article Berlioz gives a very interesting episode from the early life of this composer.

> His studies at the Conservatoire della Pieta [in Naples] were fruitful and, like the others, he wrote one of those foolishly decorated Italian works with a pompous operatic title, *I Puntigli delle Donne*. I do not know if this first work was performed, but it served as an inspiration for the composer to gain confidence in his own strength and ambition to escape from the conservatory and go to Rome where he hoped, more easily than in Naples, to be produced in the theater. The fugitive was soon caught and brought back to Naples like a vagabond, and punished, for the pretensions of being inspired to escape, into writing an opera for the carnival. He was given a libretto entitled *Gli Amanti in cimento*, which he promptly put to music and which was almost immediately played with success. The public came out to hear the young maestro … his age and his escape worked in his favor and Spontini was thus applauded, acclaimed, encored, and triumphed—and forgotten two weeks later.[29]

29 *Journal des Débats*, February 12, 1851.

Part 7

On Conducting

Berlioz as Conductor

JUDGING FROM HIS OWN COMMENTS, together with a few first-hand descriptions from important musicians who actually heard Berlioz conduct, it seems clear to this writer that he may have been the first great conductor, in the modern definition of the conductor's art. One of the eyewitnesses was the English conductor, Hallé, who had the unusual opportunity to not only see Berlioz conduct his own *Roman Carnival Overture*, but, due to an oversight, saw him perform it in public without a rehearsal!

> But to see Berlioz during that performance was a sight never to be forgotten. He watched over every single member of the huge orchestra; his beat was so decisive, his indication of all the nuances so clear and so unmistakable, that the overture went smoothly, and no uninitiated person could guess at the absence of a rehearsal.[1]

1 Quoted in *Memoirs*, 597.

The journal, *Musical World*, for 17 February 1847, describes Berlioz as a conductor as follows:

> His manner of beating the measure is generous and easy to follow—and the mass of instruments follows the slightest indication of his baton, rendering even more wonderful the exactitude and delicate nuances of expression that he wishes to obtain.

One might interpret one critic's comment to suggest that Berlioz must have employed his body as much as his baton, for he observed,

> He is as thin as his baton, and no one ever knows which of the two is beating time.[2]

2 Holoman, *Berlioz*, 587.

One account, by Rimsky-Korsakov writing about Berlioz's Russian concerts, is less complementary, but it may reflect the composer's failing health as much as his being carried away by the music.

No vagaries at all in shading. And yet (I repeat from Balakirev's account) at a rehearsal of his own piece Berlioz would lose himself and beat three instead of two or vice versa.³

3 Ibid., 660.

Fortunately, we also have some very interesting discussion of conducting in Berlioz's own words which also serve to reveal what he was like as a conductor. First, in his description of his first conducting experience, his early Mass, in the Church of St.-Eustache in 1827, he also gives us his definition of the qualities needed by a fine conductor.

Apart from a few slips due to excitement, I did not do too badly. Yet how far I was from possessing the many varied qualities—precision, flexibility, sensitivity, intensity, presence of mind, combined with an indefinable instinct—that go to make a really good conductor, and how much time and experience and heart-searching have I since put into acquiring two or three of them! We often complain of there being so few good singers, but good conductors are rarer still and in the great majority of cases far more necessary and potentially dangerous to the composer.⁴

4 *Memoirs*, 58.

In another description of the essential qualities of the good conductor, Berlioz points to Nicolai, conductor of the Vienna Kärntnerthor Orchestra as an outstanding example.

I regard him as one of the finest orchestral conductors I have ever encountered, and one of those men whose presence in a town can give it a position of unchallengable musical ascendancy when they enjoy conditions which provide full scope for their powers. Nicolai has to my mind the three indispensable qualities of a good conductor. He is a skilled, experienced and at times inspired composer; he has a thorough sense of rhythm and its complexities, and an impeccably clear and precise technique; and he is a shrewd and tireless organizer who grudges neither time nor trouble spent on rehearsal and knows exactly what he is doing because he does only what he knows how to do.⁵

5 Ibid., 374.

In a newspaper article of 1848, Berlioz points to Georges Hainl, of Lyon, as another man with the qualities of a fine conductor.

He brings together all of the qualities necessary in a good conductor—he has a clear, direct, precise, expressive and warm way of conducting. He knows how to remedy problems using the musical strengths at this disposal.⁶

6 *Revue et Gazette Musicale*, October 15, 1848.

There is an extraordinary self-portrait of Berlioz as conductor of an opera chorus rehearsal in Paris, which he writes under the title, 'Letter from a member of the Opera Chorus.'

Dear Master,
You have dedicated a book (*Orchestral Evenings*) *to your good friends, the artists of 'X,' a civilized city*. This German city (we know it) is not more civilized than many others, very probably, despite the malicious intention that you had in giving it this epithet. That its arts may be superior to those of Paris, it is permitted to doubt, and as for their affection for you, it cannot be, certainly, either as lively or as old as ours. The Parisian choristers, in general, and those of the Opéra in particular, are devoted to you body and soul; they have proved it to you many times in every way. Did they murmur about the length of the rehearsals, about the rigor of your musical requirements, about your violent interruptions, about your fits of anger, even, during the studies of your *Requiem*, the *Te Deum*, the *Roméo and Juliette*, the *Damnation of Faust*, the *Childhood of Christ*, etc.? Never, never. They always, to the contrary, fulfilled their task with unalterable zeal and patience. However, you are not very flattering to men, nor gallant to the ladies, during these terrible rehearsals.

When the hour to begin approaches, if the personnel of the chorus is not totally complete, if anyone is missing, you stride around the piano as a lion in his cage at the Zoo; you grumble, biting your lower lip, your eyes darting wild lightening; someone speaks to you, you turn away your head; you strike from time to time violently on the piano dissonant chords which indicate your interior rage, and which tell us clearly that you would be capable of tearing apart the late ones, the absent ones—if they were present.

Then you always reproach us for not singing *piano* enough in the soft nuances, of not attacking together the *fortes*; you want us to pronounce the two 's's' in the word *angoisse* and the 'r' in the second syllable of the word *traitre*. And, if an unfortunate illiterate, one alone, lost in our ranks, forgets your grammatical observation, and dares to still say *angoise* or *traite*, you hold it against everyone, you pour on us *en masse* cruel pleasantries, calling us porters, loge-attendants, etc.!! Very well, we take all of that, nevertheless, and we love you just the same, because you love us, one sees it, and that you adore music, one feels it ...

But why don't you now write a book, a book of the same kind, less philosophic and more gay perhaps, to conjure away the boredom that gnaws on us in the Opéra?

You know it, during the acts or the fragments of an act that do not contain choruses, we are prisoners in the vestibules. There it is as dark as the ship's store; we smell the lamp oil; we are badly seated; we hear old, moldy stories retold in bad language, rancid words repeated; or rather the silence and inaction at the same time crush us, up until the moment when the call-boy comes to make us enter on stage again ... Ah! the profession is not beautiful.[7]

7 *Revue et Gazette Musicale de Paris*, February 20, 1859.

He admits this is a description of himself in a similar paragraph in his *Memoirs*.

> I have often been accused by the ladies of the Opéra of a want of gallantry; I have a terrible reputation in this respect, and I admit I deserve it. The moment there is a question of taking a large chorus, before rehearsals have even begun, a sort of anticipatory rage possesses me, my throat tightens, and although nothing has yet occurred to make me lose my temper, I glare at the singers in a manner reminiscent of the Gascon who kicked an inoffensive small boy passing near him, and on the latter's protesting that he had not 'done anything,' replied, 'Just think if you had!'[8]

8 *Memoirs*, 297ff.

With regard to opera choruses, Berlioz seems to have observed some very poor conductors. He warns the reader to beware especially of the older members of this profession.

> Not all has been said as yet about those dangerous auxiliaries called chorus masters. Very few among them are really able to direct a musical performance so that the conductor can rely upon them ... Most to be dreaded are those whom high age has deprived of their energy and skill. The maintenance of any somewhat rapid tempo is impossible to them. However fast the initial tempo of a piece entrusted to their direction, little by little they slacken its pace until they have reached a certain degree of moderate slowness which corresponds with the blood circulation of their enfeebled organism. It must be added, however, that old men are not the only ones with whom composers run this risk. There are men in the prime of life, but with a sluggish temperament, whose blood seems to circulate *moderato* ... These people are the born enemies of all characteristic music and the greatest destroyers of style.[9]

9 *Treatise*, 417.

In a description of one of his rehearsals of the four brass bands in the *Tuba Mirum*, in his *Requiem*, Berlioz pictures himself just as frustrated with the trombones as he was with the opera chorus mentioned above.

> In the middle of the *Tuba mirum* is found a passage where four groups of trombones sound the four notes of the G major chord successively. The time is very lengthy; the first group must sound the G on the first beat; the second, the B, on the second; the third, the D, on the third; and the fourth, the octave G, on the fourth. Nothing is easier to conceive than such a succession, nothing is easier to play, also, than each of these notes. Well!! when this *Requiem* was presented for the first time in the Invalides, it was impossible to obtain the performance of that passage. When I then had excerpts played at the Opéra, after having uselessly rehearsed

for a quarter of an hour that single measure, I was obliged to abandon it. There were always one or two groups that would not attack; it was invariably those on B, or those on D, or both. On casting my eyes, in Berlin, on that spot in the score, I thought immediately of the disobedient trombones in Paris: 'Ah! Let's see,' I said to myself, 'if the Prussian artists will succeed in crashing through that open door!' Alas, no! Vain efforts! Neither rage or patience accomplished anything! Impossible to obtain the entrance of the second or third groups; the fourth, even, not hearing its phrase, which was to be given by the others, did not start either. I take them individually and I ask number 2 to sound the B—they do it very well. Addressing myself to number 3, I ask of them the D—they sound it effortlessly. Let's see now: the four notes, one after the other, in the order in which they are written!—Impossible! Completely impossible! I had to give up! Can you understand that? Doesn't that make you want to go smash your head against a wall?

And when I asked the Paris and Berlin trombonists why they were not playing in that fatal measure, they did not know what to answer; they did not even know themselves: those two notes fascinated them.

I must write to H. Romberg, who has performed this work at St. Petersburg, in order to find out if the Russian trombones were able to break the spell.[10]

10 *Journal des Débats*, November 8, 1843.

Berlioz describes the helpless frustration of the conductor in rehearsal again in a letter to Franz Liszt. How lucky, he says, is the great solo artist who controls every aspect of his performance, compared to the composer who must depend on other performers.

For the composer who would attempt, as I have done, to travel in order to perform his works, how different! The never-ending, thankless toil he must be ready to endure, the sheer torture that rehearsals can be—no one can know what it is like who has not experienced it. To begin with he has to face the chilly looks of the whole orchestra, who resent being put to all this unexpected inconvenience and extra work on his account. The looks say plainly, 'What does he want, this Frenchman? Why can't he stay where he belongs?' However, each man takes his place; but the moment the composer glances round the assembled company he is aware of alarming gaps. He asks the kapellmeister to explain. 'The first clarinet is ill, the oboe's wife is in labor, the first violin's child has the croup, the trombones are on parade, they forgot to ask for exemption from their military duties, the timpanist has sprained his wrist, the harp isn't coming, he needs time to study his part,' etc., etc. None the less one begins. The notes are read after a fashion, at a tempo more than twice too slow (nothing is so dreadful as this devitalizing of the rhythm!). Gradually your instinct gets the better of you, your blood begins to glow, you get carried away and involuntarily quicken the beat until you are giving the correct tempo. The result: chaos, a raucous confusion to split your ears and break your spirit. You have to stop and resume the original pace and work your way laboriously, piecemeal, through the long phrases that so often before, with other orchestras, you were wont to sail through swiftly and without hindrance. Even then it is not enough; despite the slow tempo, strange discords are discernible among the wind instruments. You try to discover the reason. 'Let me hear the trumpets by themselves ... What are you doing? I should be hearing a third, you're playing a second. The second trumpet in C has a D, give me your D ... Good. Now, the first trumpet has a C which sounds F. Let me hear your C ... Hey! What the devil! You've given me an Eb.'

'Excuse me, I'm playing what's written.'

'But you're not, you are a tone out.'

'I'm sorry, I'm playing a C.'

'What key is your trumpet in?'

'Eb.'

'Ah, that's what it is—you should be playing an F trumpet.'

'Oh yes, I hadn't looked properly. Sorry, you're quite right.'

'Timpani, why are you making such a frightful din over there?'

'I have a fortissimo, sir.'

'You haven't, it's mezzo forte—*mf*, not *ff*. In any case you're playing with wooden sticks when you should be using sponge-headed ones. It's the difference between black and white.'

'We don't know them,' the kapellmeister interposes. 'What do you mean by sponge-headed sticks? We only know the one kind.'

'I suspected as much, so I brought some with me from Paris. Take the pair on the table there. Now, are we all ready? ... For Heaven's sake—its ten times too loud. And why aren't you using mutes?'

'The orchestral attendant forgot to put them out on the desks. We will have them tomorrow,' etc., etc.

After three or four hours of this anti-musical tug of war they have not been able to make sense of a single piece. Everything is fragmentary, disjointed, out of tune, cold, flat, loud, discordant, detestable! And this is the impression you leave on sixty or eighty musicians, who finish the rehearsal exhausted and disgruntled and go round saying that they have no idea what it's all about, it's a chaotic, heathenish music, they have never had to put up with anything like it before. Next day little progress is visible. It is only on the third day that the thing takes shape. Only then does the poor composer begin to breathe. The harmonies, correctly pitched, become clear, the rhythms leap to life, the melodies sigh and smile; the whole ensemble acquires cohesion, confidence, attack. The stumbling and stammering is forgotten: the orchestra has grown up. With comprehension, courage returns to the astonished players. The composer asks for a fourth trial of skill, and his interpreters—who when all is said are the best fellows in the world—grant it with alacrity. This time, *fiat lux!* 'Watch for the expression. You're not afraid now?'

'No. Give us the right tempo.'

Via! And there is light! Art is born, the whole conception becomes manifest; the work is understood! And the orchestra rises to its feet, applauding and acclaiming the composer, the Kapellmeister congratulates him, the inquisitive people lurking in the hall emerge and come up onto the platform and exchange exclamations of pleasure and surprise with the players, with many a wondering glance at the foreign maestro whom at first they took for a madman or a barbarian. At this point you feel the need to relax. Do no such thing! It is now that you must intensify your vigilance. You have to return before the concert to supervise the arrangement of the desks and inspect the orchestral parts so as to make sure none of them have got misplaced. You must go meticulously along the ranks, red pencil in hand, writing German key-indications for French in the wind parts, altering *ut, ré, ré bémol, fa dièse*, to C, D, Des, Fis. You have to transpose a cor anglais solo for the oboe; the orchestra does not possess the instrument in question and the oboist is inclined to be nervous about transposing it himself. If the chorus or the soloists are still unsure of themselves, you must rehearse them separately. But the audience is arriving, it is time; and shattered in body and mind, you stagger to the conductor's desk, a wreck, weary, stale, flat and unprofitable, scarcely able to stand—until that magical moment when the applause of the audience, the zest of the players, and your own love for the work transform you in an instant into a dynamo of energy, radiating invisible, irresistible rays of light and power. And then the recompense begins. Then, I grant you, the composer-conductor lives on a plane of existence unknown to the virtuoso. With what ecstasy he abandons himself to the delight of 'playing' the orchestra! How he hugs and clasps and sways this immense and fiery instrument! Once more he is all vigilance. His eyes are everywhere. He indicates with a glance each vocal and orchestral entry. His right arm unleashes tremendous chords which go off like explosions. At the pauses he brings the whole accumulated impetus to a sudden halt, rivets every eye, arrests every arm, every breath; listens for an instant to the silence—then gives freer rein than ever to the harnessed whirlwind:

Luctantes ventos tempestatesque sonoras
Imperio premit, ac vinclis et carcere frenat

[The rearing winds and roaring tempests
He subdues to his dominion, and curbs and confines them]
   (*Aeneid*, I, 53–54)

And in the long adagios, the bliss of floating cradled on a lake of serene harmony while a hundred soft voices intertwined chant his love songs, or seem to confide his present sorrows and past regrets to solitude and the stillness of the night! Then often, though only then, the composer-conductor becomes oblivious of the public. He listens to himself and judges his own handiwork; and if he is moved and the same emotion shared by the artists around him, he takes no further heed of the reaction of the audience: they are remote from him. If he has felt his heart thrill to the touch of the poetry and melody of the music and has sensed within him the secret fire which is the flame of the soul's incandescence, his goal is attained, the heaven of art is opened to him, and what signifies earth?

When the concert is over and he has triumphed, his joy is multiplied a hundred times, shared as it is with the gratified pride of every member of his army. You, the great virtuosos, are princes and kings by the grace of God; you are born on the steps of the throne. We composers must fight and overcome and conquer to reign. But the very dangers and hardships of the struggle make our victories the more intoxicating, and we would perhaps be more fortunate than you—if we always had soldiers.[11]

11 *Memoirs*, 283ff.

In recounting his experiences guest conducting in Berlin, Berlioz gives us yet another vivid rehearsal description, this time in the role of the guest conductor of a foreign orchestra.

For sheer ludicrous ferocity there is nothing to compare with a fanatical German nationalist fully roused. This time, too, I had a section of the Opera orchestra against me, having forfeited their good will by my letters on Berlin, which had been translated by M. Gathy and published in Hamburg a few years before. The letters contained nothing offensive to the Berlin players, as the reader of these memoirs may see for himself. On the contrary, I had praised them comprehensively, merely adding a few carefully qualified criticisms of minor points of detail. I called the orchestra magnificent and declared it exceptional in point of precision, unanimity, power and delicacy. But—and there lay my crime—I made a comparison between some of its principal players and those of Paris, and actually stated (perish the thought!) that where the flautists were concerned, ours were superior. These innocent words had planted a rancorous animosity against me in the breast of the Berlin first flute; and as far as I could make out, he had persuaded many of his colleagues to believe that I had wantonly traduced the entire orchestra. Fresh proof of the risks you run in writing about players, and of the advisability of not standing to leeward of their self-esteem when one has had the misfortune to wound it in the slightest degree. When you criticize a singer, you do not have his colleagues up in arms against you. Indeed, they generally feel that you have not been severe enough. But the virtuoso instrumentalist who belongs to a well-known musical organization always claims that in criticizing him you insult the whole institution, and though the contention is absurd, he sometimes succeeds in making the other players believe it. Once during the rehearsals of *Benvenuto Cellini* I had the occasion to point out to the second horn a mistake in an important passage. I did so in the mildest and politest manner; but the player, Meifred, though an intelligent man, rose in wrath and, losing his head completely, shouted, 'I'm playing what is there. Why do you suspect the orchestra like this?' To which I replied, even more mildly, that it had nothing to do with the orchestra but only him, and that secondly I suspected nothing, for suspicion implied doubt, and I knew he had made a mistake.

To return to the Berlin orchestra, it did not take me long to notice a certain lack of geniality in its attitude to me during the rehearsals of *Faust*. The glacial reception I was given each day as I came in, the hostile silence which followed the best numbers in the score, and the irate glances, especially from the quarter of the flutes, made it only too obvious, and it was confirmed by what I learned from the players who had remained friendly to me. They were too much intimidated by their comrades' antagonism to applaud me, and it was in a furtive aside that one of them who spoke French let slip discreetly, as he passed near me on the stage at the end of a rehearsal: 'Sir, ze music—it is vonderful!' Perhaps I may be permitted to suspect that some of those who hissed the ballad were not unconnected with the incomparable, not-to-be-criticized flutes of the Berlin orchestra.[12]

12 *Memoirs*, 440ff.

On two occasions Berlioz openly writes of his pride in his accomplishment as a conductor. The first was an early concert he organized in the Theater Italian in Paris, when one of his goals was clearly to establish his ability to conduct his own music.

It is a shame and almost unbelievable that my success excited so many people filled with miserable envy. They even looked for a fight concerning the title, *Festival* … How little we can be in certain cases.

Be that as it may, let them talk. I wanted to do it and I did it. I wanted them to hear the two big pieces of my Requiem and the effect was incredible. I wanted to prove that I could make 150 musicians play with the greatest precision and without getting in the way—AND WITH ONE ONE REHEARSAL and I did it. Habeneck insisted that it was impossible, crazy, absurd—I proved it was possible. The performance was magnificent. I wanted them to see me at work like a great conductor of the Paris Opéra, in charge of the biggest musical army that was ever assembled together. I did it. Now let the dogs bark! That is their job.[13]

13 Letter to his Sister, Nanci, Paris, November 13, 1840, in *Correspondance*, 736.

Another occasion when he had to depend on his own ability in conducting, was one which included the premiere of the *Roman Carnival Overture*. In a letter before this concert he expresses his concern that there will be only one rehearsal.

I have given my first concert at the Conservatoire and I have organized another one for next week in a concert hall you don't know, called the Herz. For this concert I have composed a new overture, a scene with chorus and two other pieces. I have my usual orchestra, but I am worried nevertheless, as we must put together the program in only one rehearsal. Will I find the patience in Paris which I had from the Darmstadt artists so often? We worked well and worked miracles. The first concert we rehearsed everything only twice and everything went so well and energetically. Maybe we will have the same luck in escaping danger this time, but I am sure you also realize the potential danger.[14]

14 Letter to Louis Schlosser, Paris, January 28, 1844, in *Correspondance*, 881.

And potential danger there was! Not only was there only one rehearsal, but Berlioz found that he did not have all the players present.

A few years later, when I wrote the Roman Carnival Overture … Habeneck was in the artists' room at the Salle Herz on the evening of the first performance (February 3, 1844). He had heard that at the morning rehearsal we had played it through without the wind instruments (the National Guard having relieved me of part of my orchestra), and he had come to witness the catastrophe. One sees his point, Indeed, when I arrived in the orchestra, all the wind players crowded round me, appalled at the thought of giving a public performance of an overture that was completely unknown to them.

'Don't worry,' I said. 'The parts are correct and you are all excellent players. Watch my stick as often as you can, count your rests carefully, and everything will be all right.'

Not a single mistake occurred. I started the allegro at the right tempo, the whirlwind tempo of the Roman dancers [of the saltarello]. The audience encored it; we played it again; it went even better the second time. On my return to the artists' room, I saw Habeneck standing with a slightly crestfallen air, and said casually as I went past, 'That's how it goes.' He did not reply.

I was never more blessedly aware of the advantages of being able to conduct my music myself. My delight was the greater for the thought of what Habeneck had made me endure.

Unhappy composers! Learn to conduct yourselves (in both senses of the word); for conductors, never forget, are the most dangerous of all your interpreters.[15]

15 *Memoirs*, 244.

Regarding this last statement by Berlioz, that a conductor can be the worst enemy of the composer, he also observes that the composer who conducts his own music, if he is a poor conductor, can also be his own worst enemy!

No one will accuse a composer of conspiring against the success of his own work, and yet there are many composers who unknowingly ruin their best scores because they fancy themselves to be great conductors.

Beethoven, it is said, more than once spoiled performances of his symphonies, which he liked to conduct even at the time when his deafness had become almost complete.[16]

16 *Treatise*, 410.

If all the problems of performance Berlioz has enumerated above were not enough, in Paris during the time of Berlioz one had also to contend with rowdy audiences and even trouble makers planted by ones enemies. Berlioz describes such a concert where someone was sent with a whistle to disrupt the concert.

> Actually, this harmonic mass was incredible, the room trembled with the effect of the voices and thunder of the trumpets. This painting of the last judgment crushed them and three times in the middle of the piece the applause and cries from the audience covered up the sounds of my people who were singing. At the end of the piece, a dear enemy had the stupidity to blow a whistle and I would have paid one thousand francs to buy it. At that very moment, the room stood up with cries of fury and applause. The women applauded with their programs, the violins and basses with their bows, the drummers with their sticks - one could say that it was a great success.
>
> The lesson was a good one. The enemy once thrown out ...[17]

17 Letter to his Sister, Adele, Paris, November 2, 1840, in *Correspondance*, 734.

There are several interesting extant letters by Berlioz in which he asks for sectional rehearsals. In one case, regarding preparations for an 6 April 1845, concert in the Cirque Olympique in Paris, he requests for one day separate rehearsals for violins and violas (9:00 AM), basses (1:00 PM), and harps (3:00 PM), and on the following day separate rehearsals for the male and female chorus members (9:00 AM and 12:00 PM) and for winds and percussion (3:00 PM). The same letter contains some interesting comments about the percussion.

> Please let Bernadel know that we are talking about a triangle and have him tell you how much 20 pair of good cymbals would cost. Tell him to bring only seven pair of timpani.[18]

18 Letter to James Ferriere, Paris, February 22, 1845, in *Correspondance*, 944.

With rehearsal schedules like that, together with his descriptions of his experiences as a conductor, one can understand his state of total exhaustion by the end of a concert, as in this case following a performance of his *Requiem* in Berlin.

At the conclusion of the concert a great many people spoke to me and congratulated me and wrung me by the hand, but I could only stand there dazed, not comprehending, feeling nothing. My brain and nervous system had over-taxed themselves and craved rest, I was stupid with fatigue. Only Wieprecht contrived to bring me to myself with a hug like a cuirassier's. The worthy man positively cracked my ribs, interspersing his exclamations with Teutonic oaths.[19]

19 *Memoirs*, 339.

On Conducting Technique

IN HIS *Memoirs*, BERLIOZ DISCUSSES the fundamental principles of the conductor's art from the viewpoint of its essential technical demands.

It will hardly be disputed that the conductor who does not have a thorough grasp of the technique of orchestration is not worth much, musically speaking. He should at least know the mechanism and exact range of each instrument as well as the player knows it, if not better. In this way he will be in a position to assert himself, especially when it is a question of some unusual combination or some daring or difficult passage which provokes the lazy or incompetent player to announce that 'It can't be done' or 'The note doesn't exist' or 'It's unplayable,' or any of the other magic phrases invoked by ignorant mediocrity on these occasions. Instead of meekly accepting it, the conductor will be able to reply: 'You're wrong, it can be done. Try it in such and such a way, and you'll find you can manage it;' or, 'I don't say it isn't difficult, but if after working at it for a few days you still find it impossible, we shall have to conclude that you don't know how to play your instrument properly, and engage a more capable player.' In the opposite instance—admittedly all too common—of the composer who through lack of technical knowledge makes cruel demands on the players and asks for things that are genuinely unattainable even by the most puissant virtuoso, the conductor who knows his business can take their part against the composer and point out to him his mistakes …

The vulgar assumption that every composer is a born conductor, ie., knows how to direct an orchestra without having to learn, is a fallacy. Beethoven was a celebrated witness to the fact; and I could name many other composers held in general esteem each of whom, the moment he takes up the baton, becomes the most helpless greenhorn, not merely unable to indicate the time with any precision, let alone vary it, but actually capable of bringing the whole performance to a standstill but for the players' swift appreciation of his talents and consequent determination to pay no attention to the frantic convulsions of his arms. A conductor's work has two distinct aspects. The first, and easier, consists in directing the performance of a work which the players already know—a work in the repertory, as they say in the theater. In the second instance, he has the much more arduous task of rehearsing an unfamiliar score, which means discerning the author's intentions and transmitting them clearly and vividly to the orchestra, working until he has achieved the accuracy, ensemble and expression without which there can be no music, and once these technical problems are mastered, identifying the orchestra with himself and animating and infusing it with his own enthusiasm and inspiration.

It follows that, quite apart from the working knowledge of his craft which a conductor acquires by study and practice, and the qualities of feeling and instinct which he has by nature or not at all—the presence or absence of which makes him the composer's most vital ally or his most dangerous enemy—there is a further skill that is essential to the conductor-trainer-organizer: the ability to read a score. The man who makes use of a simplified score or of a mere first violin part, as is often done, especially in France, cannot detect half the mistakes that are made; and when he does point out an error, he is open to counter-attack by the player in question, who may riposte, 'What do you know about it? You haven't got my part there.' And that is the least disadvantage of this deplorable system.

Whence I conclude that to become a real conductor a man must at all costs be thoroughly taught how to read a score. He may be expert in orchestration, a composer too, and proficient in the technique of rhythmical changes, and yet have mastered only half his art if this skill still eludes him.[20]

20 *Memoirs*, 405ff.

Berlioz published the very first treatise on the art of conducting. Following is his description, in that treatise, of several basic fundamentals of conducting technique.

The orchestral conductor generally uses a small light stick, about 20 inches long … He holds it in his right hand and distinctly marks with it the beginning, the divisions and the close of each bar. Some concert-masters use the violin bow for conducting, but it is less suitable than the baton. The bow is somewhat flexible; this lack of rigidity and the greater resistance it offers to the air because of the hair make its movements less precise.

…

Even with music in strict time, the conductor must generally insist that the players look at him as often as possible. *An orchestra which does not watch the conductor's baton has no conductor.* For instance, frequently after a pause the conductor is forced to wait before marking the re-entry of the orchestra until he sees the eyes of all performers fixed upon him …

The obligation on the part of the performers to look at the conductor implies an equal obligation on his part to make himself visible to all of them … His stand should not be too high lest the board carrying the score hide his face. For his facial expression has much to do with the influence he exercises.

…

We now come to the question whether the conductor should stand or sit. In theaters, where works of tremendous length are performed, it is rather difficult for the conductor to endure the fatigue caused by standing the entire evening. On the other hand, it is obvious that the conductor loses part of his power by being seated and that he cannot give free course to his temperament (if he has any).

Furthermore, should he conduct from the full score or from the first-violin part, as is customary in some theaters? He should doubtless use the full score. Conducting from a single part containing only the principal instrumental cues, the melody and the bass requires a needless effort of memory on the part of the conductor. Moreover, if he tells one of the performer's whose part he does not have before him that he has made a mistake, he exposes himself to the risk of being answered: 'what do you know about this?'[21]

21 Quoted in *Treatise*, 411ff.

One interesting technical question he addresses in his treatise on conducting needs some explanation for the modern reader. He speaks of the problem of the orchestra seeing the second beat of 3/4 meter, if it goes to the conductor's left and *if his back is to the orchestra*. There was a time during the late eighteenth and early nineteenth centuries when conductors faced the audience rather than the orchestra, as strange as that might seem today. The reason had to do with social etiquette in the old aristocratic world; simply put, one was not permitted to turn one's back on the royalty seated out in the hall.

If the conductor has his back turned to the orchestra, as is customary in theaters, the latter method [second beat to the left] has a disadvantage in that only few players can see this very important marking of the second beat since the body of the conductor hides the movement of his arm

One successful technique which Berlioz did not address in a formal way, but certainly practiced himself, was the well planned rehearsal. There are a number of extant letters before engagements when he sets out details for sectional rehearsals, special instrumentation needs, etc. A typical example is a letter of 1852 in which he lists the days and instruments, giving specific persons by name, needed for sectionals, a list of unusual instruments, and a final worry:

For Thursday, we also need a Tam-Tam (Gong)—Beale promised that I would have one, but please see that I do.[22]

22 Letter to Henry Jarrett, London, April, 1852, in *Correspondance*, 1373. Letters Nr. 1486 and 1487 deal with similar requests for four bassoons and two cornets.

The Conductor's Duty to the Composer

IN HIS TREATISE ON CONDUCTING, Berlioz addresses the most important obligation the conductor has, his duty to faithfully represent the composer.

> Among the creative artists the composer is almost the only one depending upon a host of intermediaries between him and the public—intermediaries who may be intelligent or stupid, friendly or hostile, diligent or negligent. It is in their power either to carry his work on to brilliant success or to disfigure, debase and even destroy it.
>
> Singers are often considered the most dangerous of these intermediaries; I believe that this is not true. In my opinion, the conductor is the one whom the composer has most to fear. A bad singer can spoil only his own part, but the incapable or malevolent conductor can ruin everything. A composer must consider himself happy if his work has not fallen into the hands of a conductor who is both incapable and hostile; for nothing can resist the pernicious influence of such a person. The most excellent orchestra becomes paralyzed, the best singers feel cramped and fettered, all energy and unity are lost. Under such direction the noblest and boldest inspirations can appear ridiculous, enthusiasm can be violently brought down to earth; the angel is robbed of his wings, the genius is transformed into an eccentric or a simpleton, the divine statue is plunged from its pedestal and dragged in the mud. Worst of all, when new works are performed for the first time, the public and even listeners endowed with the highest musical intelligence are unable to recognize the ravages perpetrated by the stupidities, blunders, and other offenses of the conductor.
>
> ...
>
> Often a conductor demands from his musicians a certain exaggeration of the nuances indicated by the composer, either from a lack of delicate musical feeling or from a desire to give emphatic proof of his zeal. He does not understand the character and style of the work. The nuances become distortions, the accents turn into outcries. The intentions of the poor composer are completely disfigured; and those of the conductor, however honest they may be, are like the caresses of the ass in the fable, who killed his master by fondling him.
>
> ...
>
> The performances obtained by the old method of rehearsing are never more than approximations of correct interpretations. Yet the conductor puts down his baton, after ruining another masterpiece, with a smile of satisfaction.[23]

23 Quoted in *Treatise*, 410, 419 and 420.

In an address to the Academy of Fine Arts of the Institute of France on 11 September 1861, Berlioz spoke of the fundamental question the conductor must consider, regarding his duty to the composer, is the limits of his own artistic freedom. Where do the conductor's rights as an interpreter and performing artist end vis-a-vis the authority of the score? Berlioz addresses this question through a story about a solo artist.

> One of our most illustrious virtuosi has thus expressed himself upon this subject:
> 'We are not the mere staple by which the picture is suspended; we are the sun by which it is illumined.'
> To this, it may be replied:
> In the first place, we admit this modest comparison. But the sun, in lighting up a picture, reveals its exact design and color. It does not cause either trees or weeds to grow; or birds or serpents to appear, where the painter has not placed them. It does not change the expression of the figures; and render the gay faces sad, or the sad faces gay. It does not enlarge certain outlines, and reduce the extent of others. It does not make black white, and white black; in short it shows us the picture as the master painted it. We do not wish for anything other than that which you propose. Be therefore the suns; ladies and gentlemen, as we shall be happy to adore you. Be really suns; and try not to make of yourselves cellar-rats and rag-picker's lanterns.[24]

24 *Mozart, Weber and Wagner*, 82.

During the nineteenth century, the liberties taken by the conductor included actually changing the music. Berlioz, of course, correctly rages against this liberty.

> We have the example of Kreutzer making numerous cuts in one of Beethoven's symphonies at the time of the last *concerts spirituels* at the Opera, after which we see Habeneck altering the orchestration of another (For the last twenty years the C minor Symphony has been performed at the Conservatoire without the double basses at the beginning of the scherzo. Habenek thinks they do not sound effective. Telling Beethoven how he should have written!). In London you hear *Don Giovanni*, *Figaro* and *The Barber of Seville* with additional parts for bass drum, trombones and ophicleide supplied by Costa. But if conductors are free to tamper with works of this kind at will and add or subtract as they please, what is to stop a violin or a horn, or any back-desk player, from doing the same? It will be the translator and the editor next, even the copyist, the engraver and the printer, who will have a fine precedent for doing the same (this is just what is happening).

Is this not the utter ruin and destruction of art? And ought not we, all of us who are in love with the glory of art and vigilant to protect the inalienable rights of the human spirit, ought we not, when we see them attacked, to rise up in our wrath and pursue and indict the malefactor, and cry aloud for all to hear, 'Your crime is contemptible—despair! Your stupidity is criminal—die! May you be scorned! May you be hissed and hooted! May you be accursed! Despair and die!'[25]

25 *Memoirs*, 92.

Part 8

On Music Education

On Music Education

BERLIOZ DID NOT WRITE EXTENSIVELY on music education, but the range of topics suggests his having given considerable thought to the subject over the years. In 1835 he published an article decrying the fact that music was not part of the education of children in France. In the following, when he says 'music is not for everyone,' he means if it were, they would be teaching it to everyone.

It is not necessary to come to [composers] to give us philanthropic theories on the popularity of the arts: music is not made for everyone because of the simple reason that everyone is not made for music. We have already said it, and we will not tire of repeating it. That is rigorously true, but it is, especially in France, desperately in evidence. With us, is music a part of the education of the people? Do they teach choral singing and playing of instruments in the public schools? Does the army participate in this teaching? Well, good Lord! Listen to the songs of our workers when they return from the gates on holidays; go into the schools, into the barracks; attend the harmonic frolics of children and soldiers, and tell us if what you hear does not much more resemble the howlings of fighting Hurons, than the song of civilized men. With us, the people only retain musical scraps, which it denatures more or less. They have never been able to sing from one end to the other even the shortest tune if it includes the least modulation, the slightest accent differing from the practices of vaudeville tunes. As an example, I bear a grudge against THE MARSEILLAISE. Out of fifty thousand individuals who think they know that famous national hymn, there are not one hundred, quite certainly, who can sing it to the end without gross errors; they sing easily the beginning and the end, but at the minor:

Entendez-vous dans les campagnes
Mugir ces farouches soldats!

the sentiment of tonality and of melodic form completely escapes them; there is no more than a horrible cacophony that stops short a part of the singers, for the others continue bravely without wondering at the fact that they are singing in three or four different tones, and who only stop at the refrain:

Aux arms, citoyens.

What does music have in common with such organizations? Musical art is a power, which, coming from the thought of the composer, addresses, through interpreters, alas too rarely faithful, to certain organs, to certain sentiments, to certain ideas of the human being, to move some, excite and ennoble others, in an aim, if not of utility, at least of noble pleasure, high and delicate. How can its action be exercised on a people in whom the organs, sentiments and ideas absolutely are lacking. Whether it is a fact of nature, a fault of education, or, what is worse, a vicious education, does not matter; it is sufficient to ascertain it to prove the absurdity of this proposition trafficked by many people in France: 'Music is made for everyone.' After that, in admitting that in the crowd that throngs to open air concerts, one can count on a great number of amateurs made for music, again I would prove, without doing my utmost to hunt for faults in the details of technique, that the principle on which these miserable attempts rest is false and not to be conceded.[1]

1 *Journal des Débats*, July 21, 1835.

We cannot know how much influence the previous article may have had, but we can see Berlioz's delight in the announcement the following year that some music would be introduced into the lower grades.

It is difficult to foresee when French art will be able to gather the fruit of the recent decision of the Minister of Public Instruction, intended to introduce singing into primary school teaching; the teachers will be lacking yet for a good while. Little by little, however, they will be formed; and when musical sentiment, developed first in the normal schools, finally can issue forth and be communicated to that immense quantity of young students, deprived up until today of the means of instruction, when musical signs have become as familiar as letters of the alphabet to a great part of the nation; then, I think, one will be able to determine the truth of this opinion, already promulgated by several eminent artists: In the wise use of great masses lies the whole future of art.[2]

2 Ibid., July 23, 1836.

During this same month Berlioz published a eulogy of a musician and teacher, Alexandre Choron (1771–1834). Perhaps his eulogy was timed to help influence the decision of the Minister of Public Instruction, mentioned above, or maybe Berlioz was simply thinking of music education at this time. In any case, he presents a loving tribute to the qualities of a great teacher of any age.

Choron, only living through the life of his school: the students were he himself: outside of that, there was no longer any Choron; he offered the most complete realization of the ravishing ideal that the genius of Hoffman could make us love so much in THE VIOLIN OF CREMONA. Uniting to the fantastic sensibility of Antonia all the oddities of Crespel, his soul was not in an instrument, but in a school of music; and, like Antonia dying at the moment when the mysterious violin is broken, so Choron was to die from the blow which struck his school. He was an artist in the highest meaning of the word, one of those fiery, fanatic, devout, jealous artists, martyrs for their faith, whose race becomes rarer every day … He loved his students, gave them his time, his money; he exalted their merit, inflated their successes, had difficulty in understanding them, and other times, when their rebellious intelligence could not rise promptly to the compass of his own, he overwhelmed them with violent reproaches, with hard epithets, he beat them, he would have killed them for one wrong note too many. He must have suffered cruelly from so many disappointments coming one after another, after such beautiful hopes; he must have died a thousand times before the last time. And yet, he would not have asked for anything better than to live: in his moments of happiness, he was so completely, so profoundly happy. How his face beamed, the poor, great artist, when at the head of his troupe of children and young people of both sexes he left Paris to go for a walk in the fields. Having arrived at the plains of Montrouge, neighboring his dwelling, often in Springtime lost in the burgeoning wheat, how many times the children of harmony astonished the crude peasants with the magic of sublime hymns that the master had taught them …

Ah! Poor Choron! What a soul! With what expansive force he was gifted! What would his intelligence been capable of, if it had been understood and appreciated! What an instrument! What a lever for the one who would have known how to make use of it! But his school, calumniated under the rubric of Utility, stricken with reprobation; during the Revolution of July [1830], by the absurd prejudice that was attached to its title as an institution of religious music, little by little, it was seen to that all means of existence were withdrawn. His principal students had already left him to go into the theaters of France and abroad to make use of the excellent method … others, retained yet for a time by sacrifices of all kinds by means of which Choron tried to stay his crumbling edifice, finally were dispersed, when the unhappy director saw the absolute impossibility of providing for their needs; and the door of the school, once closed on them, was never again opened, except to allow the withdrawal of its founder's casket.[3]

3   Ibid., July 3, 1836.

With regard to higher education, Berlioz on several occasions argued for bringing the famous Paris Conservatoire up to date. At the time he wrote his *Memoirs*, he reviews the progress and notes areas where instruction was still not available.

Our conservatoire was for long without classes in such essential instruments as double bass, trombone, trumpet and harp. These gaps have been filled in the last few years. Unfortunately many others remain …
   (3) The omission of the basset horn from the syllabus of students of the clarinet was until recently a serious error, for it meant that a great deal of Mozart's music could not be performed properly in France—an absurd state of affairs. But now that Adolphe Sax has perfected the bass clarinet to the point where it can perform everything that lies within the range of the basset horn and more (it can play a minor third lower),

and since its timbre is similar to the basset horn's but even more beautiful, the bass clarinet should be studied in conservatories alongside the soprano clarinet and the smaller clarinets in Eb, F, and high Ab.

(4) The saxophone, the latest member of the clarinet family, an instrument which will prove extremely useful when players have learnt to exploit its qualities, should be given its own separate position in the curriculum, for before long every composer will want to use it.

(5) We have no class in the ophicleide, with the result that of the hundred or hundred and fifty persons in Paris at present blowing this exacting instrument, hardly three are fit to be in a good orchestra, and only one, M. Caussinus, is a really first-rate player.

(6) We have no class in the bass tuba, a powerful rotary-valve instrument differing from the ophicleide in timbre, mechanism and range, its position in the trumpet family being exactly equivalent to that of the double bass in the violin family. Most modern scores include a part for either ophicleide or bass tuba, sometimes for both.

(7) The saxhorn and the piston-valve cornet should be taught in our Conservatoire, both being now in general use, the cornet especially.

(8) No instruction is given in percussion playing. Yet is there any orchestra in Europe, large or small, which does not possess a timpanist? They all have a functionary of that name; but how many are true timpanists, thorough-going musicians, accustomed to every complexity of rhythm, masters of the technique of the instrument—which is less easy than is commonly believed—and gifted with a keen ear sufficiently trained to enable them to tune and change key accurately, and to do so during a performance, with all the noise of the orchestra going on round them? I must positively state that, apart from the timpanist at the Opéra, M. Poussard, I know of only three in the whole of Europe—and I have had the opportunity of scrutinizing a few orchestras in the last nine or ten years. Most of the timpanists I met did not even know how to hold their sticks and were consequently helpless when it came to executing a true tremolo or roll. A timpanist who cannot manage a quick roll in every degree of loud and soft is a man of straw.

All conservatories ought therefore to have a class in percussion, in which students can acquire a thorough proficiency in timpani, tambourine and side-drum at the hands of first-rate musicians. The old convention, now no longer tolerable and already abandoned by Beethoven and one or two others, whereby the percussion was treated perfunctorily or in a crudely insensitive manner, undoubtedly helped to perpetuate its low status. Composers having till recently used it merely as a source of noise (more or less superfluous or actively disagreeable) or as a means of mechanically emphasizing the strong beats of the bar, it was assumed that this modest mission was all that it could or was meant to fulfill in the orchestra, and consequently that there was no need to go into the technique of the thing with any great care or to be a real musician in order to play it. In fact, it takes a very capable musician to play even some of the cymbal and bass-drum parts in modern scores.[4]

4 *Memoirs*, 402.

In this same discussion Berlioz also mentions problems in violin study and the fact that there were no classes in viola. He also notes the absence of classes in rhythm, music history, instrumentation, and conducting.

He approaches this subject again in a newspaper article in 1857 adding some *special* classes for singers!

> I still remember the time in the Conservatory when there were no classes in harp, trumpet, trombone, or even any class in contrabass. Fortunately we have in France in the highest degree the sense of the needs of musical art, and after having recognized that in all theater and concert orchestras there are contrabasses, trumpets, trombones, and harps, the usefulness of these four classes in our great and beautiful school of music was admitted … We only lack now in our musical instruction a half-dozen other instrumental classes, a class in instrumentation for composers, plus two or three classes in rhythm, a class in pronunciation, another of prosody, another in the French language, another in the history of music, and ten or twelve classes of common sense for singers.[5]

[5] *Journal des Débats*, February 3, 1857.

Berlioz, himself, had been a student at the Conservatoire and we can imagine the conflicts which must have resulted between student and teachers, with his free and innovative mind juxtaposed against what was surely an old-fashioned and rigid approach to theory and composition. Theory, he says in his *Treatise on Instrumentation*, understands little of actual practice.

> The old presumption of acousticians to impose the results of their calculations upon the practice of art is no longer tenable; for musical practice is based above all on the study of the impressions by tones on the human ear.
>
> It is certain that music must reject them if it wants to exist at all. It is equally certain that the customary modifications of intervals between two mutually attractive tones constitute extremely subtle shadings employed with the greatest care by virtuosos and singers and generally avoided by orchestral players, and that they require special treatment by composers.
>
> Finally, it is certain that the great majority of musicians instinctively abstain from them in harmonic ensemble playing. Consequently, tones called incompatible by acousticians are entirely congenial in musical practice; relations found by calculation to be false are accepted as true by the ear, which completely disregards these very tiny differences—the opinions of mathematicians notwithstanding …
>
> These insipid discussions, this idle talk of litterateurs, these absurd deductions of theoreticians, all of whom are possessed with a mania of speaking and writing about an art concerning which they know nothing,

can only amuse musicians. Nevertheless, it is a pity; eruditon, eloquence and genius ought always to command the admiration and respect due to them.[6]

> 6 *Treatise*, 402ff.

Finally, in an article of 1858, Berlioz brings to the attention of his readers the publication of what may have been the first band method book in France. The principle will seem very familiar to readers today who are familiar with materials for elementary school bands.

> Mr. Charles Dupart has just published a teaching work which we think is truly useful for musicians who are destined for the military bands. Usually these young people receive hardly more than ten minutes of lessons each, three or four times a week. There are too many students for the number of teachers. To remove this problem, Mr. Dupart had the bright idea to write combined exercises for all the wind instruments. These exercises will at first be in one part and then in two parts written in octave, or double octave, and even in simple harmony. They are, thus, to be played by the flutes, clarinets, saxophones, sax-horns, cornets, horns, trombones, etc. The students, instead of sharing the teacher's time, can study the lesson together, under the teacher's direction. They will also become accustomed to playing together and this advantage is considerable. Mr. Dupart, in composing his *Methode polyphonique*, has thus rendered a true service to the study of wind instruments, and his work can not but encourage the development and progress of military bands in France.[7]

> 7 *Journal des Débats*, December 21, 1858.

Part 9

Music in Society

France

IN THE COUNTRIES IN WHICH BERLIOZ TRAVELED he could not help but notice the correspondence between a nation's musical culture and the civilization of its society at large. He envied especially Germany, where he saw a love of music throughout all levels of society.

During 1836–1837, when his thoughts were on music education, as mentioned above, he began to have hope for the future of society in France, if only the movement toward the musical education of the population continued.

> If the extraordinary movement that we notice in today's music education, whether in Paris or in the provinces, is upheld for only about twenty years, an immense and beautiful revolution will be accomplished in our manners, which are so barbaric concerning the art of music. This judgment of barbaric will perhaps offend many people and have me condemned as being pedantic. It is, however, easy to be motivated towards such a judgment. Do ignorance of the primary principals of an art, the inability to feel its effects and the indifference of its power suffice to constitute the barbaric in this comparison? I think it is difficult to contest.[1]
>
> ...
>
> One hardly can refuse to see ... the rapidity with which musical taste is spreading in the lower classes of the population: one may enter on the account ledger line the choral teaching already introduced into a great number of primary schools, and the influence that societies like those of Toulouse, Marseille, Dijon, and Douai exercise on their surrounding areas, and the hope of seeing us become within a few years an essentially musical people will cease to seem chimerical.[2]

1 *Journal des Débats*, September 18, 1836.

2 Ibid., January 31, 1837.

During this same period he published an entertaining account of his joining a group of citizens on the street to sing. His aim, no doubt, was to demonstrate the power of music for the masses.

> I can cite an impression, due only to the power of voices, that I myself received. It was in 1830, some days after the Revolution; I was crossing the courtyard of the Palais-Royal when I thought I heard, coming from a group, music well-known to me. I approach, and I recognize, to my grand surprise, that ten to twelve young people were singing, actually,

a war hymn of my own composition, whose words, translated from the IRISH MELODIES by Moore, were by chance exactly right for the circumstance.

Delighted by the discovery, as an author very little accustomed to this type of success, I enter the circle of singers and ask their permission to join them. They accorded it to me by adding to it a part of the bass that, for this chorus at least, was perfectly useless. But I was careful to guard my incognito, and I remember even having had quite a lively discussion with the one of these gentlemen who beat the time, regarding the tempo that he gave to my piece. Fortunately, I regained his good graces by singing correctly my part in *The Old Flag of Beranger*, to which he had written the music and that we performed the moment after. In the entr'actes of this outdoor concert, three national guardsmen, our protectors against the crowd, went through the rows of the audience, their shakos in their hands, and begged for the wounded of the past three days. The act seemed so bizarre to the Parisians that it assured the success of the receipts. Soon we saw coins of the one hundred sous falling like hail, which doubtless would have remained very comfortably in the purses of the owners, if there had only not been public commiseration and the charm of our music to draw them out. But the crowd was becoming more and more numerous, and the little circle reserved to the patriotic Orpheus shrank every instant and the *armed force* that was protecting us was startled to see itself powerless against that rising tide of curiosity seekers. We escaped with difficulty, but the wave followed us. Having arrived at the Colbert Gallery that leads to the Rue Vivienne, surrounded, tracked like a bear at a fair, they summoned us to start our songs again. A pretty salesgirl, whose store opened onto the glass rotunda of the gallery, offered then to let us climb to the second floor of her house, from where we could, without running the risk of stifling, *pour torrents of harmony on our admirers*. The proposition was accepted, and we begin *The Marseillaise*. At the first measures, the noisy throng that was milling about under our feet, stops and grows silent. The silence is not deeper on Saint Peter's Plaza, when from the height of the pontifical balcony the Pope pronounces the benediction *urbi et orbi*. After the first couplet, they were yet quiet; after the third, the same silence. This was not what I wanted: at the sight of that immense concourse, I remembered that I had just arranged the immortal song of Rouget de Lisle [La Marseillaise] for large orchestra and double choir, and that in place of the words 'tenors, basses,' I had written on the tablature of the score: *Everyone who has a voice, a heart, and blood in his veins*. Ah, ha! I said to myself, this is my business. I was, then, horribly disappointed by the obstinate silence of the listeners. But at the fourth strophe, not able to stand it any longer, I shout to them: 'Well, heavens, come on now, sing!' The people then finally hurl their '*Aux armes, citoyens*' with the ensemble and the energy of a rehearsed chorus. Imagine that the gallery leading to the Rue Vivienne was full, that the one which opened into the Rue Neuve-des-Petits-Champs was full, that the rotunda of the area was full, that these four or five thousand voices were piling into an echoing place, closed to the right and left, and above, by the glass partitions, and below by reverberant stone floor tile, consider that the majority of the singers, men, women and children, still were hot from the breath of the cannons, and imagine, if possible, what the effect would be of that thundering refrain … As for me, not using a metaphor, I dropped to the floor, and our little troupe, terrified by the explosion of voices, was stricken mute, like birds after a clap of thunder.

There, there were neither drums, nor bells, nor artillery; it was the power alone of a great mass of voices, which a fortunate chance allowed to happen.[3]

3 Ibid., July 23, 1836.

Another topic of personal interest to Berlioz was the parsimonious attitude of the government in its support of public concerts. This was a problem Berlioz faced with all the concerts he organized in Paris.

This [element of economy] is especially the case in France, where music is so far from forming a part of national life, where the government does everything possible for the theater but nothing for music itself, where capitalists readily pay fifty thousand francs and more for a painting by some great master (*because it represents a value*), but will not spare fifty francs to organize an annual music festival worthy of our nation, which would display the numerous musical resources which we own but do not use![4]

4 *Treatise*, 407.

The failure of the government to build concert halls was, to Berlioz, a hallmark itself of the quality of society.

The dimension of concert halls is in general proportional to the love that one supposes in the public for music, and their interior arrangement is in relation to the type of music that is to be played there. So we do not have any large concert hall in Paris. We have banquet halls, halls for balls, halls for the drawing of conscripts' numbers, etc., but we do not have a single concert hall worthy of that name that one may rent when one needs to do so.[5]

5 *Journal des Débats*, February 14, 1847.

Another way in which the government inhibited concerts was the imposition of a special tax, something Berlioz attempted to ridicule in the following newspaper article in 1849.

Why do they still make musical instruments?, you may ask. Because musicians are still being formed in the Conservatories and elsewhere. But why, you will add, do they persist in teaching music to those unfortunates? My God, because the habit has been formed a long time ago, because certain theaters still have their doors open, because a small number of individuals do not want to renounce the enjoyment that the art of music produces, and who are always more or less devoted to the study of this beautiful art. Doubtless the moment will come when these *characters* will be terribly rare in France, when all the lyrical theaters will be closed, when the Conservatories will no longer exist, when those musicians who are not dead of hunger will have embraced a *useful* career; but the instant of this beautiful triumph of practical ideas over the hollow dreams of poetry and art has not yet arrived; nothing is as tenacious as old customs. Moreover, Athens, Babylonia, and Memphis were not demolished in a day. Everything takes a little time. As for the rest, the Opéra is already closed, and to believe the public rumor, it hasn't many chances in its favor if it does succeed in reopening this winter. No one knows if the Theatre-Italien will manage to give any performances. As for concerts (I do not call concerts these more or less numerous collections of the indolent before whom one comes to spill out a few chromatic scales on a clavier and to mince through some bad drawing room songs); as for concerts, I say, their number doubtless will be extremely restricted, and it will be a true misfortune for the tax collector among the poor, who, aside from the satisfaction that he has felt up to now from collecting a part of the product from the work of musicians, has always been pleased to honor with his presence the large musical gatherings, and so to encourage the serfs working for him. Perhaps, taking into consideration the interests of this estimable protector of our art, the government will oblige musicians to give concerts anyway; but this useful ordinance, is not capable, after all, of forcing the public to attend, and they are more and more determined not to pay to hear music, and our Lordship, the tax collector, I do fear, will hardly collect anything, and will no longer smile in such good grace at our efforts—this is really serious! Slavery of the blacks has been abolished, and so ruined, in that way, a crowd of good fellows who liked very much to get rich without doing anything; yet, there did remain the slavery of French musicians, who brought in, good years or bad, a few miserable hundreds or thousands of francs to our tax collector, and, without their having liberated us, however here we have our good Lordship reduced to the state of a colonist in Guadalupe!!—this is really very serious!

Authority should owe, it seems to me, a little comfort to the administration of the hospices and to our Lordship, the tax collector. The concerts bringing in almost nothing to him, the lyric theaters being either dead or dying, why not replace the legitimate part that our Lordship collects from the gross receipts of the concerts and theatrical productions by an equal tax on the sale of musical instruments, since the manufacturers continue to produce? This is a very easy means, and I am surprised that no one has yet dreamed it up. Without a doubt, this legitimate *dime* will be paid with the liveliest eagerness. Mssrs. Erard, Pleyel, Boisselot, Sax, Vuillaume, Gand, and twenty others, will even be proud to pay it. One will see at their plants inspectors of their work and of their receipt books, and, the inspection finished, these gentlemen will say to M. Erard, or to M. Sax, for example: 'You have sold pianos for 160,000 francs, or sax-horns for 80,000, we have a tax-right to an eighth, even a fourth, of your gross receipts; give us 20,000 francs, M. Erard, and you M. Sax, 10,000. Very good! The tax collector is satisfied! And he *will* be satisfied. Those who would doubt his satisfaction do not know our good Lordship and his gentle ways. No one is more gentle than he. The law authorizes him to take a fourth of our gross receipts, and yet he only collects an eighth. Thus, a musician gives a concert whose expenses rise to 1,000 francs; he makes 800 francs in receipts; the law authorizes our lordship to take 200 francs from these receipts, and he only takes away precisely 100. Can one press farther disinterestedness?[6]

6 'Exposition de l'Industrie,' in *Journal des Débats*, August 21, 1849.

There was a great growth of amateur music in Paris during Berlioz's lifetime, but this also had the result of the appearance of concerts filled with literature of a more popular nature. Berlioz makes fun of this in the form of a review in the style of some of his fellow critics.

Concerts! ... When we are organizing concerts, you know how it is allowed to talk about them ... It is always like this, 'Sir, someone played a Fantasie on the clarinet which thrilled the crowd. Sir, A certain fellow possesses a wonderful talent. Miss ***, the one who performed variations on the piano which took all the prizes. The talent of this young person is really remarkable. The art of singing is making incredible progress each and every day. We had proof of this once again with the remarkable and gracious voice of Miss ***. One of Miss ***'s best students sang the famous Cavatina (*au claire de la lune*) accompanied by a bassoon. The bassoon part was superbly (or admirably, or wonderfully, or sublimely, for some such adverb ending in 'ly') sung by Mr. ***, father of the interesting singer. The place of Mr. *** is assured in the Institute. They say that this great artist has finally decided to publish his complete works for the bassoon. There is a concert to end all concerts!'[7]

7 Letter to the Director of the journal *La Sylphide*, Paris, December, 1842, in *Correspondance*, 790.

Finally, in an article of 1846, Berlioz notes the foundation of an Association of Artists designed to give artists the power of numbers in their struggles. In this article Berlioz also makes an eloquent plea for France to awake and strive toward its great potential in the arts.

The artist-musicians, in forming a society, seem to have taken as a motto, 'Help yourself, Heaven will not help you.' After years of protests, pleas, complaints, useless individual efforts, the day came when they understood that what was impossible for one, for two, for four, for twenty, for a hundred, would become possible for ten thousand, and that by acting with unity, as a compact group, they worked with the firm conviction that Heaven would not help them, that they would be obliged to use so much force, intelligence, activity, that there would be hardly any obstacles capable of resisting them or of defeating their determination. Musicians in France are the pariahs of the Arts: they alone are subjected to ruinous, crushing taxes, which make, for them, almost unworkable any somewhat daring effort, and so many dangers are sown by even slightly ambitious attempts that have as their aim making known to the public new talents and new productions.

Their Association, therefore, has as its moral aim the creation of resources in case of the misfortune that only too easily can strike its members, and as its artistic aim to do in music those great things which the Germans and the English have set us uselessly as an example for such a long time. The second of these propositions converges naturally from the resolution of the first, and produces yet another result not less important from the point of view of Art: it tends to create the musical education of the people, to give to them the sense of the poetry of sounds, to awaken in them higher tastes than those that were theirs up until now. Unfortunately, the major part of the forces that the Association expends in such a circumstance has just been broken and lost against the material obstacles that French musicians are condemned to encounter at every step ...

And why should we, as Frenchmen, allow ourselves to be surpassed in anything that there may be, by neighboring peoples? What do we lack to equal them, even to surpass them? We have a lively and rapid comprehension of things, we have the sensitivity, we have the heroic will, that will, stronger than iron and steel, that neither bends nor breaks, we are numerous, we are active, we are adroit and strong. What are we lacking then? We lack seriousness, gravity, serenity, we are lacking the qualities that make the adolescent superior to the child, the young man superior to the adolescent, and the man superior to the young man. We lack the scorn of small passions, small ideas, small things. We lack examining, rather than glimpsing, listening, rather than hearing, thinking before speaking; we lack the disdain of mockery and of the miserable success that it attains; we lack believing and firmly believing that the mind that creates is superior to that which destroys, that the instinct of the beaver is much higher than that of monkeys; we lack being ashamed, confused, blushing, humiliated, confounded, for having erected into a very school, cynicism ... But I am convinced that in repudiating the use of that tongue that knows only how to mock, insult, and curse; of that shameful slang, that, descended from the theater boards into the artisan's shop, the artist's studio, the writer's study, seems to threaten, in Paris anyway, to replace the French language ... Let us sever the head of the boa constrictor, and let its skin serve us as a defensive armor against so many other reptiles that our passage through the virgin forests of art will not fail to startle. Let us think that we are great, that we must walk, our head held high and our gaze fixed ahead, instead of exhausting ourselves in grotesque capers and in bending towards the earth, hunting the pebble that envy and stupidity love to throw with vapors at powerful and careful workers. Let us dream about what we are, about the name that we bear, and we must say: 'That people who waged the wars of the Republic and of the Empire, that one that, in three days, overthrew an ancient dynasty and razed the thick walls with which they wanted to encircle it, the people towards whom, in social crises, all the peoples of the world turn, whether they fear or admire them, whether they want to combat or imitate them, this people is manifestly destined to be as great in art as it is great in war; as it was great in our noble obstinacy when, bearing throughout an astonished Europe the torch of civilization, it had the constancy to let itself be burned rather than abandon or extinguish it, as great as it is in science and industry.' And moreover, we shall recognize, we who fear so much the weapon of ridicule, that the moment approaches when, if it were different, if we remained for art in an inferiority or even relative position, an immense laughter would come from the four corners of Europe, the *young America* itself *would dare to whistle from the edge of the Oceans*, and that they would give us at last a festival of ridicule.[8]

8 *Journal des Débats*, August 21, 1849.

Germany

As mentioned above, Berlioz was envious of the love of music, and the importance given to it, which he found in all levels of society in Germany. He imagined that through the practice of music over many centuries the love of music had become a fundamental part of the very character of the German. To illustrate how important music was even at the peasant level, he provides this touching review of a concert in Paris by a traveling German family of musicians, the Grassl family.

> I was comparing ... different races of traveling artists by listening recently to the Grassl Family at the Gymnase Musical. Certainly the German people were there with their love, serious and calm, but profound and religious, for music. For those people, it is not a voluptuous relaxation, not a frivolous toy, nor a more or less painful occupation, as with the Italians and the French, it is a divine art whose sublimity they understand and which they place in the rank of the holiest things. This sentiment of respect for music makes itself felt even with those poor devils who chase about Europe without any other resource than their voices or their instruments. Examine them, they always do their best; but it is rather less to obtain applause and money from the public than to obey that interior voice that tells them to honor the art which enables them to live, the more so as they are making it fall even more from its high mission. On receiving the offering from their listeners, they usually thank them while smiling sadly, as if, supposing that everyone shares their enthusiastic opinions, they wished to say to them 'Pardon me, Sir, for making music to earn my living; it has no need of me, but I need it, and I am aware of everything that I owe to it.' See Grassl enter into the orchestra pit with his six children. By that flattened hair that falls foolishly around his temples and even over his eyes, by that pale face, cold, apathetic, by that clumsy and heavy gait, you would take him to be a thick peasant who has barely enough intelligence needed for the cultivation of his field.
>
> This man, actually, was only a simple woodcutter in Schenau in Bavaria a few years ago; then having inherited a distillery, he would go into the highest mountains to gather the plants and roots necessary for his use. In the intervals of this daily work, Franz Grassl tried to learn music. Without a teacher, without a method book, without a guide, and without an instrument, he succeeded by the strength of his will alone, by his perseverance, and by his very Germanic patience, aided by an irresistible musical instinct, in conquering the apparently insurmountable difficulties.

He did not have an instrument so he succeeded in making himself a clarinet, for better or worse; with no method book, he hunted for the fingering and discovered it. Having arrived at the point of performing popular tunes on his imperfect instrument, his passion grew from all the obstacles that it had overcome as much as from the conquests that it had managed. He wanted to learn to read music and musical theory; a few pages of elementary principles and his reflections sufficed for him to unveil the mystery. His ambition always growing, he learned to play progressively as he could procure them, almost all the instruments. The trombone, the horn, the flute, the natural trumpet, the valved trumpet, the violin, the contrabass soon became as familiar to him as the clarinet. But he could not make harmony all alone, and everyone knows how much charm this branch of art has for the Germans. Grassl has four children, they will be his students, and so a quintet is founded. What happiness for him, on returning from his Alpine jaunts, to sit down surrounded by his young family on the threshold of his cottage, intoxicated at leisure with rest and harmony, making the mountains resound with energetic chords, or bidding a sweet and melancholy farewell to the evening's twilight, ready to disappear, and he can tell himself without too much exaggeration: this orchestra is my work, I made it all myself, the instruments, the music, and the musicians.

The Grasssl Family having grown in the midst of these artistic studies that were not, as one might certainly think, without having harmed very much the industrial work, he thought of calling music to the aid of his little colony. To be sure, never would a muse have been more thankless if she had rejected such a request. So, far from there, Grassl saw his attempt crowned with all kinds of success. His two youngest children had taken their place among the concert performers, whose number then was raised to seven; he himself and his older sons had acquired more firmness, more brilliancy in their performance; they could tempt fortune. The instruments then were carefully locked into the knapsacks, and leaving his cottage under the care of his poverty, the patriarch of harmony descended from the mountains followed by his wife bearing on her back the youngest of his daughters, while the other children walked *non passibus aequis* [with unequal steps] beside their parents. First, almost all of the cities of Germany, and then those of Italy and of Belgium welcomed with as much astonishment as pleasure that interesting little troupe of symphonic players. Money came with fame, and the proof is that Grassl travels today in a good carriage with two horses, where the entire orchestra lolls about, flouting the summer showers that no longer dampen clothing, the sun that no longer burns their faces, and the stones that no longer bruise their feet.

Engaged for twenty evening performances in the Gymnase Musical, Grassl and his children received from the Parisians a no less welcome reception than from the Venetians and the Belgians. Each concert is a new occasion for encouragement for some of them, and a true success for the others. Setting aside all considerations foreign to art, one can say that two from among them totally merit the applause that they elicit; one plays the trombone in a very remarkable manner; if some low notes sometimes lack good pitch, this is not the lack of a virtuoso ear that must be blamed, but the lack of length of his arm which does not permit the poor youngster to take certain positions where the slide of the instrument must be pushed out to the end. The other draws from the trumpet sounds as in tune as they are full of power and brilliance, and I know some orchestras in Paris that would be very happy to have a half-dozen brass instruments of that strength. The part whose high pitched timbre and melodic role placed the most in evidence, that of the piccolo, was not as well played, not by a long shot. It seems at first that this instrument presents fewer difficulties than many others, but that is only true of the fingering, the pitch and the purity of the sound are not obtained as easily, and I would have believed the little boy who was scraping my tympanum with so much intrepidity was less well organized than his brothers and sisters, if the following instant he had not very properly accompanied a brass group on the valved trumpet. Because, it is necessary to say that they all play, as does their father, several instruments; one (13 years old), plays seven; another (12 years old) four; another (11) seven; one (5) four; a little girl (8) four; the last, who is only three years old, carries suspended around her neck several small tubes with whose interior mechanism I am not acquainted, sounding out the song of the cuckoo on different tones. The sounds that she draws from them are far from being irreproachable relative to pitch; however, I confess that I can hardly conceive of how they succeeded in familiarizing a child of that age with the difficulties of rhythm and time to the point of making her sure of all her entries, even after a quite great number of rests, and starting on the off-beat.[9]

9 *Journal des Débats*, September 5, 1835.

And, at the opposite level of society, he was astounded to witness a leading German aristocrat who could perform as a pianist. This same aristocrat, by the way, also composed marches for band.

Toward the end of the evening Meyerbeer, fine pianist though he is—or perhaps because of it—grew tired, and made way for—can you guess whom?—the King's head chamberlain, Count Redern, who accompanied Madame Devrient in Schubert's 'Erl-King' with the greatest technical and artistic assurance! Proof, if you like, of an astounding pervasiveness of musical culture.[10]

10 *Memoirs*, 335.

The love of music in German society was particularly noticeable to Berlioz in the great German music festivals of the nineteenth century.

In Germany, where music is honored, festivals are organized with a sort of religion; everything happens properly, everything is disposed there in the most perfect and logical order. Hence, the response is commensurate to what one has the right to expect from the means that are used; these are true harmonic banquets, given to a population that enjoys them fully, worthily, and with all the happiness of a beautiful passion satisfied. We imagine in France that all Germans are calm and cold; this is a great error. One only need see the public of Vienna and Prague, especially, when a powerful work elevates and illuminates them, when musical vertigo seizes them, when the breath of inspiration drags them along, one only need see all those arms waving, hear those trembling voices, feel those halls tremble under the tempest of applause, in order to conceive an idea of true enthusiasm, and of the joy that the spectacle of the emotions that they can cause, gives to the heart of artists. That is when they are proud to belong to the family of those who move souls by stirring up ideas; that is when they feel themselves capable of being patient, of waiting, of suffering, of dying, rather than abandoning the task that fell upon them by nature, the constant exercise, total, complete, of their intelligence and their genius, a sublime task, which is to other endeavors of human life what love, the great love of heroes and poets, is to the honest and respectable ties that have as their aim only that of perpetuating the species and of increasing the strength of the States.[11]

11 *Journal des Débats*, July 29, 1846.

Even where music was organized for the entertainment of the public, Berlioz found the same characteristics of quality, interest, and organization.

You hear, besides, superb German military bands, because in this German city [Baden], there actually are Germans. In the evening, at midnight, when the gaming rooms are closed, bursts of laughter, songs, triple horn fanfares descend from the villa Benazet through the woods of firs which surround it. Perhaps it is Vivier [a horn player famous for his ability to play chords on the horn] who is up to his pranks. Why, of course! Who else would it be then? Who can make people laugh like that? Who is playing the horn this well? And you go away, and you stop to dream an instant on the bridge of the Oos, and you return, and you go to sleep dreaming that you could have lost so much money that you didn't actually bet, and which, therefore has been earned; and you think about tomorrow's rehearsal, because at Baden, you have a great number of rehearsals with a beautiful orchestra when one directs the Festival that is organized there every year, and you say to yourself: How attentive, and patient, and polite these artists are! How quickly and well they understand what you ask of them! They never look at their watch during the rehearsals. They have lungs, lips, and arms of iron; with them, you can push musical studies to the furthermost reaches; these are musicians who have the time to make music! And they make it![12]

12 Ibid., July 3, 1861.

Finally, whereas in France Berlioz found the government placing obstacles in the path of the musician, in Germany he found support for music at all levels of government. To support this observation, he republished an extraordinary notice from a newspaper in Köln.

> Music flowers in Germany because it is respected there, and because the opposite of music generally is rejected there. I find a new proof of that German hatred for sonorous horrors in Police Order published recently at Köln as follows:
>
>> It is forbidden for wandering musicians, organ-grinder players, persons who show exotic animals with musical accompaniment, and in general, for all individuals who make music in the streets or on public squares, *to make use of discordant or untuned instruments*. Violators, if they are foreigners, will be expelled immediately from the city: if they are natives, they will be deprived of the authorization for themselves obtained from the police; and that authorization will not be given back until after they have replaced their faulty instruments by new instruments in good state or after they have repaired properly the old ones, an operation that, in all cases, must be witnessed by means of a certificate delivered by two competent and well-known men of the art.
>
> Fine! that is worthy of a civilized people. In France, that order would seem comical. We would find it completely natural, however, to forbid in our streets the habitual traffic of vehicles which spread infectious fumes there; but for infectious sounds, which certainly are not lacking there, the interdiction would seem funny, and we should resign ourselves to stand in Paris, day and night, hearing a thousand frightful noises which would suffice to cause among musicians cases of hydrophobia, and which, brutalizing the ears of the people, make them indifferent to the most atrocious monstrosities in the combinations of sounds. I shall go even farther: the administration of a civilized people, and which has pretensions to a sentiment of the arts, should inquire also, and principally, into the anti-musicality that is being committed in the theaters, in the churches, everywhere that hundreds of individuals are called to meet. It should admit that imbecilic singers without a voice, the incapable performers, the conductors who tear apart a masterpiece, break its four members; extinguish its flame, make its physiognomy ignoble and grotesque, are beings incomparably more destructive than if they were spreading infectious odors in the room where they worked.[13]

13 *Journal des Débats*, January 7, 1852.

Italy

BERLIOZ'S WRITINGS which date from his residence and travels in Italy are filled with his condemnation of various performances he heard there. In reflecting later on the place of music in the Italian culture, he arrives at the interesting conclusion that it was a genuine love of the art of music that the Italians lacked.

> It appears that the Italians do sometimes listen. I have been assured by several people that it is so. The fact remains that music to the Milanese, as to the Neapolitans, the Romans, the Florentines and the Genoese, means arias, duets, trios, well sung; anything beyond that provokes only aversion or indifference. It may be that such antipathies are mere prejudice, due above all to the feebleness of their orchestras and choruses, which prevents them from appreciating any great music outside the narrow circuit they have ploughed for so long. It may also be that they are capable to some extent of rising to the challenge of genius, provided the composer is careful not to disturb entrenched habits of mind too rudely ... If you observe people in towns under Austrian domination, you will see them flock to hear a military band and listen avidly to its rich German harmonies, so unlike the pale cavatinas they are normally fed on. Nevertheless, in general there is no denying that the Italians as a nation appreciate music solely for its physical effect and are alive only to what is on the surface.
>   Of all the nations of Europe, I am strongly inclined to think them the most impervious to the evocative, poetic side of music, as well as to any conception at all lofty and out of the common run. Music for the Italians is a sensual pleasure and nothing more. For the noble expression of the mind they have hardly more respect than for the art of cooking. They want a score that, like a plate of macaroni, can be assimilated immediately without their having to think about it or even to pay any attention to it.[14]

14 *Memoirs*, 208ff.

Bibliography

Bibliography

Berlioz, Hector. *Mozart, Weber and Wagner*. Translated by Edwin Evans. London: W. Reeves, n.d. Originally published as *A travers chants* (Paris, 1862).

Berlioz, Hector. *Les Grotesques de la musique*. Paris: Grund, 1969.
   "La Librarie nouvelle is going to publish a volume of M. Berlioz, entitled *Les Grotesques de la musique*, destined to form a companion to his *Orchestral Evenings*. Under a frivolous appearance, it is a bitting criticism of the ideas, the wide-ranging prejudices of today's Parisian musical world, mixed with true anecdotes, although hardly believable, which make known the strange opinions, the clownish aberrations of taste of amateurs.
   Many things in this book remain implied; one must discover serious thoughts under the ironic form in which they are clothed and through the bitter jokes where the author delights in hiding them." [*Revue et Gazette Musicale de Paris*, February 20, 1859]

Berlioz, Hector. *Evenings with the Orchestra*. Translated by Jacques Barzun. New York: Knopf, 1969. Originally published as *Les Soirées de l'orchestra* (1852).

Berlioz, Hector. *Treatise on Instrumentation*. Translated by Theodore Front. New York: Kalmus, 1948. Originally published as *Grand Traité d'instrumentation* (Paris, 1843).

Berlioz, Hector. *The Memoirs of Hector Berlioz*. Edited by David Cairns. London: Gollancz, 1969.

Berlioz, Hector. *Beethoven by Berlioz*. Translated by Ralph De Sola. Boston: Crescendo, 1975. Originally published as *Voyage musical en Allemagne et en Italie* (Paris, 1844).

Berlioz, Hector. *Gluck & his Operas*. Translated by Edwin Evans. London: Reeves, 1915. Originally published as *Voyage musical en Allemagne et en Italie* (Paris, 1844).

Citron, Pierre, ed. *Berlioz, Correspondance Générale*. Paris: Flammarion, 1972.

Holoman, D. Kern. *The Creative Process in the Autograph Musical Documents of Hector Berlioz, c. 1818-1840*. Ann Arbor: UMI Research Press, 1975.

Holoman, D. Kern. *Catalog of the Works of Hector Berlioz*. Kassel: Bärenreiter, 1987.

Holoman, D. Kern. *Berlioz*. Cambridge: Harvard University Press, 1989.

Macdonald, Hugh, ed. *Hector Berlioz New Edition of the Complete Works*, vol. 19. Kassel: Bärenreiter, 1967.

Searle, Humphrey. *Hector Berlioz, A Selection from his Letters*. London: Gollancz, 1966.

About the Author

Dr. David Whitwell is a graduate ('with distinction') of the University of Michigan and the Catholic University of America, Washington DC (PhD, Musicology, Distinguished Alumni Award, 2000) and has studied conducting with Eugene Ormandy and at the Akademie für Musik, Vienna. Prior to coming to Northridge, Dr. Whitwell participated in concerts throughout the United States and Asia as Associate First Horn in the USAF Band and Orchestra in Washington DC, and in recitals throughout South America in cooperation with the United States State Department.

At the California State University, Northridge, which is in Los Angeles, Dr. Whitwell developed the CSUN Wind Ensemble into an ensemble of international reputation, with international tours to Europe in 1981 and 1989 and to Japan in 1984. The CSUN Wind Ensemble has made professional studio recordings for BBC (London), the Köln Westdeutscher Rundfunk (Germany), NOS National Radio (The Netherlands), Zürich Radio (Switzerland), the Television Broadcasting System (Japan) as well as for the United States State Department for broadcast on its 'Voice of America' program. The CSUN Wind Ensemble's recording with the Mirecourt Trio in 1982 was named the 'Record of the Year' by The Village Voice. Composers who have guest conducted Whitwell's ensembles include Aaron Copland, Ernest Krenek, Alan Hovhaness, Morton Gould, Karel Husa, Frank Erickson and Vaclav Nelhybel.

Dr. Whitwell has been a guest professor in 100 different universities and conservatories throughout the United States and in 23 foreign countries (most recently in China, in an elite school housed in the Forbidden City). Guest conducting experiences have included the Philadelphia Orchestra, Seattle Symphony Orchestra, the Czech Radio Orchestras of Brno and Bratislava, The National Youth Orchestra of Israel, as well as resident wind ensembles in Russia, Israel, Austria, Switzerland, Germany, England, Wales, The Netherlands, Portugal, Peru, Korea, Japan, Taiwan, Canada and the United States.

He is a past president of the College Band Directors National Association, a member of the Prasidium of the International Society for the Promotion of Band Music, and was a member of the founding board of directors of the World Association for Symphonic Bands and Ensembles (WASBE). In 1964 he was made an honorary life member of Kappa Kappa Psi, a national professional music fraternity. In September, 2001, he was a delegate to the UNESCO Conference on Global Music in Tokyo. He has been knighted by sovereign organizations in France, Portugal and Scotland and has been awarded the gold medal of Kerkrade, The Netherlands, and the silver medal of Wangen, Germany, the highest honor given wind conductors in the United States, the medal of the Academy of Wind and Percussion Arts (National Band Association) and the highest honor given wind conductors in Austria, the gold medal of the Austrian Band Association. He is a member of the Hall of Fame of the California Music Educators Association.

Dr. Whitwell's publications include more than 127 articles on wind literature including publications in Music and Letters (London), the London Musical Times, the Mozart-Jahrbuch (Salzburg), and 39 books, among which is his 13-volume *History and Literature of the Wind Band and Wind Ensemble* and an 8-volume series on *Aesthetics in Music*. In addition to numerous modern editions of early wind band music his original compositions include 5 symphonies.

David Whitwell was named as one of six men who have determined the course of American bands during the second half of the 20th century, in the definitive history, *The Twentieth Century American Wind Band* (Meredith Music).

A doctoral dissertation by German Gonzales (2007, Arizona State University) is dedicated to the life and conducting career of David Whitwell through the year 1977. David Whitwell is one of nine men described by Paula A. Crider in *The Conductor's Legacy* (Chicago: GIA, 2010) as 'the legendary conductors' of the 20th century.

> 'I can't imagine the 2nd half of the 20th century—without David Whitwell and what he has given to all of the rest of us.' Frederick Fennell (1993)

www.ingramcontent.com/pod-product-compliance
Lightning Source LLC
Chambersburg PA
CBHW081347230426
43667CB00017B/2744